WILLFUL SHADOWS

The Account of

SONNY JAMES

AND THE SOUTHERN GENTLEMEN

By Gary Robble
with Barb Day

Clovercroft Publishing

Willful Shadows: The Account of Sonny James and The Southern Gentlemen

©2019 by Gary Robble

Published by Clovercroft Publishing, Franklin, Tennessee

Copy Edit by Adept Content Solutions

Cover Design by Greg Robble

Interior Design by Suzanne Lawing

Printed in the United States of America

978-1-948484-51-0

To all those Sonny James fans who not only loved his music but hoped he was the kind of person they thought he was: be assured—he was.

INTRODUCTION

Don McKay

Chances are, if you are reading this, you are a Sonny James fan. If not, I feel certain you will be by the time you finish. In addition to finding out more about him, you will learn about the amazing twists and turns of fate that prevented him from being known only as a "one hit wonder" because of "Young Love," his first chart-topping hit, in 1957. You will also learn about his uncompromising principles and standards that formed the foundations of his personal and professional lives. They were centered around his strong faith, and although they helped guide him through his public musical career, to him, like most everything in his life, they were very private; he never wore them on his sleeve. Always very conscious and selective about the types of songs he sang and the venues where he sang them, he was without exception soft spoken, neatly dressed, and personable; traits that in 1952 led legendary Capitol Records producer, Ken Nelson, to change Jimmie Hugh Loden's professional name to Sonny James, The Southern Gentleman. It was the perfect moniker for the friendly, well-mannered Alabama native.

I must start by saying I was very surprised when asked to do this. There are so many people much more qualified than me to pen this introduction, but none who could feel more honored to do so, and although I am the self-proclaimed "World's Biggest Sonny James Fan," I'm sure I share that title with many, many others. Through my friendship with Gary Robble, the author of this book, I have experienced things that would be the envy of any other Sonny James fan, and I will always be grateful to him for the relationships and priceless memories resulting from them. Being at the right place at the right time allowed me to see and do things so many others would loved to have done, and though they occurred many years after his retirement, in some ways that made them even more special. Gary asked that I tell my story not just from the musical perspective of a life-long fan, but also about the personal things Sonny did that touched my life and family. Since I am not a writer and have never attempted anything like this, I do it with the hope that Sonny would be proud of the final result, and keeping that in mind, each of my words will be written as though he were looking approvingly over my shoulder.

This book will also provide an insight to just how unpredictable the music profession can be. You will learn how the last-minute selection of a song made in a Nashville recording studio the last week of October, 1956, resulted in the hit record that suddenly ignited Sonny's career and sent it skyrocketing to the top of the country charts...a place where many of his songs would eventually peak. On the other hand, you will see that even for someone with Sonny's talent, continued success could not be taken for granted, and one hit song did not automatically insure others would follow. Because they didn't, after several soul searching years following his giant hit, and realizing the landscape of country music was changing, in part due to the rising popularity of the newer, softer, less twangy, "Nashville sound," Sonny realized he needed to find a way adapt to the trend. What he found... rather WHO he found, would create and provide the background vocals that he would later refer to as "an identifiable sound" that helped reinvent and propel his enormously successful "second career," while making country music history in the process.

Known to many as a consummate showman, Sonny also had the reputation of being somewhat of a perfectionist. For example, in order to insure the rich, mellow tones of his classic Martin D-28 guitar that was so recognizable, he went to the extreme measure of changing its strings before every performance. That's right, he changed them before EVERY performance...EVERY time! That striving for perfection would eventually lead him to find the men who would help provide the change he was searching for, and in doing so establish the sound that would become his trademark. There is no doubt in my mind the leader of that group, Gary Robble, knew Sonny as well as, if not better than anyone, and that every word he has written in the following chapters comes from his respect and admiration for the man. In addition to providing insights about Sonny's career, he also offers unique "inside" glimpses at the often perceived glamorous, but sometimes not so glamorous, account of life while traveling the roads across the United States and Canada.

Although I grew up in Tullahoma, Tennessee, both sides of my family are from, and I was born in Hamilton, Alabama, about twelve miles southwest of the place Sonny loved most ... his hometown, Hackleburg. My first exposure to his music occurred during a trip back to Hamilton in 1965. While overhearing his second #1 hit, "You're The Only World I Know," as it played on my uncle Kenneth Jeffreys' stereo turntable, something about the music coming through his hi-fi speakers caught my ear and I became an instant fan. I vividly remember my family's conversation that night focusing not only about his music, but also about the type of person Sonny James was. He was known as "the boy from just up the road" who had been very successful, but had not let his popularity negatively affect him. There also was a bit of a family connection because my uncles Kenneth and Leon, along with many other men from the Marion County area, had served in the same Alabama National Guard unit with Sonny and were deployed together during the Korean War, in 1950.

Years earlier, at age thirteen, my mother first saw Sonny perform at the local county fair when he was only eight years old. Singing with his parents, Mom and Pop Loden, along with his sister, Thelma, their act was known then as "Sonny Boy and The Loden Family." Sonny's makeshift "stage" that night was the dusty wooden boards of a flatbed farm wagon. Who would have thought then that he would go on to have a stellar country music career, and how could that young teenage girl have imagined that seventy-seven years later she would receive an amazing surprise from him, on her 90th birthday?

My family also had a somewhat comical connection to Sonny, one that involved a vehicle. Sometime during the late 1930s my grandfather, Earlie Jeffreys, purchased a "well used" car in Hamilton. After returning home, and while showing it to my grandmother Nell, the sun's rays hit the side of the door panels at just the right angle. To their surprise, faded white letters spelling "Sonny Boy and The Loden Family" bled through the dull black paint! It had obviously been owned by Pop Loden at one time, and used for their travels to performances around the southeast. It always remained a funny family story, one that my grandmother never let my grandfather live down!

After hearing Sonny's music, and a little about him personally, I became interested in finding out more about him and the other men singing with him. In those days my friends were listening to their favorite artists and bands such as The Beatles, Elvis, The Supremes, The Beach Boys, or The Rolling Stones, and had the advantage of being able to actually see them perform from time to time on one of the three major television networks. On the other hand, although Sonny's songs were getting airplay around the country provided in part by Hall of Fame disc jockeys such as Joe Rumore at WVOK in Birmingham, Ralph Emery on his all night show at WSM in Nashville, and Terry Burford at KFDI in Wichita, Kansas, there were very few television programs showcasing country artists ... one reason why I had never actually gotten to see Sonny. An exception was the National Life & Casualty Insurance Company sponsored *Grand Ole Opry*, a 30 minute television program emceed by Jud Collins. It was on that show, which aired the night of June 18, 1965, that I first saw Sonny James perform, as he and his vocal group, The Southern Gentlemen, sang his most famous hit, "Young Love." Finally, there were faces to go along with his music!

I couldn't put my finger on one specific thing that intrigued me as I watched his performance from the stage of the historic Ryman Auditorium that night, because actually it turned out to be more than just one. As he sang, Sonny sat front and center on a stool holding his classic guitar with the letters S O N N Y spelling his name diagonally across its face, while his backup singers crowded in closely behind, without instruments. At that time most country artists were primarily solo performers who stood alone at a microphone, with their band, usually consisting of a fiddle, rhythm, electric, steel guitar, and a standup bass situated in the background, while harmony, if any, was supplied by a single band member occasionally stepping in to help. So what I saw and heard during Sonny's performance that night was something different … very different. Many others realized it too, and that fresh new sound would soon dominate the country charts for years to come. In fact, from 1967 to 1971 Sonny would have sixteen consecutive Billboard #1 hits. Think about it, folks … SIXTEEN #1's in a row!

At this point I need to take a minute and shine the spotlight on Gary Robble. In one of his chapters he will tell how he began his career with Sonny after being approached by him backstage between Opry performances at the Ryman Auditorium. Recognizing the talent of The Chordsmen, a quartet Gary was performing with there that night, Sonny envisioned blending their harmonies with his in order to create a new, unique sound. After a brief "interview," which lasted no longer than five minutes, a win-win agreement was consummated without the need of an agent, manager, or signatures on a legally binding con-tract...just a firm handshake. The firsthand story he told me about that meeting is not only remarkable, but is another example of being at the right place at the right time.

During the following seven years Sonny and his vocal group would travel hundreds of thousands of miles together in a thirty-five foot long, diesel powered, 1964 model Flxible tour bus. In those days before most interstate highways had been completed, they traveled mostly on two lane roads in order to reach venues ranging as far as southern California to Nova Scotia, and from Miami to the northwestern prov-inces of Canada. And yes, it's true that one of those shows really was located, as one of Sonny's biggest hits indicated … just a little bit south of Saskatoon!

In June, 1971, after years on the road, having sung on 180 recordings, 1,500 live performances, and at the height of Sonny's career, this close knit band of brothers peeled away and embarked on new careers in the "real world." Gary chose to start his own insurance business, having no idea that one day years in the future he would once again be teamed up with Sonny.

After a hit-filled decade, by the mid-1970s Sonny's music began to disappear from country radio playlists, and except for his occasional guest appearances on *Hee Haw*, and autograph signings at Fan Fair, he began to fade into obscurity. It was though the industry had simply forgotten him. I had long given up on the possibility of ever meeting him, and to be quite honest, had decided I wouldn't want to even if the opportunity presented itself. I had formed my opinion about the man based on things I had heard over the years, so why would I want to do anything to find out differently? What a huge disappointment it would be if I found out he was not in "real life" the way I had always perceived him to be. What if I were to meet him and he turned out to be rude or standoffish? I had heard stories of people finally getting to meet athletes or other celebrities they had long admired, only to be very disappointed after doing so. Well, there was no reason for me to be concerned about that because there was just no way I would ever have a chance to meet him. Or was there?

Fast forward to Wednesday, August 30, 2006. It was on that day the Country Music Hall of Fame announced Sonny had been selected, along with George Strait and legendary recording session guitarist Harold Bradley, to become its newest inductees. Immediately, I began trying to find as much information about the upcoming ceremony as possible. Turning to the internet, a quick Google search revealed the official induction would take place a few weeks later during the *Country Music Association Awards Show*, on the night of November 6, at The Grand Ole Opry House, only a short distance from Sonny's Nashville home. Interestingly, Sonny had co-hosted the very first *CMA Awards Show* thirty-five years earlier, sharing the podium that October night in 1967 with Bobbie Gentry, singer of her then-current Billboard hit, "Ode to Billy Joe." I knew the induction was much deserved and long, long overdue, coming some twenty-three years after his final performance, and knew how much the honor would mean to him, but I had no way of knowing how much the events surrounding it would eventually affect my life!

Eager for more information, the next night another Google search led me to a site that would allow me to be introduced to some very special people. There was someone in Alabaster, Alabama, who claimed to be just as big a Sonny James fan, and like myself, had been for over forty years. His name was Terry Dillard, and the information on his website indicated he was the host of an internet radio show ... whatever that was, and his guest for his next show was Gary Robble, one of Sonny's Southern Gentlemen backup singers. Realizing I would never have another chance to hear his first-hand experiences about time spent with Sonny, I knew what I had to do, but there were two glaring problems. First, I had absolutely no clue how to find the program, and second, it was scheduled to begin in less than thirty minutes! With my very limited computer skills, I frantically searched the internet once again, hoping to find a way to access the webcast. Luckily, after several minutes, I stumbled across what appeared to be a link to the show. Excitedly, I clicked on it, but nothing happened. Just my luck! Frustrated to have come so close, I assumed I would miss the interview, but just as I was about to give up Terry's voice came through my computer speakers as he began to welcome Gary to the show!

As he began the interview, Terry invited his listeners to email him their questions about Sonny. He, in turn, would direct them to Gary, who was linked to the show from his home, just outside Nashville. Taking advantage of the format, I submitted several, wondering if they had any chance of actually being chosen—and to my surprise, they were! Without telling Terry beforehand, Gary had conspired with fellow Southern Gentleman Glenn Huggins to also call in and join the show from his home in Greely, Colorado. "Huggins," as he was known to those close to him, had provided the deep bass "umba unga" background vocals so recognizable on Sonny's classic #1 hit,

"Running Bear," from 1969. As Terry read each question, Gary and Huggins answered in great detail, and both genuinely seemed to have fun doing so. The hour passed much too quickly! Terry was an excellent host, and his two special guests left no doubt in anyone's mind about the mutual respect they both felt for the friend they had performed and traveled with.

Sometimes incredibly good things can happen to us just by being at the right place at the right time, and by the conclusion of Terry's webcast, I felt very lucky to have found him and his show. Gary and Huggins were the real deal and my good fortune had allowed me to interact with two people I had watched and listened to for almost fifty years. Plus … and this is a big plus … it had shed some very positive light on some of my questions about the "real" Sonny James. The friendships born over our computers that night would soon lead to some very amazing things for everyone involved, and would eventually provide me the answers to all my questions.

One night early the next week my home telephone rang and as I glanced at the caller ID screen, I was surprised to see it was Gary Robble calling! With Terry Dillard's help, he had gone to the trouble of finding my phone number and where I lived. The sole purpose of his call was to thank me for listening and submitting my questions during the interview, and to tell me how much he and Huggins enjoyed answering them. He was thanking me, when actually, I should have been thanking him! Taking advantage of this second unexpected opportunity, I started asking Gary more questions, and over the next two hours I began to find more and more things about Sonny. Without realizing it, Gary's words were reinforcing my opinion of him, but still there was that little shred of doubt.

The selection of Sonny to the Hall of Fame was announced by Kris Kristofferson during the CMA telecast in late October; however, his official induction would not take place until six months later. Meanwhile, Gary and I continued to communicate regularly, with him always patiently taking time to answer my constant barrage of questions. To my surprise, one of the most interesting things I learned was that none of the group, including Sonny, ever totally realized the full significance of what they had been part of. According to him, they were all just doing what they had always done, and in a business where money and fame are so often the motivation, they simply loved singing, harmonizing, and performing … things they had done many times in the past for free. When I asked Gary what it was like being famous and traveling across America in a tour bus while song after song after song reached #1, he said "We really never thought about it that way. Then, when we were off the road for a few days, we were just regular guys, all happy to get back home." That was not the answer I was expecting, and I quickly learned Gary not only did not realize it back then, he was still oblivious all these years later! Terry and I couldn't understand why, but we were determined to open his eyes!

As time grew closer to the induction ceremony, Gary, Terry, and I continued with our many emails and telephone conversations. None of us had ever met in person, but we were beginning to feel as though we had known each other for years. We had mentioned several times that it would be great if we ever had the chance to meet in person, and now the perfect time had presented itself … the weekend of the Hall of Fame induction. Living just outside Nashville, Gary would be hosting and coordinating some of the events during those hectic few days and graciously invited us to town. Gladly accepting, plans were made for Terry and his wife, Fredia, along with my wife, Marissa, and I to meet him and Huggins for breakfast at The Loveless Café on Saturday morning, the day before the induction. During a telephone conversation Terry and I had a day or so before the trip, once again we both were sharing a familiar concern. We were about to meet two men who sang with Sonny for years and had played such an important part of his career. What if we had been wrong about them, too? If so, that sure would make for a very uncomfortable breakfast! Oh well, we were about to find out!

On a beautiful Middle Tennessee spring morning, everyone arrived at the restaurant, and immediately Terry and I both knew we had nothing to worry about. As soon as we all met it became obvious the friendships initiated from the font characters on our respective computers had now seamlessly changed to real-life characters who were joking, laughing, and becoming the loudest table in the crowded restaurant. It really did feel like we had known each other for years, and before we knew it, two hours had passed and we had long finished our breakfasts.

Just as we were finishing our last extra cups of coffee, Gary told us about a free perk (no pun intended) he had arranged for us. In those days the Hall of Fame offered free complimentary passes for members and their guests, and we were being invited! We quickly learned that in Nashville, knowing people connected to the music business certainly had its privileges. As we prepared to leave for the short fifteen-minute drive, Gary and Huggins had another surprise for us. During a dinner the previous night, Sonny overheard Gary mention we were all meeting for breakfast the next morning. Understanding we were coming to town to celebrate his induction, he did something very special. Incredibly, during the busy weekend that was so meaningful to him, he had taken time to autograph some gifts just for us! Little by little we were confirming our thoughts about who Sonny James really was.

Sonny's musical journey that began at age four when his father converted a used molasses bucket into a stringed "instrument" was now, almost eighty years later, about to culminate with his induction into the Country Music Hall of Fame. There were many stops along the way in places very familiar to those who followed their favorite artists of his era … places like the Big D Jamboree, in Dallas, Texas; The Ozark Jubilee, in Springfield, Missouri; and the Louisiana Hayride, in Shreveport. While so many talented artists were searching for something "magical", or a big break that would lead them to their goal of performing on The Grand Ole Opry, I think it is ironic that's exactly where Sonny was when he found his. The magical "something" he found backstage that hot August night in 1964 would not only change his career, but also his life and the lives of each of the men who would become his vocal group, The Southern Gentlemen.

Together they reached the pinnacle of their musical profession, and the next day would be a very special one for each of them.

******

The day of the induction was sunny and unusually warm in Nashville. With the temperature reaching into the mid-80s, the concrete walkway leading up to the entrance got very warm during the three-hour wait, but none of us were complaining. About an hour before the first guests and honorees were to arrive the traditional red carpet was rolled out and barricade rails installed. The rails were designed for crowd control, yet close enough to allow fans to obtain autographs. Right on schedule, limousines carrying current and future members started arriving, and as the celebrities exited the vehicles, each was introduced. Then they proceeded up the red carpet while being applauded by fans on both sides of the walkway. Legendary stars such as George Jones, Randy Owen, Porter Wagoner, and George Strait each stopped to sign hats, shirts, magazines, and even a guitar belonging to one lucky fan!

Finally, the black stretch limo we had waited for arrived. The door opened, and out stepped Sonny, his wife Doris, his sister Thelma, and some other very special guests. After traveling all those miles together, Sonny had invited his Southern Gentlemen to join him for one last trip, this one to 222 5th Avenue South, home of the Country Music Hall of Fame, only a few short blocks from where they first met forty-three years earlier! Sharing the honor with those who had been so instrumental to his success, Sonny insisted they all walk the ceremonial red carpet just as they had always performed. TOGETHER!

After almost fifty years of listening to his music, I was now close enough not only to see Sonny James in person, but also close enough to hear him speak as he chatted with the Hall dignitaries who welcomed him. Then, the most amazing thing happened. As he started to make his way up the red carpet, Sonny suddenly turned to his right, went around the barricades, and made his way to the surprised but appreciative fans! Making his way toward the television reporters at the top of the steps, he took time to acknowledge everyone who had been waiting and shook our hands. How special it was, after so many years, to have that experience, and have it happen as he was about to enter the Hall of Fame!

When Sonny retired from performing in the early '80s, he did so with no fanfare. There was no press release, no good-bye tour, just one final show somewhere hundreds of miles away and then one last bus ride back home, this time with an old trusted friend sitting silently at his side. On the seat next to him, a road-weary case contained his famous Martin guitar, by then with one of the letters missing that once spelled its proud owner's name. And unlike hundreds of times before, Sonny had not restrung it in preparation for the next show. Both understood there was no need. The illustrious performing career that began so long ago back in Hackleburg when he was barely kinder-garten age, was over.

Thirty-two years passed, and although fully retired and spending much of his time out of the public eye, Sonny had definitely not been forgotten by his fans or others in the music business. Although he maintained an office near Music Row for business purposes, he had no staff, which required him, along with Doris' help, to respond to requests for things such as autographs, interviews, and general fan mail. Meanwhile, Gary's insurance agency had been very successful, and when Sonny happened to contact him about a project he was working on, without being asked, he once again stepped in to offer Sonny his "back-up" skills. This new chore did not require harmo-nizing, loading and unloading sound equipment, driving a tour bus hundreds of miles at a stretch, or selling records to fans after personal appearances as his old job had, but this one was equally important. As a trusted, long-time friend, Gary not only understood the need, but more importantly, he knew without a doubt *how* Sonny wanted such things handled. In addition, Sonny also knew the confidence he had placed in Gary that night long ago at the Ryman Auditorium had never, nor would ever, be compromised. So the new "position" was filled, and unlike last time, without even a handshake. Once a Southern Gentleman, always one, so Sonny knew Gary Robble was the perfect person for the job!

Now here's when things really started to get interesting. As Memorial Day 2009 approached, Gary was looking forward to the group's reunion, a tradition which began in 1989. Getting together every five years, this one was to be even more special because Gary and his wife, Thelma, would be hosting everyone for a private dinner at their home, and from our recent conversations, it was obvious Gary was excited because everyone would be there. Gary and I usually spoke by phone during evenings, so I thought it a little unusual when I received a call from him at work on Wednesday morning, two days before the special event. I could tell he was looking forward to it when we talked about the upcoming weekend for a few minutes, when suddenly, and in an almost nonchalant manner he said, "You know, Thelma and I are having Sonny, Doris, and the guys over here Friday afternoon, and we were wondering if you and Marissa would like to join us?" After almost dropping the phone, I quickly accepted Gary's invitation before he could change his mind!

Gary made the same call to Terry, and immediately the four of us started making plans for the trip. Realizing the reunion only happened every five years, and not wanting to impose on their limited time together, we came up with an idea. Everyone was supposed to drop by early in the afternoon for dinner, except Sonny and Doris who planned to arrive at 5:00. Our plan was to meet in Nashville at noon, stop at a bakery and pick up a cake for them to have later for dessert, arrive at the Robble's at 2:00, spend time with everyone, and finally, meet Sonny and Doris. To insure we would not be imposing, we included a very important part of our plan. Whenever dinner was almost ready, a prearranged signal would be our cue to excuse ourselves, leaving the remainder of the evening for our hosts to enjoy their special time together.

With our plan in place we drove to Gary's and were immediately treated to an unexpected surprise. Milo Liggett, Sonny's long-time friend, bass player, and prolific songwriter, was singing some of his original songs, while Gary, Lin, and Huggins harmonized with him. What amazing talent, and what a thrill to have The Southern Gentlemen performing just for us! Time flew, and before we knew it Sonny and Doris were due to arrive. I was nervous about meeting him because of *who* he was, but even more apprehensive about finding out *what* he was. Once again … what if I had been wrong? Well, I was about to find out because I glanced out a living room window and saw Sonny's white SUV, with an American flag decal on the driver's door, turn into Gary's driveway!

After parking behind the house, Sonny made his way up the multi-level steps to the top of the deck, and entered through a back door. Our wives were in the kitchen helping Thelma when Marissa got a big surprise. With her back to the door, hearing footsteps approaching, she turned around and found herself face-to-face with a tall man carrying a large container of barbecue! Realizing he had stunned her, and before she could speak, with a big grin he said, "Hi there, I'm Sonny!" That warm, friendly introduction broke the ice, and the two of them became instant friends. I had waited almost fifty years to meet Sonny James, and my lovely wife had just beaten me to it!

After a few minutes, Sonny and Doris made their way through the house to the living room. After Gary introduced them to Terry and Fredia, finally it was my turn. As soon as we shook hands and said our hellos, I knew I had not been wrong about him. Even though the room was full of his long-time friends, some of whom he had not seen in several years, he and Doris made me feel like I was the only other person present. As if he knew the situation might cause me to be a little nervous, he immediately reversed it and made the moment about *me*, not about *him*. When introducing us, Gary had mentioned my family was from Hamilton, so he started asking me questions about them, leaning toward me so he could hear my responses over all the other conversations. His attention was centered on me, and he and Doris put me totally at ease.

Also included in our plans was something else that was very

important to Terry. He brought along his own Martin guitar, one his father had given him years ago. As a teenager, he learned to play Sonny's songs on it while listening to them on the radio and playing his records, and he hoped to get Sonny and each of The Gents to autograph it. So at just the right moment, Terry approached Sonny, guitar case in hand, and asked if he would do the honor. Carefully, Sonny removed the instrument, took an ever-present pick from his pocket, positioned himself on a kitchen stool, just as had done during that 1965 Ryman Auditorium performance, and with a broad smile masterfully played a few bars. Making sure that special moment was captured, I snapped pictures of the three of them: Sonny, Terry, and Terry's now priceless possession! Later, when he returned it to the case, it certainly was one of a kind, its face bearing five very special signatures!

As the afternoon passed, everyone was having a wonderful time, especially Terry and myself. Both of us had met Sonny, and Terry not only had his musical hero's signature on his guitar, but he also had the unforgettable memory of watching and hearing Sonny play it. I remember thinking our day couldn't have turned out any better, but I was wrong! As the dinner announcement was made, just as planned, we started gathering our things to leave. Seeing that, Sonny and Doris nearly in unison said "Y'all can't leave now! Dinner is almost ready, and we want you to stay and eat with us." It was an unexpected surprise and one we weren't about to refuse.

While final preparations were being made for the meal, I felt someone tap my shoulder. Sonny wanted to continue our conversation, especially wanting to know more about my family in Hamilton, and while we were talking the most incredible thing happened. Terry had his unforgettable memory with Sonny and now I was about to experience mine! Gary announced dinner was ready and then asked Sonny if he would ask the blessing. Asking everyone in the room to join hands, Sonny reached over and took mine as he began to pray. I vividly remember that his prayer was humble and sincere, and his words seemed to touch everyone present. That was a moment I will remember the rest of my life, and right then I knew who Sonny James was, and I had not been wrong about him!

During dinner we were treated to hearing funny "road stories" from so many years ago, and it was obvious how much they still cared for each other. Time may have faded their memories of those days a bit, but all of us watching and listening had no doubt they would loved to have jumped on a bus and headed out to headline one more show.

Finally, it was time for us to say our goodbyes and leave the remainder of the evening to our special friends. As we prepared to leave, Sonny quietly and hurriedly made his way back through the kitchen and out the back door. As we made our way back to our car, we had one more surprise awaiting. Sonny had slipped out to his SUV and had gifts for each of us! As each of us thanked him, I realized and mentioned we had forgotten to take any pictures of us with him. His immediate response was "Well, let's take some!" So once again, focusing all his attention on us, he patiently allowed all the time we needed, joking and laughing with us until we finished. As we left Gary's house that night each of us knew we had just been part of something very special … with some very special people!

A few weeks later I received another important call from Gary. He had just completed updating Sonny's sound system, and afterward Sonny asked him if he knew anyone who might be interested in the old speakers. Gary suggested me, and when he called to see if I wanted them I jumped at the once-in-a-lifetime offer! My friend Terry had his prized possession autographed by Sonny, now I would have mine … the old, but like new set of beautiful walnut paneled stereo speakers Sonny and Doris had used in their home for over three decades. After writing a personal note and autographing the back cover of one speaker with a silver Sharpie, Gary suggested he might want to sign the other. Taking his advice, Sonny wrote a funny note on it and also autographed it. Those speakers now sit in a prominent place in my home, just like Terry's guitar occupies a very special place in his. Later, after receiving my thank you note, Gary told me

Sonny had a big laugh when he read the part explaining the speakers sounded a little "muffled," because I have them facing the wall backward ... so visitors can see his signatures. Like Terry's guitar, my speakers are priceless!

As special as those things are, the most meaningful thing Sonny did for me was actually something he did for my mother, Nina McKay. As her ninetieth birthday approached in October, 2014, I thought of something to do for her, but it would require Gary and Sonny's help. The plan was simple: I would pick out the perfect birthday card and then have Gary hand deliver it to Sonny. Sonny would sign the card then Gary would return it to me. On her birthday, I would give her the card, without telling her who it was from. I called Gary to get his thoughts, and he immediately knew it would be something Sonny would enjoy doing. So after finding the card I thought Sonny would have chosen, I sent it to Gary, and the plan was in motion. A few days later Gary called to tell me about his "card signing" meeting with Sonny. Wanting to make sure everything was perfect, Sonny took several minutes thinking about just the right birthday message. Then he not only signed the card, but included his wishes for her on an autographed picture as well.

Gary returned the items to me and told me to be sure to let him know Mom's reaction. Realizing she would love the picture, I had it framed and gift wrapped. Now, the final part of the plan was all set ... or so I thought. After she opened what she thought were all her gifts on the night of her party, as our entire family watched, I handed her one more, only telling her it was from someone special. After unwrapping it and reading his birthday wish, she stared at the picture for several long seconds. Then, with an astonished look on her face she looked up at me and asked, "Is this from the real Sonny James?" Just as I assured her it was, I suddenly had the strange feeling of someone being behind me. Turning around, I had a big surprise, too! Gary had secretly arranged, with Marissa's assistance, to sneak in just in time to see Mom open her special gift. He had driven sixty-five miles to Tullahoma and parked outside until Marissa signaled him at precisely the right moment, to personally wish her a happy ninetieth birthday and surprise me on behalf of himself and Sonny!

We took several pictures of Mom that night and one very special one showed her holding the framed photograph Sonny had signed. After seeing it, Gary instantly had another idea. Knowing Sonny as well as he did, he said, "Don, you know Sonny has signed thousands and thousands of autographed pictures for fans, but he has never had a fan sign one for him!" As soon as he said that, we both knew what needed to be done. Using a silver Sharpie, I had Mom write a short thank you note on a lower left hand corner of one of the pictures and then "autograph" it. After identically framing it, I returned that special picture to Gary, so he could "redeliver" it! He took it to Sonny and Doris, placing it on a stand right next to their kitchen table. Doing so, he told them, "Now every morning when you wake up you'll have the best reason in the world to smile."

That's who Gary Robble is.

On February 25, 2016, I made the nearly three hour drive to Hackleburg High School, the place Sonny had chosen for his funeral. I arrived two hours before the service was to begin, and expecting to be the first car in the parking lot, I found I was mistaken. As I parked in a space next to an earlier arrival, I noticed the car's tags were from out of state, and glancing over, I saw an elderly gentleman motioning for me to roll my window down. After asking me if he was at the right place, he introduced himself and told me he had driven all night from his home in Florida in order to pay his respects to his favorite singer and guitarist, adding, "I just had to come." He said he had attended one of Sonny's shows many years earlier, and after it was over, like many others, he stood in a long line to meet him. His main purpose, he explained, was not to get an autograph, but to do something much more personal and important. When they were finally face-to-face they shook hands, and he told Sonny that he was the reason he had started playing guitar, and although he would never be able to afford an expensive Martin, still he hoped to be able to play like him some-day. With emotion in his voice, he then told me he had never forgotten

Sonny's response: "It doesn't matter how much or how little your guitar costs; it's true worth is determined by the amount of enjoyment you get from playing it."

A short time later, the parking lot began to fill, and as I made my way inside, my thoughts turned to the many nice people I had the privilege of meeting and becoming friends with because of our mutual respect for Sonny and his music. I had the honor of sitting with four of them during the service; Terry and Fredia Dillard, and Sonny's cousin, Ginger Chaudron, and her husband, Leon. Although never meeting in person until minutes before the service, Ginger and I had exchanged many, many emails, enabling me to learn so much about Sonny's early years growing up in Hackleburg. Without knowing her, I never would have enjoyed the honey Leon sent me after robbing his bee hives on their farm in Foley, Alabama. Another great gift! And had it not been for Terry's interview with Gary, none of us would have met and this amazing book might never have been written.

Since meeting Gary Robble twelve years ago, I am convinced he was Sonny's closest, most trusted friend, and understandably so. From all of our conversations, and there have been many, I have been privileged to learn things that not only increased my admiration and respect for Sonny, but for each of the men he respected most: his Southern Gentlemen brothers. Without doubt they supplied the wind for Sonny's sail. Sonny knew that, and proved it when he unprecedentedly asked them not only to accompany him to the Hall of Fame, but to also sing that evening at the Medallion Ceremony.

One sure way of finding out about a man's reputation is by talking to people in his hometown. Gary and I had the opportunity to visit Hackleburg and Hamilton recently and spent time with several of Sonny's long-time friends. What we found there was the same as everywhere else. The first reaction when his name is mentioned is not about his string of #1 hits, his star on the Hollywood Walk of Fame, or being a member of the Country Music Hall of Fame, but rather about the kind of person he was. After all the places his amazing career had taken him, once again, he was happiest when spending times with his family and friends in the place he loved most … his hometown, Hackleburg, Alabama.

That's exactly who Sonny James was.

Now it's your turn. Sit back and enjoy the story that nearly didn't happen: *The Account of Sonny James and The Southern Gentlemen.*

PROLOGUE

February 24, 2016

Sonny James and The Southern Gentlemen (Milo, Gary, Duane, Lin, and Glenn) together were like peas and carrots, biscuits and butter, turtle wax, and a '57 Chevy! Those two halves made a whole lot of legendary music and timeless memories. Sometimes you don't realize what you had until it's gone. I pray history recognizes the legacy. God speed, Sonny Boy!

Rick E. Hall *Fame Recording Studios*
Muscle Shoals, Alabama

Contents

Somewhere in the mystery of life, we arrive at a place where our eyes are able to adjust as the fog lifts and the shadows move, allowing the concealed things to become clear—where, as the haze clears, we finally can admit to what we could not see and see what we were not able to admit. The great revealer moves across our landscape, turning profiles into people and using what has been allotted to all of us: a precious limited supply of: *the hands of time.*

So having nothing to lose at this point, I can afford to tell the engaging truth as I see it, limited only by a clear conscience and a mindfulness of good taste.

CHAPTER 1

THE BOXED SET

"The obscure takes time to see, but the obvious takes longer."
—EDWARD R. MURROW, AN EARLY PIONEER
IN AMERICAN BROADCAST JOURNALISM.

History rides ahead on a gray stallion, waiting to decide where the hoofbeats of the past will lead. It's the selfless soul that can sense the impending outcome, who can rein himself in and change direction in order to rewrite the future.

It was the third Saturday night in August—August 15, 1964 to be exact—a date long forgotten by those that it affected, that is, until now. At that one brief moment in time, three pieces representing six people clicked effortlessly into place without any fanfare. Its effect on country music history has occupied a front seat in the shadows of time for all of these years.

On that night, something quite unconventional occurred: Sonny James, a thirty-six-year-old singer, whose career had been on a slow downslide for seven years, asked an acapella quartet of Yankee boys, average age of twenty-two, whose dreams had been going south, to join him and his thirty-year-old bass player whose good fortune was also on its way to evaporating. There must have been serious magic in the air at that moment because the gentleman from Alabama recognized the potential in this most implausible combination.

It's a new story. It's an unimaginable story that can only occur in one of life's wildest dreams. Inspired by Rick Hall's personally worded statement of condolences, as the spokesman for Sonny James' vocal group The Southern Gentlemen, I am about to document this improbable account for the very first time.

However, even though I decided to start our story going back to 1964, none of what I was intending to say would be relevant to anything unless I jumped ahead to 2002 to a most unexpected circumstance — not to a window that would allow us to see north and south or east and west. No, nothing quite as clear as that. For me, it would start at a most unusual place—in a CD boxed set. Yes, you heard it right—a boxed set— and it still seems unbelievable.

It was 2002, thirty-one years since the last of those college boys that started with Sonny in 1964 had performed "Young Love" with him for the final time in mid-1971. The former Southern Gentlemen (Lin, Gary, Duane, and Glenn) were into their next lives. When I left in 1971, Sonny's bass player, Milo Liggett, would stay on for another couple of years before their times together became just so many mental souvenirs.

As for me, I had started my own insurance business, and those music days had been locked away in a cabinet for some potentially far-off time. Over the years, I had given away all but one of the albums we had recorded with Sonny. The remaining one was the Astrodome album, with the vinyl disc looking like something my boys had used for a Frisbee while on a month's vacation (which, to be truthful, I think they had). At the time, my oldest son, Greg, born just three months before we had joined Sonny, was in his second career as a self-employed website developer. My middle son, Dale, was deep into his second life as the founding pastor of Highland Park Church here in Nashville. Our third and last son, Page, born just three months after we had left Sonny, had received his bachelor of science degree and as a CPA was working for Faulkner, Mackie, and Cochran, a public accounting firm also here in Nashville.

So here I was in early 2002, enjoying my insurance life far removed from the frenzied days of the music business when the phone rang. It was Sonny. I hadn't really kept up with his life much after moving on with mine; in fact, on a personal basis, I really didn't know very much about what was going on with him.

What was Sonny wanting in that call? Well, he was asking me to do him a simple favor, although I knew nothing with him was ever simple. Bear Family Records, an independent record label that specializes in reissuing vintage music in CD format, a company that I'd never heard of, was going to do a boxed set on Sonny that they were going to call *Young Love*. It would include CDs of all of the songs he had recorded from 1952 to 1962, along with what would turn out to be a sixty-eight page, 12 x 12 inch booklet that would have not only pictures of Sonny (sixty-nine in total) but also a biography. In June of 2002, after completion of the project, Bear Records, to my surprise, sent me a complimentary boxed set that they were selling for (best I remember) about $250, giving me credit on the set for my help. Though I didn't know it at that moment, my help turned out to be much more than my helping them—they had no idea how much my helping them was about to eventually turn my life around.

Sonny's call was to ask me to be the man in the middle between himself and Dave Samuelson, a writer from Indiana that Bear Records was using to write Sonny's first official bio. My involvement would be simple (he said with a smile). Dave would call Sonny and record an interview with him. Then Dave would type up a first draft and get it to Sonny for corrections. And here's where I was to come into that scene. Though Sonny understood performing and songwriting, guitars and fiddles, fishing and fishing poles—he didn't own, nor did he care to own a computer or fax machine. Samuelson would email me his Word document, and I would print it and then drive ten miles to drop it off at Sonny's place. Sonny would then spend time correcting it and then I would drive ten miles back over to Sonny's house, pick it up, bring it back to my place, scan it, and send it to Samuelson. Sonny and Samuelson and I went through that process five or six times before they got what Sonny considered his accurately finished biography.

I didn't pay very much attention to what was passing through my hands each time — I had a business to run and I thought I would probably catch the final product somewhere along the line anyway. So fast forward to June 2002 when, following the completion of the project, the boxed set arrived at my home. It was beautifully done, and even though our vocal group wasn't with Sonny during the years Bear Records was promoting, they used a number of pictures of us from the mid-60s, most of which were from our live performance in Phoenix, Arizona. Why, I asked myself, after Sonny had been retired for eighteen years was a company spending this amount of time and money on someone who hadn't recorded or performed since 1983? (This is excluding, as I later learned, the unfortunate 1986 MCA/Dot Records album release).

So I started playing the songs on the Bear CDs, 147 in all, songs I had never heard. Back in the mid-1950s, Sonny had recorded "For Rent," "'Til the Last Leaf Shall Fall," and "You're the Reason I'm in Love" —three songs that he would record again with us after we joined him in 1964, but in typical Sonny James fashion we were not aware, nor made aware that he had cut them some ten years before. (This is a statement that needs to be etched in your mind as we move along in this story.) When we joined Sonny there was no internet and no YouTube. In the beginning of our time with him, he didn't hand us a collection of his old recordings to listen to, nor did we run out and try to find a bunch of his old records in a record shop. When we went with Sonny James in 1964, there were no CD compilations for sale. In 1964 for us, outside of that clear, bright window, it was dark.

The boxed set lit a fuse. It made me realize that after all this time Sonny James hadn't been forgotten, so after spending some time in it I made a call to Sonny and then went by his house with one thought in mind—to thrust him into the electronic age.

With both of us being very efficient, if I said one o'clock, I was always there at one, and Sonny would always be waiting just inside the door in their time-capsule home. After the hug, we would mosey through the living room, passing by and off to the left an area that was always ready for Christmas. Then we would take a right into a spot adjacent to the kitchen where we usually met, spending many hours over the next years on a comfortable bench seat with our shoes sunk deep into shag carpet, just being what you might expect: two old friends carrying on and laughing as we shared old road stories that made us young men again, if only for just a couple of hours.

In an interview Sonny gave in 2001 to Walt Trott of *Country Music Magazine* he said:

> We've had the same house for twenty-five years. If you come to see me, you'd never know I was in the music business. Don't get me wrong: I appreciate beautiful things, but our home is livable and our friends are everyday people that we know.

But on this day, I was in their home for a different reason—technology. The no-computer, no-fax machine world Sonny lived in was about to be earthquaked to pieces. The first tremor of the earthquake was explaining "internet" and "website"—keeping it as uncomplicated as I could for him. For me, back in 1985, I had purchased a computer language and developed all the programs that ran our business, ultimately becoming twenty-six different integrated databases, calculating as best I could that I had spent over 7,000 hours just writing the programs. For the next couple of hours it was to be Q&A—Sonny was the Q's, and I was the A's, and there were a lot of them.

Enter my oldest son, Greg, who had been born just three months before we joined Sonny. Greg had spent his early adult life primarily working for tour production manager, Jake Berry. When Greg left the road to get married and start a family of his own, he moved rapidly into computers, writing programs and then ultimately setting up his own website development and hosting company. So the next transition was strikingly obvious—get Greg and Sonny together to let Sonny see technology in action from someone who understood avenues of the music business beyond his own comprehension.

So here was Greg sitting with Sonny, trying to explain the reach and importance of the internet and websites and how they work to a man who had absolutely no understanding of the internet and everything else that went along with it. Immediately they started working together on the website that became www.sonnyjames.com, which would go online about a year later on August 6, 2003. But between those two dates were two men working closely with each other, two men who are at entirely opposite ends of the technology spectrum, and thirty-six years apart in age.

Rather than Greg leading the way, Sonny grabbed the bull by the horns and set off with his own thoughts, leading to the second rattle of the earthquake. Sonny got a 2 ft. by 3 ft., what Greg referred to as the "big book," and went at it. He scotch-taped selected pictures in the big book, adding captions typed out by his wife, Doris, identifying each. Particular as he was, it had to be just the way Sonny envisioned it, but Sonny's vision, as you might imagine, was based on old-school shaggy carpet concepts.

When he finally got what he wanted in that "big book," Sonny and Greg got together for the moment of truth. "Here's how I want it, Greg." "Well, Sonny, it works really well in your 'big book' but we have to go by the format that regulates websites." Sonny, never one to be deterred by mere elements of speech, pushed ahead as if it was only a simple word obstacle that could somehow, just by willing it so, be easily overcome.

After a few tough concessions, everything was finished and online. It only took about four months before Sonny was hearing some positive news about the number of visitors going to his website, and he was audibly surprised by it. There were so many people whose lives his music and touring had been a part of, and a great many of those same folks were still very interested in him. In retrospect, this seemed to give Sonny a renewed sense of fulfillment in his later years and the confidence to once again see himself as others saw him—the successful but enormously modest entertainer he had always been known to be. That is because Sonny, after all these years, was still Sonny, and that was something people just seemed to enjoy.

It was at this point that I seriously started to read the bio and incredibly, I didn't know but just a few bits of it. Sonny hadn't talked much at all about all the things that he and Samuelson had written. I hope you get the picture — on a table at my house in a boxed set called *Young Love* was a Sonny James *I literally knew nothing about.*

So you have to ask yourself, as I have asked myself many times since 2002, how can this be? I traveled with him for seven years at the height of his popularity, logging hundreds of thousands of miles together on the road, performed about 1,500 shows; and recorded 184 songs. How could I have known no more about Sonny James than I knew about my great-great grandfather?

I accepted Rick Hall's words as a challenge. I was determined to research everything I could find in order to properly document Sonny James' legacy.

TERRY BURFORD SNIPPET

As you know Sonny James and Doris sent very unique Christmas cards with the picture of the two of them on the front, and they sent them to members of the media and to radio stations. This had gone on for years but in the late '70s everyone at country giant KFDI in Wichita, Kansas, received their Christmas card, and I didn't. I just thought it was an oversight, but I did mention on the air that I did not get my usual card from them. So, the ranch hands at the station began mentioning it on their shows—well, that was about all that happened that first year. But then when I didn't get one the next year, I mentioned it again on the air. Well the cards started coming in: "Merry Christmas, Terry." Our listeners took it upon themselves to send and then sign them Sonny James (I didn't know Sonny could sign his name so many different ways). From that point on this became the running joke at Christmas when I continued to not get my card.

So one Christmas, this card shows up in our mailbox at home from

Sonny. It was addressed to my wife, and it said, "Merry Christmas, Joye, and tell ole what's his name I said hi"—and it was signed Sonny James.

Well, the next year, their card came, showing Sonny and Doris sitting outside their home roasting marshmallows. So I took it and inserted my picture on it, so you can see me standing outside the family circle. I showed it to all the ranch hands and, of course, they did not believe it was real. We had fun with that one. I never went anywhere in our listening area around Christmas time that the first thing I was asked was: did I get my card from Sonny. It was a running joke that went on for years—a Christmas card from Sonny, addressed to my wife, telling her to say hi to ole what's his name.

TERRY BURFORD — *Magnolia, Arkansas*
(Hall of Fame Country Music DJ at KZHE)

Now I, Gary, will tell the "rest of the story" as Paul Harvey would say:

Life had taken its toll, and 2014 would be the last year Sonny would send out his highly-anticipated, personally signed Christmas cards, and he was a bit down about it. I got to thinking and came up with an idea that might turn the tide — I knew where we could get a 2 ft. by 3 ft. tall Christmas card, and knowing the story about Sonny, Terry, and Joye, I ordered it.

When I took it by Sonny's, he was all excited and thought about what he wanted to write. He went to a kitchen cabinet and pulled out a brown paper bag and began to practice writing in big letters. After a bit, practice having been completed, came the big-letter moment of truth, "Making up for forty years" followed by the largest autograph Sonny James had ever signed. Terry told me the card now occupies a place of honor in their home — the last Christmas card Sonny would send.

CHAPTER 2

SPLITTIN' THE DIFFERENCE

"What chance combination of shadow and sound
and his own thoughts had created it?"
—Patricia Highsmith

Rick's six words, "I pray history recognizes the legacy," would quickly take me to a place I had never even thought about, in fact, to a place that I didn't even know existed.

The reason why I knew so little about who Sonny really was, how and why he thought as he did, and why all of us Southern Gentlemen had such a sketchy understanding of him—hear me here—was because as time went along, he treated us like more than friends.

I knew, as I moved along in my writing, that this chapter would need to be someplace in the book. I struggled with that thought a lot, and finally decided that it needed to be right near the beginning, so here it is as the second chapter. If it wasn't up front there would be so much I would have to repeat over and over to clarify what I meant when I said, "I didn't know much."

American poet and writer Carl Sandburg (01/06/1878 — 07/22/1967), probably best known for his biography of Abraham

Lincoln, which I had read during my high school years back in the late '50s, wrote a line that has stood the test of time: *"Nothing happens unless first a dream."* But when you find yourself in the place where I was at that moment, the initial dream that Sonny James might have had years before was something I would have to backtrack into; not the dream of a career, but a vision of how he would handle his life and how he would present himself throughout it. Let me explain in the best way I can. The footprints left on the sands of time tell us more about ourselves than the dreams for tomorrow we fashion in our minds.

Follow me if you will, as we start with the most recent impressions, retracing them along their trail. There's a certain word that will stand out in the illustrations that will be placed here. It's an important word, and it will present us with an opportunity right up front that will prepare us to better understand Sonny James. So let's step into a footprint he left a few years back.

While researching for this book I came across author Peter Henriques presenting his thoughts on the biography *Realistic Visionary: A Portrait of George Washington* that was published in 2008. Henriques stated that when Washington wrote letters, he would address them for example as: "Sir, Dear Sir, My Dear Sir." Said he, "You had to be a really close friend of Washington's to be addressed as 'My Dear Sir.'"

Hanging on my office wall, just to my right is the last likeness that Sonny had decided to use if fans and admirers were to ask him for an autographed picture. If fact, in a box just to my left are the last seventy-five of those pictures — given to me by Sonny's niece and nephew, Donna and Chuck, to distribute to any fans desiring some piece of Sonny James memorabilia. The picture hanging on my wall was not a picture I requested, or even expected. Sonny knew, because I had told him on many occasions, that I probably had more Sonny James stuff than anyone alive. After the boxed set had arrived at my door and the website went online, I set out on a mission to get my hands on anything and everything Sonny James. And I succeeded; I mean, I *really* succeeded.

On that particular day when I went by to visit, out of the blue, Sonny said, "I've got something for you." Now maybe at age eighty-three, he realized his remaining days were slipping away, or possibly he wanted to relate a very personal message to me that he had never expressed before — I don't know his reason, and I won't even attempt a guess. But whatever it was, he handed me one of those pictures. In the lower right corner and written in his own hand was this: "Gary, Thelma—Part of our family."

I am certain that there are stacks of pictures Sonny signed over the years. Sonny, as I became aware in my research, had developed this graduated scale when referring to people he knew. You could be a "new friend," "a friend," a "good friend," a "dear friend," or a "close friend." On occasion I have come across other designations such as "a special person" and the like. As this became clearer to me I couldn't help but wonder what his criteria were for moving folks along in that personalized sequence — I am sure nobody other than Sonny would know, and as I would learn over and over about so many things in his life: *it would remain only his to know.*

If he moved you into one of those personalized niches, you would never know if you had joined a select group of a hundred or a handful. But once he promoted you into one of those special categories, there was one thing you could be assured of — you would not be privy to discuss the professional side of Sonny James with him. He drew a line in the sand he would not allow you to cross, a line that kept you from seeing into his professional life. He would no longer want to be Sonny James to you; he would prefer to be just Sonny or "Son" as I called him, and occasionally, he would return the favor by giving you some personal designation.

One person who was special to Sonny was Margie Bowes Wilburn, the widow of Doyle Wilburn of the Wilburn Brothers. She was one of the youngest female artists to become a member of The Grand Ole Opry, joining in the late '50s. She had a number of country-charted hits, but her career was cut short when she was involved in a serious automobile accident.

I first met Margie in person in 2016. She and I had talked on the phone a couple of times before that when she called to ask me if it was OK to go by and visit with Sonny and Doris — she had that much respect for them. I cleared her request with Sonny, something she didn't need to do, but that was Margie; she would never have thought of just barging in on him unannounced. That's where our relationship started and continues to this day. She must have been special to Sonny because she told me he had tagged her as "Little Marge." That tradition has remained steady to this day because that's what I call her.

Tracking back further down that road, we come to a moment on May 6, 2007. Sonny, The Southern Gentlemen, and Milo had walked the red carpet together at the Country Music Hall of Fame on their way into the Ford Theatre, where Sonny, along with guitarist Harold Bradley and singer George Strait, would be inducted officially as the newest members. When the four songs Sonny had chosen had been sung by Vince Gill, Connie Smith, Ray Stevens, and Randy Owen, with The Southern Gentlemen supplying the vocal background on all four, and the medallion had been placed around Sonny's neck by his long-time fishing friend Porter Wagoner, Sonny stepped up to the microphone and spoke. After a few minutes reading from some care-fully-chosen remarks, he put the note away, looked over at us sitting just off to his right, pointed, and with a rare display of emotion, said, and I quote: "My Southern Gentlemen: they're super. They came up with a sound for me … that's the deep sound that you hear on all of my records. I know it sounds simple, but it was an identifying thing. I told them at the start, I said, 'Guys, we've got this group together and we've got a good sound, but we are friends first. And that's the way that it started. And today we're closer, we really are.'"

As I have mentioned, Sonny's scale seemed to begin at the "friend" level, and that's where he put us at the beginning. Those terms of endearment were very private places Sonny had developed, and only he knew why he had placed you there. I really feel quite secure in thinking that nobody really gave it a whole lot of thought when he referred to them in his own special way, I know I didn't — but of this

I am quite sure — *Sonny did.*

Now I never really thought about the graduated concept he had developed, but it was just his way. And there's one thing that really began to surface as 1 + 1 started coming together, one thing I hadn't ever identified as I started looking back to our time with him from 1964-1971, and even at the five reunions we would have starting in 1989, Sonny never let us see into his professional life. Let me try to explain without being the least bit critical or disparaging in any way. Here's a few examples:

- When we did the Ed Sullivan show for the first time in 1969, and Michael Jackson came into Sonny's dressing room to introduce himself, Sonny never called us in to meet Michael — in fact he didn't tell us about the incident until years later at one of our reunions.

- When Stuart Roosa, command module pilot of Apollo 14, came to a show in Houston, Texas, to present Sonny with an American flag that he, along with Alan Shepard and Edgar Mitchell, had carried on their flight to the moon in February 1971, Sonny never invited us to join him to meet Stuart, and never told us about it until years later. When Sonny did interviews, he never invited us to join in. In fact, in the seven years we were with him, we were never interviewed by anyone.

- When a dignitary or well-known sports figure came backstage to one of our shows, we were not made aware or were ever invited to be in on the conversation, nor were we ever introduced to them.

These examples are just facts, not complaints in any way.

Now don't gasp. We were not aware at the time that all these folks were meeting Sonny, which meant we never felt left out. It wasn't until years later that we became apprised of all of that. And it was at that point, starting at the reunions, that Sonny occasionally let a few of those long-hidden private things slip out. And it was then that the questioning in our minds was piqued — what was that secrecy all about, and why had Sonny not invited us in?

You see, we all are who we are, and to Sonny James, each one of us meant something very special to him even if we didn't realize it. There was this unknown disclaimer that came along with it - Sonny's professional life would be just out of reach to you. From our, that is from The Southern Gentlemen's standpoint, Sonny didn't want us to be looking up to him as anything special — he just wanted to be one of us. When he went back to his hometown he just wanted to be part of the Hackleburg family — not Sonny James the Country Music Star. It wasn't until I made the decision to write this book that my research started to uncover information about who he was and why he was what he was that my understanding of him became clearer. One of our research gurus, Long Islander Suzanne Cummings, came across an online article in the September 1973 issue of the magazine *Country Music* that for me brought it all to light. Suzanne even went a step farther and found an issue of that magazine for sale on Ebay and sent it to me. The article, written by Robert Adels, is titled "Sonny James: At All Times, In All Ways, "The Southern Gentleman."

Uncharacteristically, and I really mean uncharacteristically, Sonny had invited the writer of the article into his home here in Nashville. In the article, there are pictures of Sonny at his desk, and Sonny on the floor with tapes and records and all sorts of music paraphernalia scattered all about, and Sonny on the phone, and Sonny in his home office with awards decorating the walls and some awards that hadn't been hung yet laying haphazardly on a table with Sonny holding a hammer, and Sonny sitting on the grass in his yard surrounded by fishing tackle boxes with a dozen rods and reels and — well, to me it was all so un-Sonny. Let me give you just one example of why it was so not like him: I had never been in that same office in his home where all those awards were — not one time — not ever. The entire article was so unlike the Sonny James I knew. For some reason, I guess Sonny decided to let down his guard, which explained everything I have said so far in this chapter. Let me quote from Adels's interview:

Sonny began to sum up his understanding of the relationship between the public eye and the mind's eye… 'I don't want to be a mystery, but I don't think that I should become so wrapped up in entertainment as to bring the family into it. They aren't a part of it. I want the public to know enough about me to be fair, to know that I'm not an oddball, and I'm not using lack of publicity as a gimmick. But I'm also feeling freer if I don't include my daily activities in my professional side.'

"So if Sonny James seems to be hiding from all but his closest friends, it's only to maintain that degree of privacy he deems essential to his lifestyle. 'Some people like to keep everything secret,' Sonny observes 'others want everything they do known to the public. I guess you might say I'm splittin' the difference.'"

So there I was: writing a book about Sonny James and The Southern Gentlemen, and realizing I was pretty much half in the dark. Marshall Grant, the bass player in Cash's The Tennessee Three, had published a book in 2006 titled, *I Was There When It Happened — My Life with Johnny Cash.* The title was an old gospel song that Johnny had recorded with the last two lines of the chorus being "I was there when it happened, and I guess I ought to know." Well, like Marshall, I was there when it happened, and to be perfectly honest, there was no guessing about it — I didn't know very much and I had to admit I needed help. Let me explain it this way:

Take the Good Book, specifically the books of Luke and John. John was an eyewitness, there from the beginning, having transferred his loyalties from the Baptist to the Baptist's Supreme Successor. John didn't need anyone to tell him what happened. He saw it all with his own eyes. He knew what he knew and sensed what he sensed. John didn't need to do research—all he needed to do was to recall what he already knew and write from that perspective.

On the other hand, we have the physician Luke. He knew nothing from personal experience, understood nothing because of it, but somewhere along the line as a companion of Paul's on his journeys, was determined or even inspired to unearth eyewitnesses and verify their recollections. So Luke starts his book with an admission that stands out with the honesty of a pure-cut diamond.

> Forasmuch as many have taken in hand to set forth in order a declaration of those things which are most surely believed among us, even as they delivered them unto us, which from the beginning were eyewitnesses, and ministers of the word; it seemed good to me also, having had perfect understanding of all things from the very first, to write unto thee in order, most excellent Theophilus, that thou mightest know the certainty of those things. (Luke 1:1–4, KJV)

John didn't need a human being to remind to him of what he saw and experienced, whereas Luke needed everyone he could find to explain to him what they saw and experienced.

If you have caught that comparison then let me explain my position in this writing. I was trapped somewhere between John and Luke's experiences. I was an eyewitness to what I saw and experienced between 1964 and 1971. I was fortunate to sit with Sonny in his home for hours and hours and hours of conversations, starting in 2002 and continuing for the next thirteen years.

My actual account started in mid-1964 when our vocal group originally connected with him — however at that time he was thirty-six, and our average age was twenty-two. As you saw in the first chapter, I had no awareness and had not even thought about Sonny's first thirty-six years of life until 2002. Then Sonny was seventy-three, and I was sixty. And for the next fifteen years, until Rick Hall wrote those six words in his condolence, I hadn't done any research, or even tried to find eyewitnesses to fill that thirty-six year gap. After Rick's words woke me up, I realized that too many of the first-hand-observers had already left us. I would find myself on a lonely backroad headed toward somewhere, someplace. My work would be cut out for me as it was for Dr. Luke.

My first impulse was to read the scores of comments left on every obituary notice that could be found on the internet following Sonny's passing in 2016, and when I found one that seemed like it was from a personal experience that individual had had with Sonny, I did everything I could to find a way to contact those folks. I was very lucky. Tracking them down and getting them to talk was well worth the time and effort and gave me a much deeper insight into the private, guarded, and understated values of this good man.

As this book started taking shape in mid-2016, my son Greg shared many personal experiences with Sonny. Starting in 2002, they spent a serious amount of time together working on the website. Then when I got into my writing, Greg and I had frequent discussions about what was becoming apparent in our research. One advantage my son had over me during that period of time was that I had worked for Sonny, but Greg, born just three months before we joined him in August 1964, had in reality known Sonny since birth. Greg could say things and ask questions of him I would have never felt comfortable asking. Something my son gave me was as revealing of Sonny as anything anyone could have ever written. Greg sent me this poetic insight into the private side of Sonny James:

> The secret of the man we knew and cherished was that there were none. The gift he gave was supremely simple. When you were with him then you were everything to him. Nothing and nobody else seemed to matter except for you and those you care about. Life for Sonny wasn't a contest but instead was an ever-present homecoming where he got to see and speak with those he and Doris treasured—everyone who ever knew him; family, friends, associates, fans, everybody. He kept each of us in high regards and protected us deep in his heart.

> We were all his *willful shadows*.

GINGER CHAUDRON SNIPPET

My parents were from Hackleburg, Alabama, with Sonny's mom being my great aunt. My folks lived and worked on the Loden Farm after they were married. Sonny told me in later years that even though everyone called him Sonny Boy, my mother always called him "My Boy." My dad served as the first announcer for the Loden Family group when they appeared in small local shows. This was around the time Sonny played the homemade mandolin that his pop made for him, an instrument formed from the bottom half of a molasses bucket. In 1936 or 1937, my parents left the farm, so Daddy could attend Auburn. After Daddy's graduation, we moved to Andalusia, Alabama, but made trips back to visit family in Marion County. That is where I remember going to Uncle Archie and Aunt Della's (Sonny's parents) for "Singings." They still lived in their white farmhouse south of town and would invite friends and neighbors to those musical gatherings.

Of course, the family played several instruments and always invited anyone else who wanted to take part.

Shortly after this, the Loden Family began to make appearances in other locations. They came to Andalusia and stayed with us while they performed in area school auditoriums. When school was out in the afternoons, Sonny would sometimes go and practice basketball, allowing me to tag along and watch as he and some of the local boys would shoot hoops. I can imagine that they have great memories knowing they played basketball with Sonny James.

As the years went by, his parents moved into town and opened Loden's Department Store in Hackleburg but still kept the farm. In later years, Sonny had cattle on it. When we attended Sonny's funeral service in Hackleburg, I met the lady whose family now owns the farm. I wish I had been able to talk more with her about it; however, we rode by the place for old time's sake.

The last time we visited Sonny's sis, Thelma Lee, who was living in Hackleburg, Sonny and Doris were there. Knowing Sonny, he never talked about himself and always seemed to get you to talk about yourself. As we were leaving, with a mischievous smile, he said, "I am going to write a book." And we thought finally, nobody has put out a book about Sonny's life and here he was letting us in on it for the first time. Then he went on to say that the book wouldn't be very long because it would be all about Leon (my husband) and the things Leon hadn't done. Then it hit us—this was so Sonny, the book was going to be all about us and not him, which, if you knew Sonny, was not at all surprising.

When Sonny's death was announced, a number of my classmates called to offer condolences. "Young Love" was a hit when we were seniors in high school, and to this day, it remains my favorite song that he ever recorded.

GINGER FREDERICK CHAUDRON —*Foley, Alabama*

CHAPTER 3

TREE OF LIFE

"Take up your life and do business with it."
—Lee Roberts

Life is a twinkling gift, and we have no say-so about the moment we will be packaged up in ribbons and bows and presented to the world under the Tree of Life.

Born on the front row of a dream, the gift known as Jimmie H. Loden arrived on May 1, 1928, 100 miles northwest of Birmingham in the "Friendly City" of Hackleburg, Alabama (population 600), on a 300-acre farm located about six miles south of town and about eight to ten miles, depending on which crow was doing the flying, from Hamilton, the Marion County seat.

Along with his "Sis," Thelma Lee, born five years earlier, Jimmie Hugh grew up listening to music as both of their parents were musicians. "Pop" (Archie Lee Loden) and "Mom" (Della Burleson Loden), Jimmie Hugh, and Thelma Lee were a closely knit family. The one common thread that kept them tightly strung together throughout their lives was music; not the recording side of it because they never recorded, but the performing side of it.

On Saturday nights, as time would allow, the local pickers and singers would congregate at each other's homes for some old time pickin' and singin' while the coal-oil lamps flickered to the beat of the music. Jimmie Hugh, not quite three at the time, was experiencing his first real taste of music. Pop decided that the least he could do was give his son a musical instrument to play around with — so Pop took a molasses bucket, cut it in half, turned it upside down and stuck a neck on it. It became something of some kind of a little banjo thing, but Pop tuned it like a mandolin. In no time little Jimmie Hugh was pickin' and singin' on his own with Pop re-christening him "Sonny Boy."

By the age of six Sonny was also playing the fiddle well enough to join the neighborhood gatherings. Long-time Hackleburg resident, Mr. J. H. Sullins, two years older than Sonny, beamingly told me about some of those shindigs. One of them stands out as a real grinner. Sonny's grandmother, known to the folks around town as "Aunt Mary," had a favorite fiddle tune. She always requested "The Old Hen Cackled (and the Rooster's Gonna Crow"). Mr. Sullins laughingly recounted that during the song "she would always rare [sic] back and crow like a rooster!" By the time Mr. Sullins had finished telling that and a few other stories, I felt as if I had missed out on a real part of life by not having been raised in Hackleburg.

Sonny was eventually given a precious family heirloom—his great-grandfather's (1835-1880) fiddle that had survived the Civil War. Sonny cherished it and used it to become a master fiddler.

When Sonny was four and Sis was nine, they recorded a song at a local radio station. Standing on a box so he could be closer to the microphone, he took the vocal cords he was born with and sang and yodeled away (it's a real hoot). This recording is on the website www.sonnyjames.com. It's a must-listen.

The guitar came a bit later. Everything about Sonny's ability to play came from hands-on experience. Like most country pickers of the day they didn't go somewhere to take lessons — it was sit down and figure it out yourself. In Sonny's case he had a great advantage — even though Mom and Pop played on their shows, Sis was the real guitarist in the family. Sonny told me that the runs he played originally came from copying what she did and he just built on them.

In 1933 Pop Loden decided to take his little family group, at first called "Sonny Loden and the Southerners," on the road as professional musicians. Pop would contract to get the family a regular fifteen-to-thirty-minute spot on a radio station anywhere that would have them. Then he would contract for personal appearances at venues in a fifty or so mile radius of the station. As Sonny's talents got him noticed more and more, Pop renamed the group "Sonny Boy and the Loden Family."

I have a letter dated March 25, 1946, that Pop wrote to the program director of station KMBC in Kansas City, Missouri, that he signed A. L. Loden. I quote a couple of sentences from it here:

> If you still have an opening there and would like to have a No. 1 act, please advise and quote aprox. terms and ect. . . . This act is strictly nice in every respect and guaranteed to please the audience, whether over the air or on personal appearances.

In the next chapter you will see in more detail stations WMSD, WAPL, KLCN, WJDX, WNOX, WPTF, WSGN, and WMPS — stations and towns ranging from Arkansas in the west to North Carolina in the east that they worked out of.

From the family's act, he learned about the value of humor in a performance. Sis was the comedian on stage playing the part of freckle-faced Arta Vee, with Pop bouncing comedic shtick off her. As Sonny put it, "Sis was just a natural at it." No, Sis wasn't loaded down with freckles, but she made herself up to be the character.

He also learned from Pop how to manage the family singing group as a business because, long and short of it, that's what it was. Up front, it was singing and performing, but before the show began and after the show was over, it was business and that's where you would certainly find Sonny in later years. He was always the point man when it came to his career.

On occasion he told this story about Pop, with this "hand-in-the-cookie-jar" look on his face as he was getting close to the punch line: There was a promoter who contracted with the Loden Family to sing on the shows he was putting together. The price for admission at the time was all of ten cents. At some point in the 1930s, the promoter raised the price from ten to fifteen cents to which Pop responded, "He's ruin' the business, ruin' the business." It's laughable to think about now, but it was a time not far removed from the Depression and raising the price another nickel might have kept some folks from attending.

Schooling was important to the Lodens but difficult to maintain as they moved from place to place, only coming back to the farm temporarily as needed. Sonny fell somewhat behind during their touring days. When Pop folded up the Loden Family group in 1947, they returned to Hackleburg to stay. Sonny was finally able to get caught up, ultimately graduating from high school after completing his senior year at the age of twenty.

Now back home, at last he had the chance to participate in two sports—football and basketball. We've come across a posed photo of Sonny with the rest of the Panthers basketball team; hopefully, some-day we will find one from his football days. His coach in both sports was thirty-two-year-old Emmitt Ray whose twelve-year-old brother, Max Ray, and similarly-aged friend, Max Burleson, were the desig-nated managers for the teams. I got to spend some quality moments with Max Ray ("Coach" to me) as I was doing my research, finding that he followed in the footsteps of his older brother, spending four-teen years in the football program; the first twelve as head coach and the last two as an assistant.

Coach Ray shared two great stories that revolved around his older brother Emmitt as Sonny's football and basketball coach. The Panthers were playing Vernon in a regular season football game. Sonny, as one of the tallest players on the team, was positioned at end. They had the ball right down near the goal line, and Emmitt, because of Sonny's height, decided to put him in as halfback for the critical play with these instructions, "Just fall straight ahead and hold on to the football." Sonny did as instructed, wrapped his hands tightly around the ball, fell forward six feet three and a half inches, and scored the winning touchdown.

Emmitt, as mentioned, also doubled as the basketball coach, with his two tallest players being Sonny, and Billy Joe "Stackpole" Kennedy. The Panthers were in the playoffs in the spring of '48 and had won their first game on Friday, April 30, with their next game scheduled three days later on Monday, May 3.

Saturday, May 1, would change everything. Sonny would turn twenty, and the rules stated he would be ineligible to play. Suddenly one tall player was gone. Also on the first, Stackpole got married. Uh-oh. When the second round of the playoffs rolled around two days later, apparently Stackpole's head was still in the clouds. Following the loss, Coach Emmitt Ray was quoted as saying, "He'd a been just as well off if he'd a been too old, too." These good people just had a down-home way of sayin' things.

After spending some time with these wonderful folks you realize there's something genuinely real and down-to-earth about them — it's no wonder Sonny loved his hometown like he did. But it was more than that. It seems that from the beginning, Sonny was in love with Hackleburg — and as the years rolled by, Hackleburg seemed to fall more and more in love with him.

We all are, every one one of us, made up of little bitty pieces of life's experiences, and Sonny James was no different. He took all of the wisdom gained from them and skillfully blended all of it into one gentlemanly package. Starting with the Loden Family at age four and continuing on until he retired some fifty-one years later, it was obvious that he was **born to perform**—that's what Sonny James was naturally gifted to do. He had grown up performing with the family and the public loved their music. Up onstage performing was where Sonny was professionally most comfortable. Yes, for certain he took life and did business with it, but **performing**—that sums up Sonny James perfectly.

The Roots of the Tree of Life

There is something that happens to nearly all of us as we slide into our formative teen years. We come face-to-face with an inspiring person or read a book that really moves us, and we unconsciously begin the process of re-christening ourselves.

- In 1922, Harold Bell Wright's book had a lasting effect on eleven-year-old Ronald Reagan.

- In 1952, C. S. Lewis wrote a book that twenty years later would strike at the heart of Chuck Colson.

- In 1896, Charles M. Sheldon wrote a book that in 1956 would have a profound effect on a fifteen-year-old boy living in Endicott, New York. That book, given to me by my mentor, Rev. Homer M. Smith, now stands as a monument to the power of words in a teenager's life.

- In the spring of 1958, Rev. Smith brought in nineteen-year-old Sheila Graham from New Brunswick, Canada for a speaking engagement. She spoke to the heart of this young man. In 2017, she wrote her biography, *My Journey by God's Design*.

- In 1748, at the age of sixteen, George Washington copied by hand *110 Rules of Civility & Decent Behavior in Company and Conversation*. These were based on a set of rules composed by French Jesuits in 1595. The first English translation of the rules appeared in 1640, ascribed to Francis Hawkins, the twelve-year-old son of a doctor. (See the end of this chapter for a selection of thirteen of the rules.)

What does this have to do with a book about Sonny James and The Southern Gentlemen? Everything; as you will see. From being teamed with Sonny for seven years to our reunions every five year, starting in 1989 until 2002 when Sonny added "family" to the relationship the two of us had, I am willing to state that I have no positive proof, but I firmly believe that I have a very strong sense of the man Sonny

James, and am inclined, self-persuaded if you will, that Sonny's life was influenced dramatically after reading Washington's *110 Rules of Civility*. I am convinced that Sonny sat down one day with the 110 and proceeded to write out his own version of those rules.

The one rule in Washington's list that to me most identifies with Sonny is #10. I have asked a lot of people about that one, and they all agreed — not one person could remember ever seeing Sonny do that. However, he did slip up one time. There is a YouTube video of the *Glen Campbell Good Time Hour* from the '70s. Glen, Jerry Reed, and James Burton were there with their instruments. Sonny was introduced; he came out with fiddle in hand, and they began playing the bluegrass song, "Uncle Pen." For about fifteen seconds, there at the beginning Sonny unconsciously crossed his legs. Then he suddenly sat up straighter and repositioned himself. Watch the video and see for yourself. It's a simple thing, I know, but it is a big clue into the mind of the man. I really think that this was one of his own *Rules of Civility*.

You can easily tell by watching Sonny just how much he enjoyed that performance. It seems to me that it was as if he was back in Hackleburg with friends and family at a Saturday night gathering. It is obvious to those of us who were close to him, just by the beaming expression on his face. They always say you can never really go back home again — but when he put his hands on that fiddle and started sawing away, his countenance revealed another Sonny from a long time ago - he was back home again just having fun.

On August 17, 2017, Philip Smucker, a fifth-great-grand-nephew of George Washington was on PBS talking about his newly-published book *Riding with George*. Smucker's work looks into the inner-George during his formative years, taking note of a number of vital lessons and life experiences necessary for Washington to become a successful 18th-century gentleman. The one-hour program was followed by a question-and-answer session. This one question and its answer were most intriguing:

Q: "I understand that George Washington was fairly aloof, except with his friends, and I was wondering if perhaps his interest in etiquette might have been a way that he could maintain that aloofness from not being so familiar with other folks."

A: "Washington observed people very closely — he observed people in the theater — he observed people in real life. But he also decided, I think in his own mind, [that] to be the Father of the Country, he had to maintain a certain amount of aloofness. He could not be overly familiar with friends and kin. And so, essentially, it was a bit of acting. I think he loved everybody — but did and famously remained aloof."

To me the word *aloof* would be too extreme for Sonny. In retrospect, it easily could have been a bridge too far in trying to explain Washington. I would have liked to have asked the questioner if he had read *The 110 Rules of Civility,* and where in them he could feel that Washington had determined to act aloof. *Reserved* might have been a better choice of words.

I once read that Abigail Adams, after first meeting Washington, wrote to her husband, John, saying, "The gentleman and the soldier look agreeably blended in him." I have no hesitation in saying that "The gentleman and the country music star look agreeably blended in Sonny James."

So I leave it at this — if Sonny chose a Virginia Gentleman as a pattern for life, well, The Southern Gentleman couldn't have chosen a better man to emulate.

Thirteen of Washington's 110 Rules of Civility

- 1st Every Action done in Company, ought to be with Some Sign of Respect, to those that are Present.

- 10th When you Sit down, Keep your Feet firm and Even, without putting one on the other or Crossing them.

- 49th Use no Reproachful Language against any one neither Curse nor Revile.

- 50th Be not hasty to believe flying Reports to the Disparagement of any.

- 56th Associate yourself with Men of good Quality if you Esteem your own Reputation; for 'tis better to be alone than in bad Company.

- 59th Never express anything unbecoming, nor Act agst the Rules Moral before your inferiours.

- 63d A Man ought not to value himself of his Atchievements, or rare Qualities of wit; much less of his riches Virtue or Kindred.

- 65th Speak not injurious Words neither in Jest nor Earnest Scoff at none although they give Occasion.

- 79th Be not apt to relate News if you know not the truth thereof. In Discoursing of things you Have heard Name not your Author always A Secret Discover not.

- 81st Be not Curious to Know the Affairs of Others neither approach those that Speak in Private.

- 89th Speak not Evil of the absent for it is unjust.

- 108th When you Speak of God or his Atributes, let it be Seriously & wt. Reverence. Honour & Obey your Natural Parents altho they be Poor.

- 110th Labour to keep alive in your Breast that Little Spark of Celestial fire Called Conscience.

MARK RAY SNIPPET

During the late 1960s and early 1970s, many of our friends and family were regulars at the annual Tennessee Valley Fiddler's Convention held at Athens University campus in Athens, Alabama. On our first year, we learned that Sonny James had, during a prior year TVFC event, made a surprise appearance on this popular fiddler's event stage. As it turned out, James' utterly unanticipated appearance became a showstopper.

According to our source, Sonny James *not* been known as a "fiddler" or violinist virtuoso, but rather for his well-known skill as a "pop country" vocalist, bandleader, and (somewhat less so) for his electronic studio wizardry.

This totally unanticipated occasion occurred at the close of the Tennessee Valley Old Time Fiddler's Convention evening after all the contestants had performed.

Sonny James entered the stage right at the close of it. The contest winner had not yet been announced. James, already a professional musician, had no desire to compete with his fans.

James was introduced to the audience. There was a roar of approval. After the cheering subsided, James casually picked up his violin, aka "fiddle," and placed his bow across the strings. What actually came out of that instrument was so unexpected, so ethereal and sensational, that it held the entire Athens university audience *spellbound* in rapturous disbelief. James performance was so pure and velvety-smooth that his instrument acquired a life of its own, transcending the idea of mere fiddling to an entirely new plane. At the close of the performance, the audience reacted with such thunderous applause that it must've continued unbroken for two to three minutes—a very long time for *any* performer.

After James' first encore, the applause and whistles continued unabated. They quickly rose to a roar, begging James for still more. According to our source, the audience wouldn't let him exit quietly. Sonny had to make at least two more curtain calls before finally exiting.

The undersigned has written the AU administration regarding whether or not anyone may have captured this once-in-a-lifetime Sonny James performance on tape, but alas, no one had any knowledge of anyone who had recorded that spectacularly momentous occasion.

This is to issue an appeal to anyone having any knowledge of a recording that may have been made of Sonny James' performance at the Tennessee Valley Old Time Fiddler's Convention during the mid-to-late 1960s at Athens University. Hopefully, with any luck at all, one will eventually be discovered so that this epochal moment in time will be preserved for all to share.

MARK RAY - *Madison, Alabama*

CHAPTER 4

THE OPENING YEAR—1952

"Life is one grand sweet song, so start the music."
—Ronald Reagan

Whether we care to admit it or not, life is more trial and error, hit and miss, guess and guess again than we are probably willing to admit. Sometimes, as Shakespeare wrote, "To be or not to be ..." unfortunately is not always up to me. That decision so often ends up in the seasoned hands of Grandmasters moving us around like so many pieces on a chessboard. We understand, don't we, that in this life, there are kings and pawns. Often we are left wondering how we unwittingly became the pawn and someone else the king — moving us completely out of sync with our dreams. The shell game of life spins us dizzily around until we wobble in place barely able to tell one direction from another - and often that is done by others with the best of intentions. The moves they end up putting us through are to fulfill their dreams, not ours.

On the other hand, sometimes circumstances infused with an influence far beyond that of any mortal moves others aside and simply replaces those people with a dream — the dream I have for my life and how can that desire be fulfilled without losing myself in the process.

I have often used the example of the blacksmith who was the man in town to go to whenever a horse needed shoeing. There was no one better than ole "Tom Cagle." The trade had been passed down from his grandfather through his father and onto him. Then one day Henry Ford rolled into every American town, and years later what had once seemed like just an overnight fad turned into a mighty leap — and for every "Tom Cagle" in the USA suddenly everything changed. In the First World War, one million horses were sent overseas to help with the war effort. Only 62,000 of them returned. Henry Ford, with his mechanical horse, would even change the way future wars were fought. Such is progress; the ground breaking discoveries and inventions that dominate our future years.

In 1952 nobody had any idea of anything, yet at that moment the **adolescent pieces** of Sonny's future **team** puzzle were, unknown to him, scattered all over kingdom come. Would it happen? Could it happen? Should it happen? And when you have no idea when the major creative moment is waiting to take place somewhere down the timeline there is no fear or anxiety. None!

So in April 1952, into that ever inconstant world of music — enter Jimmie Hugh Loden from Hackleburg, Alabama, who was the oldest piece of that future unassembled puzzle, a month shy of his twenty-fourth birthday, and just out of the Army where he served Uncle Sam while dreaming about all things music.

Enter Shirley Wilson Legate from Fulbright, Texas, who checked into life in 1934, and in 1952 was seventeen years old and about to graduate from high school as valedictorian of his senior class, a class that totaled only twelve students. We would know him as Milo.

Enter Ernest Duane West from Salisbury, Maryland, who in 1952 was eleven years old. He would take up the trumpet and be a member of his high school choir and later would sing with his siblings in a trio at church. We knew him as Duane.

Enter Gary Lee Robble from Endicott, NY, who was ten years old and getting ready to throw the first pitch (a knuckleball for sure) in the top half of the first inning as Little League Baseball made its debut in his hometown. Gary's hero, though they never met, was a twenty-nine- year-old rookie knuckleball pitcher named Hoyt Wilhelm who in 1952 went 15-3 for the New York Giants, ultimately compiling an unbelievable career ERA (earned run average) of 2.43. The guys called me Gary —Huggins called me Robble.

Enter Glendon William Huggins from East Liverpool, Ohio, who was nine years old, holding that three-valve instrument in hand and looking at a picture of Betty Grable's husband on his bedroom wall. Huggins was trying to play like her man, Harry James, one of the great trumpet players of all time. He went by Glenn — I called him Huggins.

Enter Albert Linwood Bown from North Easton, Massachusetts, who in 1952 was at the ripe old age of eight spending those formative years as a very energetic and athletic pastor's kid. He was always Lin to us.

All these rough pieces were far, far away from the *team* they would eventually become.

In that same year, Jimmie H. Loden, through Ken Nelson, signed a contract with Capitol Records. From page 133 of Ken's book, *My First 90 Years Plus 3* (published in 2007), we find:

Chet Atkins had been playing on most of my Nashville sessions and wasn't yet the producer for RCA Victor. It was the spring of '52 that he called me and asked if I would come to his house and listen to a young Korean [War] veteran friend of his who had a good voice and was anxious to get a recording contract. The young man's name was James Loden. As a youngster he had sung with his four sisters [sic: one sister] in the Loden Family group … He also performed while in the service. He accompanied himself on guitar and sang three songs for me. I liked what I heard and agreed to sign him, however, I felt the name James Loden was not euphonious. In discussing it with him he said, 'My folks used to call me Sonny.' I said, 'That's it, Sonny James.' He agreed and adopted it as his professional name.

Said Sonny about that time in his official biography written with

Dave Samuelson (2002), and located in its entirety on the website www.sonnyjames.com, "In his [Ken Nelson's] mind he knew that I cared so much about my career that he gave me leeway. **There are some things that a person does naturally.** The longer I worked with Ken, the more liberty he would give me. If he didn't think something was a good idea, he'd tell me. He had a way of doing it. He'd say, 'Sonny, you might consider this.' We just treated each other just like we should have. It's not anyone overriding. He recognized that I was doing my best. Of course, being a friend of Chet's, and we were musicians, he gave you that liberty to show what individuality that you had. That's one of the things that I think was the greatest thing to happen to me because I did work with someone like Ken. You see I love to play the guitar, and it became a part of my sound. And without that, it wouldn't have been me. By him giving me the liberty to bring out my guitar, it's a style. Without that, there wouldn't have been a Sonny James sound that people are familiar with."

So on June 11, 1952, Sonny got to record for Capitol for the first time and walked into the Castle Studio located in the Tulane Hotel at 206 8th Ave., North Nashville, Tennessee. Castle was the first recording studio in what would later become known as Music City, USA. This studio idea in Nashville was developed first in the minds of three WSM radio engineers in the mid-1940s. Of all the artists who had recorded there, the most memorable was Hank Williams, whose song "Lovesick Blues" had been cut on December 22, 1948, just one year after the studio opened. In the last session that Hank Williams did at Castle on September 23, 1952, a few months before his untimely death on January 1, 1953, he recorded a song that would become one of his most memorable recordings — **"Kaw-Liga."**

But here we are, some fifteen months before "Kaw-Liga" was recorded, and Sonny finds himself in Castle Studio surrounded by some of country music's most well-known musicians — Chet Atkins (guitar), Eddie Hill (guitar), Jerry Byrd (steel), and Lightnin' Chance (bass), with Ken Nelson assuming the role as producer of the session. In what is typically a three-hour deal, they knocked out four songs:

"It's So Nice to Make Up," "Believe Another's Lips," "I Wish," and "Short Cut."

Out of those four songs came Sonny's first single release on Capitol Records — the up-tempo tune "Short Cut" on one side, backed with "It's So Nice to Make Up" on the flip.

We need to stop right here in 1952 and step way ahead, about fifty-five years. I had been searching Ebay for about a half-dozen years for anything that had to do with our time with Sonny (1964 — 1971), and on occasion I would find something outside of that time that interested me so I would jump at it. In 2002 or so, I came across a simple piece on the internet that laid out Sonny's entire discography, and for the first time was aware that "Short Cut" was one side of his first release. On two different occasions that 78 rpm went up for sale on eBay, and I grabbed both of them. On the purchase of the first, I put it in an old record safekeeping cardboard kind of thing, the kind that my parents used to keep records safe (where I grew up it was to store polka records). A man I knew from church asked me one day if I wanted a bunch of old Edison acetates and 78s that he was clearing out, and I told him sure. In with that bunch of 78s he gave me were four of those heavy cardboard safe-storage things and also some other great old records, for instance, Gene Autry's "Back in the Saddle Again." Over time I was able to purchase around ten of Sonny's 78s and place some of them in one of those old thick things that interestingly read on the front, "Frankie Carle Comes Calling." My constant curiosity forced me to look up Frankie Carle on the internet and found that his best-known piano composition was "Sunrise Serenade" which rose to #1 in 1938. When I went to YouTube and listened to the song, I instantly recognized it. Who knows — maybe "Sunrise Serenade" was one of the 78s that was originally in this cardboard thing I now owned.

So here I was in about 2007 at Sonny's house with this Frankie Carle thing protecting Sonny's white label 78 with "Short Cut" on one side and "It's So Nice to Make Up" on the other. We chatted for a while about things as we always did and reminded ourselves again of some old laughable road stories before I decided to open Frankie Carle up and pull out "Short Cut." When I did Sonny's eyes opened wide, and he reached out, encouraging me to let him hold the white-label 78.

And there I was, handing Sonny his first record release from 1952 and expecting no more than a "you found this where?" or something like that statement. But as best I can remember, this would become the first time Sonny would crack open that door to his past and relate something he had never ever talked about, not to me or in all of the interviews I have read that he did, and I would find myself listening in amazement that he had let me into that below-the-radar stuff he was so effective in keeping to himself.

With the recording in hand, Sonny began to talk, "I would have handled this record myself." Not knowing what went into record releases back in the early 1950s, I guess I kind-of got jolted by Sonny's statement. After asking him the obvious questions I learned that when Capitol put out a promotional white label record in 1952, the artists had to take care of getting it to radio stations that they thought would play it. The total cost of mailing, packaging, and everything else would be at the artist's expense. If it got enough requests for airplay, then Capitol would release the blue-label 78, which would be for sale. On this, Sonny's first recording, the blue-label was never released—and this promotional record was all that ever went out. "I would have packaged this record up myself," Sonny continued, "and carried it to the post office and mailed it out to the stations I thought would play it."

Not long after that I found another white label 78 of that same record on eBay and purchased it. When I received it, there was a promotional piece included that had gone out with the record to those radio stations Sonny had chosen. Sonny never mentioned it to me when handling the first record, but there it was, in pristine condition. The piece was introducing Sonny James' first release on Capitol Records with a short five-paragraph bio on him. When I got to the next to the last paragraph, well, read it for yourself: "He is a member of the church, doesn't smoke or drink strong drink in any form . . ."—a most unusual way to introduce yourself to the music industry. But more than that; I found that Sonny James, The Southern Gentleman, was always understated. What I mean is he lived it—he didn't laud it.

In 2002, when Sonny wrote his bio with Dave Samuelson, I became aware for the first time that the Loden family had lived in different towns and had a weekly radio program and then worked a fifty-or-so-mile radius as a result of that broadcast. In 1933 when Sonny was just five, and before moving very far away from Hackleburg, Sonny's dad, Pop Loden, as they all called him, was given an audition for the family and secured a regular Saturday radio slot on WMSD in Muscle Shoals, Alabama. Following that the family won a Mid-South Champion Band contest against fifty-two other contestants, the prize being that they got to play two weeks on WAPI, a 5,000-watt station in Birmingham.

Over the next years, the family lived in Blytheville, Arkansas, and worked out of station KLCN. The family also did brief stints in Greenwood and Columbus, Mississippi, before securing an extended slot over WJDX in Jackson. During that period of time, Sonny added to his credits three Tri-State and two Mid-South fiddling champion-ships. (He never mentioned these to us — that was typical Sonny.) Jan Mancini, a long-time Sonny James fan originally from Jeddo, Michigan, sent me a newspaper article from late 1957. It is a full page piece from the *Hillbilly and Cowboy Hit Parade* magazine where Sonny mentions this to the reporter who is unnamed in the article.

Just before the end of WWII the Loden Family moved to Knoxville, working out of station WNOX before moving on to Raleigh, North Carolina in 1946, where they worked out of WPTF.

I said all that to say this — in 1952 Sonny had eight radio stations from the Loden Family era that he could count on to at least play his new record, and he would have mailed them the white-label promo. And sitting there in Sonny's house with him, Sonny held in his hand one of those records that he had mailed to one of those stations so many years before.

As I left his home that afternoon, I realized that I had done some-thing most of us don't ever, or maybe rarely, get to do—getting some-one to talk about a time they hadn't thought to mention before, or just connecting them to part of their past they hadn't visited in a long, long time. Just a few moments ago, I again opened that Frankie Carle cardboard thing and held the record that I had handed to Sonny on that day in 2007; again it took me back, but to something else from 1952.

Several days after that session on June 11, 1952, Ken Nelson unexpectedly brought Sonny back to the studio, this time as a sideman. Jim and Jesse McReynolds, also making their debut session for Capitol, arrived in Nashville without a fiddle player. Knowing Sonny was still in town, Nelson asked him if he might help the brothers. In his bio Sonny wrote, "I said sure, because I like them," he remembered, "I was more or less just helping out."

That fiddle, Sonny's fiddle, carries with it a long history. Its recording history, however, starts with the Jim and Jesse songs as, unfortunately, the Loden Family never went into a studio and cut a record. How old the fiddle actually is we will probably never know, but from what we do know, we can trace its history back to before the Civil War.

From the information I have been able to gather, the fiddle belonged to Sonny's great-grandfather who hid it in the chimney of his house for fear that Union soldiers, as they made their way south, might find it in his home and snatch it away for themselves. It was eventually given to Sonny's father, Archie, who turned it over to Sonny early in his life. There is much more that fiddle could relate, but sadly its entire history has now, and forever will be, lost to the fog of time.

Now some sixty-five years later, after using that fiddle on Jim and Jesse's first recordings and from there to being used on well over 1,500 personal appearances with us, that same never-refinished fiddle stares up at me from its open case as an incredible inspiration from Sonny James' past. It has been in my care and custody for some time now, floating my mind to those long-ago years stretching back for sure as far as Abraham Lincoln's presidency and even farther back than that.

Now hailed as bluegrass classics, those early Jim and Jesse Capitol releases capture a rare glimpse of Sonny James' skill as a fiddler. The five songs Sonny recorded with Jim and Jesse that day were "A Memory of You," "Is it True," "My Little Honeysuckle Rose," "I'll Wash

Your Love from My Heart," and "Virginia Waltz." But even though Sonny was a very exceptional fiddle player, that was not where his heart needed to be right there at the beginning. You can listen to the "Virginia Waltz" on a YouTube video presented by Richard Custer. As of this date, Richard has posted on YouTube every song Sonny ever recorded and all of the live shows we did.*

Sonny recorded fifteen songs at Castle Studio in Nashville (not including the five songs he did with Jim and Jesse), with the last session being on September 23, 1953. Following that first session on June 11, 1952, where four songs were recorded, of the remaining eleven songs cut over the next fifteen months, there were two real disappointments.

Back in those days, covering other artists on their songs was an accepted practice. In 1952 Sonny joined Slim Whitman's band for a two-month stretch. During that time, Capitol released Sonny's first record "Short Cut/It's So Nice to Make Up." Though Sonny never recorded with Slim, he did front his shows for thirty minutes, whipping up the crowd with songs and fiddle tunes, including his ever popular trick fiddling. Taken from Sonny's official bio on the website, "James kept his eye open for other opportunities. While visiting a Jackson, Mississippi, station to promote his first single, a disc jockey suggested the singer hear a new release by Baton Rouge singer Lou Millett: 'That's Me Without You.' He (the DJ) said, 'It's strictly territorial, and I know the writer would like to get a major label to do it.'"

Sonny called Ken Nelson, his Capitol producer, and the first song cut in his second recording session at Castle Studio on September 17, 1952 was "That's Me Without You." The four musicians on the recording were Chet Atkins ([guitar), Eddie Hill (guitar), Jerry Byrd (steel guitar)], and Lightnin' Chance (bass).

Just for those readers who would be interested in a historical piece of trivia — six days later Hank Williams Sr. would enter that same studio and record for the last time before his death on January 1, 1953. The four songs Hank recorded were "I Could Never Be Ashamed of You," "Your Cheatin' Heart," "Kaw-Liga," and "Take These Chains from My Heart." Adding to the trivia even further, three of the musicians that were on Sonny's session were also on Hank's session — Chet Atkins (electric guitar), Eddie Hill (rhythm guitar), and Lightnin' Chance (bass). Jerry Byrd played steel on Sonny's session, and Don Helms played steel on Hank's.

In 1953, when Capitol was ready to release Sonny's second single, Sonny had moved to Dallas, Texas, and joined RCA Victor artist Bobby Williamson's band. From the bio, "In addition to opening for Williamson, James became a utility player, picking up the fiddle, mandolin or guitar as needed. The group made several television appearances, worked a regular midday show over WEAA ... Even more important, the singer [Sonny] was given a slot on WFAA's *The Saturday Night Shindig*, which was simulcast on radio and television."

"While James was in Dallas, Capitol released "'That's Me Without You." Disc jockeys jumped on the song, and Billboard reported strong airplay. The next stage (at that time) in making a record a success was to grab the attention of jukebox operators. After that, record sales usually ballooned.

"James' record reached No. 9 in Billboards 'Most Played by Jockeys' country chart at the same time Marty Robbins did with his intended breakthrough ballad *"I'll Go On Alone."* James believes both songs could have sold even better had it not been for a back-to-back cover by Webb Pierce, then Decca's hottest country artist. 'He came right out with that, and he just absolutely killed us,' James said. He killed what would have been for Marty and me a good start."

But as unconventional and improper as that might seem in today's music business, that's the way the sausage was made back then. Some years later Sonny related this same story - not only to me but also to Virgil True, a band member who was with him near the end of his career in 1983, and Sonny stated it to Virgil the same way, "At that time Webb was 'hotter than a firecracker' and when he covered you, it was all but over."

To the day, exactly nine months later on March 11, 1953, the other major disappointment had to do with the song "I Forgot More," which was also recorded at Castle in Sonny's third session and about the time "firecracker" Webb Pierce was burying both Sonny and Marty.

The related story on the song comes directly from Ken Nelson's book *My First 90 Years Plus 3*. The song had come to Ken's attention from a publisher who told him he could have the song, which meant that he [the publisher] wouldn't show it to any other record producer. Quoting from his book:

> I liked the idea of the song but the melody of the middle part didn't seem quite right, so I asked [the publisher] if he would object to my changing it. I wouldn't expect writer credit. He said that would be okay. I told him I was going to Nashville the following week and would record it with Sonny James. Sonny liked the song, but when we started to record it we both realized the lyrics in the middle part didn't make sense.
>
> Knowing of his writing ability, I phoned Fred Rose, told him of the problem, and asked if he could come to the studio and see what could be done. He came immediately and within ten minutes had the lyrics making sense. Fred did not want writer credit either, he did it as a favor to me.
>
> When I returned to Hollywood I played the record for [the publisher] and told him I planned to release it in the fall. He asked if he could have a dub so he could have the revised version copyrighted, and I gave it to him. He obviously immediately sent it to Steve Sholes, who was head of and producer of country artists for RCA Victor.

And as Sonny related the story to me, some weeks later, RCA went into a studio and recorded the song with the Davis Sisters (Skeeter Davis and her friend Betty Jack). My research found that RCA recorded the song on May 23, 1953. The Davis Sisters had no idea that this action had taken place. Both releases came out at about the same time, and then the sad twist to it all—the Davis Sisters were in a terrible car accident just outside of Cincinnati, Ohio, on August 2, 1953 in which Betty Jack lost her life. This tragic event overwhelmed the song, and Sonny's cut just didn't stand much of a chance of making it the radio stations' turntables—delaying the start of his career again.

For the Davis Sisters, and especially for Skeeter Davis going forward, "I Forgot More Than You'll Ever Know" was a blockbuster hit, the only #1 country song by a female duet until the rise of the Judds some thirty years later. The song ultimately stayed at #1 on the country charts for eight weeks. According to the Wikipedia article on the song, chart historian Joel Whitburn commented that "I Forgot More Than You'll Ever Know" ranks among the top 100 country hits of all time. The article failed to mention the story behind the song that Ken Nelson wrote about in his book.

"I Forgot More" went on to be recorded by a number of artists, but Sonny never received credit for having recorded it first — a fact he never brought up. That's just the way the ball bounces sometimes, but when it bounced like that for Sonny, he just let it bounce itself out. Some of the others who recorded it were Patti Page, Johnny Cash, Bob Dylan, Jerry Lee Lewis, Patty Loveless, The Statler Brothers, Kitty Wells, and Slim Whitman.

Two major disappointments within a year would be enough to crush most of us. It is always well to remember that there is an enormous difference between a horror movie and a terrible reality. However, this had to have been a real learning experience for Sonny, that is, that the music business was not ever going to be easy. Of all the things I observed about him in my fifty-plus years of knowing him, this stands out the most — when one minute after midnight rolled around, yesterday was old news. Today was a new day: tomorrow would be another day, so let it go. Just let yesterday go.

When that second dust-up occurred less than a year into his recording contract with Capitol Records — it was old news. Today and tomorrow were all that mattered to Sonny. He was content to let the dust from the dust-up settle on its own. All he could do by getting into this storm was to keep the dust flying — and that just wasn't Sonny James. (In fact, he was actually allergic to dust.) A song on his 1967 album, *Only the Lonely,* beautifully illustrates this characteristic of his. The song, "Where Forgotten Things Belong" has as its first line, "Let me leave you where forgotten things belong." This was the Sonny

James I came to know and understand. He could take something that had hurt him, place it over there in the "forget about it" drawer, and leave it there for time and eternity. To him, that's where those things belonged.

Sonny never revealed the name of the underhanded publisher to me. He said he knew who the individual was but decided to rack one up to experience. That was his way; he would not say anything negative about anyone, even if he had been hurt by them. I will not reveal the man's name because that would be disrespectful to Sonny. However, if you really must know, read pages 113-114 of Ken Nelson's book.

In *Baggar Vance,* one of my favorite movies (from 2000), one that the Hollywood folks just had to dress up with some "pardon my French" lines and a few scenes not necessary to the plot, actor Will Smith plays the part of Baggar Vance and shows up out of the blue to caddie for Matt Damon who is Rannulph Juna in the movie, a golfer who has lost his swing, There is a young boy in town named Hardy Greaves, played by J. Michael Moncrief, a boy who is being given some putting pointers late one night on a putting green. Says Baggar:

> They say that inside of each person is one true authentic swing — something we was born with — that's ours and ours alone. Something can't be taught to you or learned. Something that got to be remembered. Over time, the world can rob us of that swing…and get buried inside us under all our woulda's and coulda's and shoulda's

It is obvious to me and obvious to any fans of Sonny James and even obvious to Sonny himself when I quoted him a few pages ago saying, "There are some things that a person does naturally," it is obvious that he was born with an ability, a talent if you will—one, as Baggar said, "can't be taught or learned" "one that got to be remembered." Sonny said in an interview he did on September 30, 1981, "If I'm ever asked . . . I always say have a recognizable style, something that you don't work on, what is naturally yours." It's as if the script writers for the movie had read Sonny's interview from 1981 and not given him credit for the quote. The heading to the section was "Style is the Most Important Thing."

*****

Over time Sonny would find that it would take a team to really make his natural style work long term. He would come to understand that for him it would take more than a guitar to accompany his voice. He hit on the combination a couple of times in the mid-1950s with "'Til The Last Leaf Shall Fall" (1955), "For Rent" (1955) that went to No. 7, and "You're the Reason I'm in Love" (1957; the flip side of "Young Love"), but the success of "Young Love" completely buried the combination of Sonny, his guitar, and a vocal chorus singing behind him for the next six searching years.

Sonny publicly recognized the combination a number of times. In January 2001, in an interview with Walt Trott of *Country Music People Magazine,* Sonny said this, "Most of the things I did — and if you recall my Southern Gentlemen — sounded so full. . . . On most of my recordings, the predominant thing you'd hear would be, I guess, the guitar that I played — which I always tried to bring out — and The Southern Gentlemen singing. Then the other thing was Millie Kirkham who began singing this high part."

On November 6, 2006, on ABC television when Kris Kristofferson announced Sonny as one of the newest inductees into the Country Music Hall of Fame, Sonny began his thirty-four-second acceptance speech with these words, "I want to thank *my* good Lord for the career *He's* given me." He then went on to thank his wife Doris, his parents Mom and Pop Loden, his Sis Thelma, Ruby Palmer, The Southern Gentlemen, Ken Nelson, Mike Curb, and all of his hometown friends in Hackleburg, Alabama. At the official Medallion Ceremony six months later, Sonny would publically state that The Southern Gentlemen had come up with that deep identifiable sound that you heard on all of his records. Rick Hall understood we were like "biscuits and butter", but that private side of Sonny kept those inner feelings deep in his heart for years and years. When those feelings finally came out he acknowledged that the team he had surrounded himself with in the mid-60s were like butter, and had put him on a country music roll. However, all of that is a long time and a lot of ups and downs away.

First comes the seven years Sonny spent in Dallas, Texas, honing his craft. In 2016, the four-lane interstate trip would be 664 miles from Nashville, taking about ten hours to drive. In 1953, the two-lane trip would have taken closer to fourteen hours. In this written piece, you can get to Dallas in a hurry—just turn the page and you're there. Oh the miracle of a word map.

*The link to the "Virginia Waltz" is https://www.youtube.com/watch?v=SrjwBlowh3o

CHAPTER 5

THE DALLAS YEARS—1953-1959

*Patience and perseverance have a magical effect before
which difficulties disappear and obstacles vanish.*
—JOHN QUINCY ADAMS

(Note: this chapter is very short and sketchy because Sonny never told us anything much about it. I was really surprised when I read the account in the boxed set. Newspaper clippings on a Dallas historical website and a connection with one family in Dallas were the only other documentation I came across in my research.)

The summer of 1952 was incredibly busy for Sonny. He was recording in Nashville, traveling with Slim Whitman, and making guest appearances on the Louisiana Hayride. In August, he performed at the Big D Jamboree in Dallas.

This performance evidently made a good impression on somebody because in October '52, Sonny joined the cast of the competing *WFAA Saturday Nite Shindig* just thirty or so miles west of Dallas in Fort Worth. He began as a member of Bobby Williamson's band, playing fiddle, guitar, or mandolin as needed. Very soon he became a headliner in his own right, and WFAA even gave him a fifteen-minute radio show that aired twice a week.

Paula Bosse, a long-time Sonny James fan ever since she heard "Running Bear" as a youngster, now a Dallas area writer and historian, wrote: "It looks like there were two distinct periods of the Shindig: the first era which began when it started in the '40s, which was more old-fashioned and "homespun" — more traditionally barndance-y — and the Sonny James era, which seems to have been a bit more Big D Jamboree-like, with more of an awareness of teenagers and young adults and the looming era of rock 'n' roll."

Sonny had two more recording sessions back in Nashville, then the next seven sessions over the course of three years were held at the Jim Beck Studio there in Dallas.

Sonny joined the Big D Jamboree in Dallas and became a regular after the Saturday Nite Shindig shut down. Then came the first really big break in his career. On January 22, 1955, ten months before he moved to Dallas, the Ozark Jubilee, a new nationally televised prime-time country music show originating out of Springfield, Missouri, premiered on the ABC Television Network. It was a live ninety-minute program hosted by Red Foley that ran until September 24, 1960. At the time there were just three television networks.

This from Sonny's official bio:

"It was originally an hour-and-a-half show," James said. "Red said, it's just too long for him to emcee — he was afraid people would tire of it." Foley opted to emcee the final hour of the show, leaving the first thirty minutes to be shared by three rotating hosts: Sonny James, Webb Pierce, and Porter Wagoner. Pierce hosted the first half-hour of the ninety-minute programs once a month beginning October 15, 1955; Wagoner and James joined him in monthly rotation from January through at least July 1956.

Every three weeks, James would board a train from Dallas to Springfield, nearly 425 miles away. "Every third week I'd emcee the first portion," James said. "I'd have to give the Rolaid commercial live and all that stuff. I just remember they'd always make sure that they manicured my fingers because they'd shoot me holding the Rolaids.

That was just one of the sponsors, but I had to do that. They'd just make sure that your nails were clean."

By early 1956, estimates placed its weekly TV audience to be as high as nine million viewers, which led to Sonny charting three back-to-back country records in 1956: "For Rent" at #7, "Twenty Feet of Muddy Water" at #11, and "The Cat Came Back" at #12. The Jubilee had given Sonny James national name recognition by the end of 1956 as a country music singer.

Suddenly, in late 1956, "Young Love" exploded onto the music scene, making Sonny James a household name. He was quickly invited to perform on *The Ed Sullivan Show* and *The Bob Hope Show* and received more and more requests for personal appearances. Now Sonny had to cut back on his shows in Dallas.

Somehow in all of this activity, Sonny found the time to quietly court pretty Doris Shrode whom he had met at Peak and Eastside Church of Christ (now known as Main Street Church of Christ) in Dallas; in July 1957 Jimmie Loden and Doris were married in a small private ceremony there. Their fifty-eight-year marriage was a glowing example of love and devotion.

If you visit www.churchofchristpreaching.com and go to the History section, you will see that Sonny is still remembered and respected there.

Another person Sonny met at Eastside was fellow musician Shirley Wilson Legate. Milo (as we would know him) would become Sonny's bass player and lifelong friend, as well as comedy partner and all around handyman. We will document more of Milo's story in another chapter.

Also, Linda Arnold and her daughter Ruth were early members of Sonny's fan club in Dallas and became his good friends. He memorialized this friendship by using "Linda Ruth" as the name of a child in his 1954 Christmas song "I Almost Forgot to Remember Santa Claus."

Paula Bosse's research also turned up an amusing story. Sonny was already becoming known as an avid fisherman and she noted that he had entered many fishing tournaments. His fellow church members even knew. On one Sunday after "Young Love" became a hit, the church bulletin included a paragraph congratulating him and expressing their joy over his good example to the young people. The note concluded with "and hurry up and get that new Cadillac—we will need it to go fishing." Couldn't help but think—Holy (freshwater) mackerel!

Probably the most revealing thing that Paula came across was an interview Sonny did with Dallas, Texas reporter Tony Zoppi as "Young Love" was riding high on the charts. Zoppi, well-known in the Dallas area, asked Sonny a question whose answer was to be as revealing as anything Sonny would ever say in his entire life, and in just a few short words would give us a deep look into the heart of the man whose life at that moment was at the top of everything. The simple two-word question was, "What's next?" Sonny's answer wasn't the name of his next record release, or that he would be appearing on a network television show in a week or two, or anything of the sort. No, Sonny's response was, as we would come to understand about the man, as true to Sonny as anything he could say, "Can't tell what's ahead, but whatever it is, I'll still be Sonny James of Hackleburg when it's all over."

Well, we're about to see "what's ahead."

Sources Consulted
1. SONNY JAMES Young Love The Complete Recordings 1952-1962 Bear Family Records
2. Flashback Dallas (website) Paula Bosse, owner
3. Sonny James—The Official Site of The Southern Gentleman

CHAPTER 6

FIFTEEN MINUTES TO FAME

"If a window of opportunity appears, don't pull down the shade."
—TOM PETERS

We need to roll back time a bit to 1955 when Sonny was into his third year of living in Dallas. At that point, he and his producer Ken Nelson had started to find minor success with songs and the simple sound that would identify Sonny James in later years. That sound was another test run for an artist searching for something, anything that might give him a chance at a lasting career. Ken, through his publishing company Central Songs, had secured some lyrics from song writer Jack Morrow that seemed to have potential for Sonny. Ken connected Sonny and Jack — Jack as the lyricist and Sonny adding the melodies. This combination produced material that really fit.

Their first combined effort was released at the end of 1955 titled "Pigtails and Ribbons." It was country all the way. It kicked off with Harland Powell playing his steel guitar, the song not only mentioning pigtails and ribbons but "freckles on your face." Then came 1956 with the first release "For Rent" co-written again by Sonny and Jack which reached #7 on the country charts. The next release was "Twenty

Feet of Muddy Water" written by Bill Smith which topped out at #11, followed by a song titled, "The Cat Came Back" that peaked at #12 country and #30 on the UK charts — the first time since Sonny had signed with Capitol four years earlier that he had three songs in a row that charted and one that charted overseas. It seemed like Capitol and Sonny had finally found his target audience and presented them with the type of songs they could identify with.

On Tuesday, October 30, 1956, Sonny and Ken Nelson would be recording for the first time at the Quonset Hut located on 16th Ave South in Nashville. Prior to this day they had walked into recording studios thirteen times in four years with great anticipation as they recorded fifty-three songs. The last time Sonny had recorded in Nashville was in 1953 at the Castle Studio. Between 1953 and this recording session, Sonny and Ken had recorded in Dallas, Texas, at Jim Beck's Studio and at the Capitol Recording Studio in Hollywood, California.

They walked into the back door of the Quonset Hut to greet some old and new faces. There was Pete Wade playing guitar, Lightnin' Chance on bass, Buddy Harmon on drums, and Sonny's steel player Harland Powell to do background singing with the Jordanaires' first tenor Gordon Stoker. They had a song in hand written entirely by Jack Morrow, and both Sonny and Ken realized it had great potential.

So at 10 a.m., the three-hour session began. All of us who have spent time in recording sessions from that era know how it could go. You might run through the song one time and have it. Other times you might never get what you wanted, and still other times you might get it in half an hour. Sessions back then always had a hopefulness about them—let's get three songs in three hours if we can—that always seemed to be the ideal. In the previous two recording sessions on August 15 and 16, which were in Capitol's Hollywood studios, Sonny and Ken had recorded six songs in each of those three hour sessions for a total of twelve in all. They were walking on air as they entered this new environment in Nashville. We have no idea how many songs they carried in, but we do know how many they came out with.

I wish I had been a little fly on the wall on that day. The first song they set out to record was Jack Morrow's song. There are varying but similar stories about what happened during those three hours. Private as Sonny was about some things, the story I am presenting is not anything Sonny, as far as I know, ever related to anyone. It is well to remember that sometimes artists and/or producers get a certain feeling for songs—the artist likes it and the producer doesn't; or the producer likes it, but the artist can't stand it. You get the picture.

There's a story in Nashville that comes through reliable enough sources that I feel comfortable relating it. Ferlin Husky, a Capitol Records artist who was also produced by Ken Nelson, cut the song "Gone" that went to #1 country and #4 on the Billboard pop charts. In 1960, Ferlin was once again recording, and Ken Nelson was producing. Ferlin had a song he wanted to cut but Ken didn't. As the story goes — Ken had to leave the session right near the end of the three hours to catch a plane and Ferlin, against Ken's wishes, held the musicians overtime in the studio and recorded the song "Wings of a Dove," which went to #1 country and #12 pop — the second and last #1 Ferlin Husky would have. Whether the story is totally accurate or not it makes the point. Sometimes not everybody knows what a hit is — in fact, most of the time nobody knows.

So here's the story on the "Young Love" session related to me by our bass player Milo Liggett who had a conversation years ago with Selby Coffeen, the recording engineer that day. Sonny and Ken were really hearing the possibilities this particular song offered. They recorded it once, then twice, then for the fifth time, and then the tenth. They incorporated in the song the vocal background style that in the future would be an identifiable piece of Sonny's sound. But they just couldn't get what they were hearing in their minds down on tape, so they went on to the fifteenth and the twentieth and twenty-fifth take. Mind you, not every attempt was a full take.

The story goes that at times they stopped before they had completed the entire song. Maybe the tempo didn't feel just right—they were recording it too fast or too slow or someone messed up so they just stopped. Finally, and I mean finally, after two hours and forty-five minutes, they got it on take number twenty-eight. That's right — take twenty-eight — that same number of takes it took to get the fifth #1 country charted hit, "Hound Dog," recorded by Elvis in 1956 (actually Elvis recorded it thirty-one times but they ultimately chose take #28 for release). So Ken Nelson, after two hours and forty-five minutes and twenty-eight takes, announced, "That's it. We got it Thanks, everybody." Sonny responded by saying that they still had fifteen minutes left, and he had this song that had come to him through Bill Lowery out of Atlanta, a song written by Ric Cartey and Carole Joyner, and it was real simple, and Sonny felt they could probably lay it down it in those last few minutes.

Ken Nelson caved in and after grinding out one song for nearly three hours recording, "You're the Reason I'm in Love," Sonny played this new song. The words to the first verse were:

They say for every boy and girl
There's just one love in this whole world
And I know I've found mine
The heavenly rapture of your embrace
Tells me no one could take your place
Ever in my heart

Sonny changed the fourth line to read: "The heavenly touch of your embrace" and they recorded it within that fifteen minute period. Let's let Ken Nelson give his side of the story from page 115 in his book *My First 90 Years Plus 3*:

That session was one of the rare times I ever raised my voice to an artist. We only recorded two songs, "You're the Reason I'm in Love" and "Young Love." When we had finished the third take on [the last song] "Young Love," I said, "That's it." I felt the background was perfect, and Sonny had the right emotional appeal. When I played it back for him, he wanted to do another take and was quite insistent. I too was insistent and in a determined voice said, "That's it, period."

Ken Nelson remembered three takes — Milo said Selby remembered it was actually two. That's what fifty years tends to do.

The record was released on December 10, 1956, with "You're the Reason I'm in Love" as the A side and "Young Love" as the B side—and why not? They had spent a grinding two hours and forty-five minutes and twenty-eight takes on the A side, and fifteen nondescript, hurried minutes and two or three takes, depending on whose story you accept, on the B side. That was a no-brainer. And because the cut of "You're the Reason I'm in Love" was considered so country-oriented by Ken Nelson, as Sonny wrote in his bio, "Five years later [after he had signed with Capitol in 1952] . . . [they] called me 'The Southern Gentleman.'" That single record release identified Sonny on both sides, for the first time in his life, as "The Southern Gentleman." Not only had Ken Nelson gotten Sonny to change his name to Sonny James in 1952, but now in 1957 had given him a defining label. Country was all Sonny ever wanted, and country was all he ever was, and "You're the Reason I'm in Love," along with being labeled as "The Southern Gentleman," was about to bring his dream to a dramatic head.

The record was pressed with Capitol expecting normal sales of a Sonny James record as they were plugging the country A side for airplay. On the way to the turntable, as they say, the disc jockeys at the stations had to accommodate other ideas when the B side started getting requests from listeners. It happened to Sonny like nothing this gifted country boy from Hackleburg, Alabama, could ever have imagined.

And then the surprise of all surprises happened. Within ten days of its release, "You're the Reason I'm in Love" fell on the floorboard of the back seat and on December 19, the B side "Young Love" dashed to #1 on the Billboard country charts and stayed #1 for nine weeks. Ten days later on December 29, it hit #1 on Billboard's pop charts.

That wasn't the beginning and the end of all that hard work on "You're The Reason I'm in Love." (Twelve years later on November 20, 1968, we recorded it for its second go-around in a faster-tempoed version with horns. Sonny held it back for three and a half more years before releasing it on April 17, 1972, where it went to #1 on the country charts during the week of June 24, 1972.)

And so, on October 30, 1956, Sonny's fifteen minutes to fame happened in a way much different from what others would call fifteen minutes of fame. Only twenty days after its release, "Young Love" turned out to be fifteen minutes that turned into fame for The Southern Gentleman, Sonny James. The dream days were over—now came the reality of managing the follow-up. I once heard it said that it takes talent to win and character to repeat. That and more were going to be put to the test.

Like the Rhinestone Cowboy getting cards and letters from people he didn't know and offers coming over the phone — now that was the immediate reality. Just five weeks after "Young Love" was released and three weeks after it hit #1, Sonny found himself in New York City. He told me it was the most amazing thing he had ever experienced. He said he couldn't turn around without hearing "Young Love" being played all along Broadway. His face wasn't all that familiar yet, but it would be in just a matter of days. His reason for being in New York City was that an offer had come over the phone to appear on *The Ed Sullivan Show* at the 8 p.m. hour on Sunday night, January 20, 1957 — an offer, of course, a man couldn't turn down.

Two weeks earlier, on January 6, Elvis made his third and final appearance on *The Ed Sullivan Show,* backed up by the Jordanaires. They did a total of three segments totaling seven songs, with the final song famously being "Peace in the Valley." I said all that just to say this — Gordon Stoker was the first tenor with the Jordanaires backing up Elvis. Stoker was also one of the background vocalists on Sonny's recording of "Young Love." And now there was Sonny James, on top of the world, appearing on the Sullivan show with actor and singer Fess Parker and with R&B recording artist Ivory Joe Hunter who would sing his hit, "Since I Met You, Baby."

Immediately Ed McLemore, Sonny's manager located in Dallas, began booking Sonny for personal appearances all over the place. In addition to Harland Powell, who had been with Sonny for three years, Sonny picked up two additional musicians — drummer Dude Kahn and Gene Stewart as a guitar player (he was Redd Stewart's brother. Redd along with Pee Wee King were the co-writers of "Tennessee Waltz" and another lesser known but very popular song "Slow Poke"). Unfortunately we have no record of most of those dates. Some have surfaced through newspaper articles and the like, but we have only a few.

On April 24, 1957, just three weeks after Elvis, accompanied by the Jordanaires, had performed in Ottawa, Canada, to a crowd of screaming girls, Sonny was there for a show. The newspaper article, which I have, is from the *Ottawa Citizen* and has Sonny posing for a picture, playing his guitar, as five female subjects are gazing at him. The caption under the picture reads, "SONNY'S SONGS SEND THEM." By that time Sonny's excellent follow-up to "Young Love" had been released —"First Date, First Kiss, First Love." The article's headline was "Sonny James not like Elvis Presley, but the fans squeal just as loudly." The article refers to Sonny as The Southern Gentleman and interestingly mentions that when Sonny went to his car to leave the show, there were lipstick prints all over the vehicle.

Another offer arrived, and a week later on May 5, 1957, Sonny was in California as a guest on *The Bob Hope Show*. Also appearing on the show were Shelley Winters, George Jessel and golfer Dr. Cary Middlecoff. Sonny sang two songs: "Young Love," and "First Date, First Kiss, First Love." Sonny once talked to me about his appearance on the Hope show. It wasn't as much about his appearance as it was that Mr. Hope invited him to stay overnight with him and his wife Delores in their home. Sonny, never one to make more of it than it was, said he had a wonderful time. As Jerry Reed would sing some years later in a song, "When You're Hot You're Hot," boy-oh-boy in 1957 this 6-foot, 3-inch handsome man with his crop of curly hair was really hot as the spring rolled into the summer.

1957 was a great year for Sonny and Ken Nelson with only one misstep, the song "A Mighty Lovable Man" didn't chart country or pop. "Uh-Huh-Mm," which was more Elvis-like than anything Sonny had ever done, went to #8 country.

	Charted Country	Charted Pop
"Young Love"	1	1
"First Date, First Kiss, First Love"	9	25
"Lovesick Blues"	15	—
"A Mighty Lovable Man"	—	—
"Uh-Huh-Mm"	8	92

But there was a strong undertow happening. This tagged Southern Gentleman from Hackleburg would be pushed really hard by Capitol Records and Ken Nelson to be a teenybopper and rock-and-roll artist along the Elvis lines. Sonny's next sixteen recorded songs after "First Date, First Kiss, First Love" would feature Elvis' vocal background group, the Jordanaires, The last three singles released in 1957, "Lovesick Blues" and "Uh-Huh-Mm," would all trend toward bee-bop/rock-and-roll. You can listen to them on YouTube and decide for yourself. That simple sound that had started to define Sonny James on three consecutive country charted songs in 1956 was beginning its early journey toward disappearing into the musical sunset.

And saddest of all, the tag of The Southern Gentleman was about to become an anchor to what Capitol and Ken Nelson saw as an opportunity for the label to really clean up by pushing Sonny into pop. On "Uh-Huh-Mm," the last single release in 1957, Ken Nelson, who had given Sonny the label of The Southern Gentleman just a year earlier, would drop the identifying tag from the record and Sonny would simply become Sonny James again. It's as obvious as the nose on your face—The Southern Gentleman "country" designation would be a distraction from being a teenybopper pop star. Along with the loss of his country identity, Sonny's talent as a master fiddler would become useless in promoting him as a rock-and-roll singer. The Southern Gentleman tag and his grandfather's violin would not identify Sonny James again until seven long years later.

The question to be asked here is: how did this happen? What brought it all about? That's the challenging question. Maybe there's a lesson in here for all of us.

Two Reviews of Sonny James' Bear Records Boxed Set on Amazon. Com:

> The first two discs are great! Sonny starts out in the popular early-'50s Hank Williams style with stronger than average vocals. By the late-'50s, he was making pure pop. Background vocals, strings, lyrics for teens, blah. James' voice is a thing of amazing beauty, and he could have set the honky tonk scene ablaze if he had stayed true. Unfortunately, Sonny and Ken Nelson headed in a different direction. Sad, sad, sad.

> Once "Young Love" comes along, you'll read about the dilemma Sonny's producers are faced with, concerning his target audience and the mistakes that were made following this success. Fascinating reading as you listen to his music evolve starting with concerning his target audience and the mistakes that were made following this success.

All that aside—"Young Love" was to be the moon shot of country music. It quickly led Sonny to become the first country artist to record a million-seller at the Quonset Hut in Nashville, to being the first country music recording artist to appear on *The Ed Sullivan Show,* and to be the first country music recording artist to have a star on the Hollywood Walk of Fame.

By the final months of 1957, Sonny James, The Southern Gentleman from the friendly city of Hackleburg, Alabama, was well on his way to losing his distinctiveness. The powers to be had been slowly pulling the shade down on his identity. Though Sonny didn't let on to anyone, going back over his career starting in 1958, it was a heart-wrenching thing to discover and even harder to write about.

CHAPTER 7

SO, WHAT HAPPENED?

*"While you're waiting on opportunity, it might be waiting
on you to come to it. Get up and go get it!"*
—FROM THE BOOK *THE DAY MY SOUL CRIED:
A MEMOIR* BY YVONNE PIERRE

I was taken back to a true story Sonny told me more than once over
the years. First let me set it up. It was in the beginning eight months of
his Capitol Records recordings. On March 11, 1953, Sonny had completed his third session here in Nashville and had been thwarted in
each attempt. His first release didn't get enough airplays from the disc
jockeys to warrant Capitol releasing the record for sale.

During that period Sonny was booked on a show alongside a man
who in September 1948 had replaced Eddy Arnold on The Grand
Ole Opry. He went on to have a monster million-selling hit in 1949
with a song that stayed #1 on the charts for three weeks. The song
was "Candy Kisses," and the country crooner was twenty-four year
old George Morgan. Through the remainder of 1949, George had six
more releases that, except for one, charted top ten country. Starting in
1950 and continuing through 1951, George had nine more singles and

not one of them went anywhere.

Sonny was a virtual unknown at the time. When he and George Morgan had appeared on that show together, George, of course with "Candy Kisses," was the most recognized of the two. As Sonny was standing talking to George, a lady came up and asked George for his autograph. In his quiet, humble way, George obliged, asking who he ought to make the autograph to, and she gave him her name. As George was signing, she said to him, "Mr. Morgan, I just knew you were going to be a big star after 'Candy Kisses.'" George nodded and smiled and thanked her for the kind compliment as he kept on writing.

"So," she continued, "What happened?"

Though Sonny and I had a hearty laugh each time he told it, I came to realize some years later that the story was no laughing matter to Sonny or any other artist for that matter; it was the fear of every one of them. One song, one two-minute and thirty-second tune and for a one-hit wonder that's all you'd be allotted ("Candy Kisses" was 2:49, and "Young Love" was 2:28).

So back to that George Morgan/Sonny James experience. It's the question every artist fears after their first hit song, the question no artist ever wants to be asked—"Mr. James, I just knew you were going to be a big star after "Young Love" . . . what happened?"

Yes, so what did happen? After such a promising start, what caused the derailment? Did the failure just happen on its own merit or was some kind of wrench thrown into a promising country music career? We can toss three names into the mix to try and figure it out — Capitol Records, Ken Nelson, and Sonny James. At this point, I feel comfortable scratching Capitol Records off the list, which will leave us with Ken and Sonny. And why scratch Capitol? Ken Nelson, Capitol Record's Mr. Country Music was the decision maker for the "Hillbilly" side of Capitol. As Ken Nelson said himself in his book, *I approved all songs to be recorded* and maybe we could also add "and that's it, period."

At this point as I write, the men I would wish to get information from are all gone. To the forefront, I bring four into focus — Ed

McLemore, Bob Neal, Ken Nelson, and Sonny. Of the four now before us Ed (1904-1969), Bob (1917-1983), Ken (1911-2008) and Sonny (1928-2016), as far as I have been able to find, only Ken and Sonny left something behind for us to dig into. Sonny's bio, as was Sonny's way, was quite surface. He didn't get into his deep feelings or into blaming or controversy or anything of the kind — that was not his way. On the other hand, Ken Nelson's 352 page book, *My First 90 Years Plus 3,* is loaded with detail.

Before we get into "what happened," here are just a couple of facts up front. The Wikipedia page on Ken Nelson strangely makes no mention of Sonny James. It states, "During his many years with Capitol's division in Hollywood, California, he produced many of the genre's most notable and successful hits, by artists including Merle Travis, Gene Vincent, Ferlin Husky, Jean Shepard, Hank Thompson and the many Number 1 country hits known as the Bakersfield Sound by Merle Haggard, Buck Owens, along with many others." Sonny had sixteen #1 singles in a row, and yet he is not mentioned by name by the contributors of Ken Nelson's Wikipedia page? WHY? We will cover that anomaly in the chapter "One Giant Leap."

On the other hand, on November 6, 2006, when Kris Kristofferson announced on ABC television that Sonny would be the newest Country Music Hall of Fame inductee, in Sonny's thirty-four-second acceptance speech, one of the seven people that Sonny thanked for his career was Ken Nelson. It begs asking the question here — was Sonny thanking Ken for signing him in 1952 or for the song "Young Love" or was there something more subtle to the thanking than that?

At this point there are some very interesting events that happened, starting in 1955; two are referenced in Ken Nelson's book, events that have never been addressed before but will be addressed here.

Ken's position as Capitol's country music A&R man was to sign new artists and develop them, as well as working with the current artists under contract. It had to be a day-in and day-out, day and night job. By 1956, he had Sonny and Faron Young and Ferlin Husky and Hank Thompson and Jim and Jesse and the Louvin Brothers and

Martha Carson and Tex Ritter and a number more, along with the near signing of a new up-and-comer on October 20, 1955. On top of that another artist he signed in mid-1956 that he didn't have to find a song for—a new singer whose song had already been demoed with the only thing that Ken had to do was re-cut it.

I am fortunate to have a small but dedicated team of Sonny James admirers who keep looking and finding interviews and documents and challenging me with opinions and observations shrouded just below the sight-line, information that is invaluable. I have already referred to Suzanne Cummings from Ridge, New York. At this point in my writing let's say hello to Don McKay from Tullahoma, Tennessee.

Don and I had been discussing the "what happened" question for quite a while. Don's ability to think out of the box forced me back to Ken Nelson's book that I had leisurely read some fifteen months earlier, a book indexed which is such an invaluable part of any written material.

So there I was again, Ken's book in hand, scouring through the seventy-eight page section titled 1951-1960 (pages 98-176) when the first of the two events I mentioned jumped off page 129. Here's the section —just five little sentences:

> I had been hearing and reading about a young singer named Elvis Presley, who was recording for Sun Records in Memphis, Tennessee. I found out that his manager, Bob Neal, was a Memphis disc jockey. I decided to try to get him [Elvis] for Capitol. I went to Memphis and met with Bob [Neal], and he told me that Elvis' contract was not for sale. A few weeks later, I read that RCA Victor had signed Elvis and his manager was Colonel Tom Parker.

Though not mentioned in Ken's book, Elvis signed with RCA on November 21, 1955.

Bob Neal was one of those men right up there near the front on the second row of music history, and he is hardly, if ever, talked about in much front-page detail. Without going into a lot of background on

Bob, he was into radio in Memphis on WMPS, a station the Loden Family worked out of in the late '40s. In mid-1954, Sam Phillips gave disc jockey Bob Neal one of the early Elvis records that would be played on the air. By the start of 1955, Bob was officially Elvis' manager, booking dates for him. Enter Col. Tom Parker and by the spring of 1956, as I understand it (there are differing stories about it), Bob sold his share of Elvis to Col. Parker and opened a talent agency (Stars, Inc.). Among those he booked were Sonny, Johnny Cash, Roy Orbison, Jerry Lee Lewis, and Faron Young. In the 1960s, he started the Bob Neal Talent Agency in Nashville and booked all of our and many other artist's shows. A couple of times he rode with us on our bus as we made our way from one show date to the next.

A few turns later on pages 136-138 the second event appeared which was a real eye-opener for me. Let's set it up. Without quoting all of it, here's the gist — it was 1956 and a demo of a rock-and-roll song called "Be-Bop-A-Lula" sung by Gene Craddock and his band was sent to Ken. On May 4, 1956, just six months after not being able to secure Elvis as an artist for Capitol Records, Ken Nelson recorded four songs by Gene and his group in Nashville at Owen Bradley's studio. The song was released in June 1956 and peaked at #7 on Billboard's pop charts. Ken wrote, *"I was impressed by the singer and the song **and felt that Rock and Roll was to become an important part of the music industry**"* (underline and bold type are mine). Ken signed Gene Craddock to a contract and changed his recording name to Gene Vincent (his middle name) in much the same way he had changed Jimmie Loden to his professional name of Sonny James.

It so happened that Gene didn't have a manager so Ken connected him up with Ed McLemore, a businessman out of Dallas who also was managing Sonny at the time. It seems obvious that Ken, feeling as he did at the time about the future of rock and roll, was caught up in the Elvis phenomenon and was looking for a young artist he could sign to a Capitol Records contract to rival Elvis (taken from the Wikipedia page on "Be-Bop-A-Lula"). In April 1957, Capitol announced that over 2 million copies of this record had been sold to date.

So with Ken missing out on Elvis, and being a savvy businessman he realized you should not put all of your eggs in one basket. If Gene Vincent didn't turn out as Ken imagined, following the success of "Be-Bop-A-Lula," then who would be Ken's next pick? Ken Nelson kept looking.

Enter the fray — Tommy Sands. He was signed by Capitol, and his first release was "Teenage Crush" that quickly went to #2 on Billboard's pop charts in January 1957 selling well over a million. Ken Nelson, Capitol's head country A&R man found himself on a "pop" roll.

Though not mentioned very often, even though Elvis was hitting it big as a rock-and-roll singer from 1956 through 1959, the country boy from Tupelo, Mississippi, had eight of his singles that reached the #1 slot on the country charts during that time. Starting in 1960 and through the end of that decade, he lost his country identity with but eight songs charting country. The average Billboard position of the eight was #44. That's for someone else to explain.

And suddenly in January 1957, following the pop success of "Young Love," there was Ken Nelson - three major recording artists in his hip pocket (Gene, Tommy, and Sonny) along with their three monster songs. How would the three of them react to their overnight successes? Would the three be up to allowing Ken and Capitol pushing them to take on RCA and Elvis? The back story on Gene Vincent was laid out clearly by Ken in his book on page 138, "A few months after that [after April 1957] he [Ed McLemore] called me and said, 'Ken, I'm dropping Gene. I can't handle him. He's too much of a problem.'" Suddenly, one was down, and two remained.

As for Tommy Sands, rather than post the entire three-paragraph and over 350-word section, let me give you the Cliff Notes version: Tommy was dating Frank Sinatra's daughter Nancy and wanted to record with The Nelson Riddle Orchestra and the June Nelson Singers. According to Ken on page 148, "He probably wanted to prove to her [Nancy Sinatra] that he could attain the same stature as her father [Frank Sinatra] by recording with Nelson Riddle's orchestra, which did all of Frank Sinatra's Capitol Records." Said Ken, "I told him [Tommy

Sands] I thought it would be a mistake and could hurt his career because they were not the type of songs his fans expected or wanted from him. He was very insistent." Long and short of it, Ken "foolishly consented," and Tommy Sands ended up recording twenty-four songs with the Nelson Riddle orchestra over the next twelve months. Half of the songs were with the June Nelson Singers with both albums having "little acceptance." Quoting again from page 148, "When his five year contract was up, I didn't renew it." Two were down, and one was left.

Just some interesting background here — Frank Sinatra was on Columbia Records from 1946–1952, and his career was starting to slump. In 1953, he signed with Capitol Records and remained on Capitol through 1962. Tommy Sands was dating Nancy Sinatra and to be sure the Capitol/Sinatra link had a lot to do with Tommy also signing with Capitol. Also interesting to note — Frank left Capitol around the same time Tommy's contract with Capitol wasn't renewed by Ken Nelson.

These many years later as I was putting this book together, I realized I knew and had experienced first-hand what Ken Nelson was about to do with Sonny James. In no way do I wish for business decisions or decisions of any kind to deflect from the sincere goodness of a man. Business decisions are business decisions period, and should ultimately be viewed totally independent of the character and charm of an individual.

Let me explain. In the chapter "The Opening Year—1952," I mentioned that as a ten-year-old in 1951, I had this inherent ability to throw a knuckleball and was using it in Little League. The following year in 1952, I finished the season with a 7–1 record and was voted the MVP. Hanging on the wall in my office is a picture of a sports writer in our area presenting me with the trophy as two New York Yankee AAA players are looking on.

As my knuckleball-throwing major league hero, Hoyt Wilhelm, stated later in his life—he did not teach other pitchers the knuckleball, believing that you had to be "born with a knack for throwing it." Hoyt should know—he pitched in the majors until he was just fifteen days shy of being fifty years old and ended his playing days with the lowest career ERA (earned run average) of any major league pitcher, which still stands till this day. As much as Sonny was born with the uncanny gift to play stringed instruments, a similar dose of ability was given to this kid from Endicott, New York, who seemed to be endowed from the beginning with the ability to throw a baseball that would do the Texas two-step all the way to home plate.

The knuckleball was my bread-and-butter pitch and my catchers (this was well before a larger glove had been developed to catch it), fought the devilish thing all the way into their chest protectors. I filed my fingernails and worked on gripping it all sorts of different ways, and it really did tricks for me. My dad, who was a great industrial league pitcher back then and who threw eighteen one-hitters in his career, relying on a fastball for his bread and butter, said my knuckleball was the best he had ever seen. My older brother John also pitched, and I watched him pitch a no-hitter in high school. My brother, like my dad, had a blazing fastball and a tenacious curve ball to compliment it, yet he also said that his younger brother had the best knuckler he had ever observed.

My dad, unknown to my brother and me, kept a scrapbook with newspaper clippings of games we had pitched. Later in life my dad gave me the book, which also included not only clippings of our college quartet singing in the Endicott area, but also clippings of a couple of shows Sonny and The Southern Gentlemen did in the vicinity.

One of the baseball clippings was from an All Star game I pitched in as a fourteen-year-old on July 6, 1955. John Wiley had started the game, and they brought me in for the last four innings. Of the twelve outs made by the opposing team, ten were strikeouts—most, I am sure, the result of my dancing knuckler.

It happens to all of us, and it happened not only to Sonny but also to me. My dad felt that for me to really be successful as a baseball pitcher, I needed to develop a fastball like he and my brother had, and my dad was insistent I throw harder. So persistent was he that in the spring of 1956 as a fifteen-year-old, I gave it my best.

I have no recollection as to how this happened, but I came across a book that "fireball pitcher" Bob Feller had written in 1947 titled *Bob Feller's Strikeout Story.* I read it excitedly, and I guess I thought that just the reading of it would be enough to enable me to throw like my dad and my brother and Feller. Bob was the strikeout king of the times and had been with the Cleveland Indians since 1936. By the time his career ended in late 1956, he would end up pitching twelve one-hitters and three no-hitters while striking out 2,581 batters. I suppose it seemed simple—if my dad and my brother and Bob Feller could throw harder than me it must just be as easy as believing I could, and Bob's book inspired me (a few years ago I came across and purchased a first edition of that same book).

So as spring baseball season rolled around in 1956, I was in a position to put my excitement and determination into practice. With my dad's encouragement I got myself fired up and pitched in a game, throwing as hard as I could and struck out twelve opposing batters in six innings, relying I am sure almost solely on a fastball. The short of it was that we won the game, and my dad was thrilled. The long of it was — in just one game I threw my arm out.

Unfortunately, my dad had determined to try to turn me into his dream, and it was not to be. In just one game, that dream would be my undoing. Whatever had happened to me, the doctors at that time couldn't fix it (Tommy John surgery didn't come along until eighteen years later), and my love of throwing the knuckleball and continuing to throw it were suddenly over in just five short years of pitching. At that time, I was too young to think beyond the moment. Trying to make it in baseball was the farthest thing from my mind, but loving to make the thing do what it did and seeing the opposing batters swing at the air and miss wildly was something I have never gotten over. Who knows for sure—maybe I was as good as Hoyt Wilhelm; I don't know. But looking back, I sure wish I had had the opportunity. I really loved baseball.

Like my dad with me, Ken Nelson had now been stymied three times: by Elvis Presley, by Gene Vincent, and by Tommy Sands in his conviction that *rock and roll was to become an important part of the music industry*. But Ken, after three disappointments, still had one player warming up in his bullpen who was waiting to be used. Ken still had Sonny James, and before he knew it, Sonny found himself, like me, standing on the music-mound trying to throw a fast ball when he should have been relying on a proven knuckler.

Don McKay sent me an email stating it perfectly, "All the artists at that time shared one common talent—they could *sing*. A few could also play an instrument, but even fewer had *mastered* it. Another few had *three* things going for them—the looks, personality, and stage presence that drew their audiences even closer to them than their music. But only Sonny had "mastered" *all three*! Ken Nelson probably never admitted it to anyone, but he had to have recognized that fact and tried to at least nudge Sonny in the same direction as Elvis and Gene and Tommy—something none of his other stable of artists could come close to doing."

And when "Young Love" hit the charts in late 1956 and stayed at #1 on the country charts for nine consecutive weeks in 1957 and immediately hit #1 on the pop charts — Ken Nelson had his Gene Vincent replacement, his Tommy Sands smooth-voiced cover, his Elvis rival — all wrapped up in one neat package and without all the baggage handling that accompanied Vincent. It just fell into Ken Nelson's lap with two or three takes in fifteen minutes and a B side hit — and all he had to do was find the follow up songs to keep it rolling.

There are many books that tell you how to be successful, but hardly any tell you how to stay that way. Sonny's "stay that way" would not be found in a book—it would be in a person who had complete control —Ken Nelson.

The list below makes it obvious. Following the success of "Young Love," and starting in August 1957 with "A Mighty Lovable Man," Sonny would record forty-four songs over the next two years. Still riding on the coattails of "Young Love" only "Uh-Huh-Mm," an Elvis-type song, charted country. As we can see, five songs charted on the pop charts. We might cheer that fact, but that wasn't good enough for the record company, not nearly good enough. Capitol, as with most record companies, was looking for another "Young Love"-type song, charting at #1/#1.

	Charted Country	Charted Pop
"Young Love"	1	1
"First Date, First Kiss, First Love"	9	25
"Lovesick Blues"	15	—
"A Mighty Lovable Man" recorded 08/1957	—	—
"Uh-Huh-Mm" recorded 10/1957	8	92
"Kathleen" recorded 01/1958	—	—
"Are You Mine" recorded 01/1958	—	—
"You Got That Touch" recorded 06/1958 Writers - Sonny James/Richard Hollingsworth	—	94
"Let Me Be the One to Love You" recorded 09/1958	—	—
"Dream Big" recorded 11/1958 Writers - Paul Hampton/Bacharach	—	—
"Talk of the School" recorded 03/1959 Writer - Sonny James	—	85
"Pure Love" recorded 03/1959 Writers - Jesse Hodges/Johnny Burnette	—	107
"Who's Next in Line" recorded 06/1959 Writer - Sonny James	—	—
"I Forgot More Than You'll Ever Know" recorded 10/1959 Writer - Cecil Allen Null	—	80

Not one time in our seven years with Sonny did anyone request that we sing any of the above songs other than "Young Love." Interestingly, we were often asked to do "A White Sport Coat" which was a #1 country and #2 Billboard pop hit for Marty Robbins in mid-1957. Sonny was not into doing other artist's hits on our shows; however, the one exception was we did Ned Miller's 1965 song, "Do What You Do Do Well" that went to #7 for Ned on the country charts.

Sixty years after Sonny and "Young Love" had exploded onto the scene, *Time Life* was presenting a new ten-disc CD collection on television in 2017 and promoting it as Oldies but Goodies. The collection included 158 songs and a thirty-two page booklet. It was proclaimed to be "the most definitive collection of '50s oldies music ever offered with teen idols, rockabilly rebels, music legends, love songs, instrumentals, and novelties." Three-fourths of the way through the thirty-minute TV program, Time Life introduced all of us viewers to Bonnie Belville who said, "This [the CD collection] is the origin of Rock & Roll. Whether it's Sonny James, which had that country flavored [Young Love], or whether it's [the] R&B of The Drifters and Chuck Berry, this is the beginning of Rock and Roll."

There's just no way to overstate that "Young Love" was simply a bridge to a new era in popular music.

During the "Young Love" success, and for a period of about six months, Sonny had added a three-piece group to perform with him. They were Dude Kahn on drums, Gene Stewart on guitar, and Harland Powell on bass (Harland was also one of the singers on "Young Love"). Before that, Harland had traveled for three years with Sonny playing steel, providing vocal harmonies, and doing eight recording sessions with him, totaling thirty-eight songs. Six of the sessions were recorded at the Jim Beck Studio in Dallas and the other two at Capitol Recording Studio in Hollywood.

Sonny cut twenty-two more singles in 1957 after "First Date, First Kiss, First Love" for Capitol Records and had nothing much to show for it. Two of the recording sessions were in Hollywood and eight were again in Nashville at the Quonset Hut with the vocal background provided by the Jordanaires. Following the successful run of "Young Love," Sonny again returned to being a solo artist — a singer without a band. Only one short year after "Young Love," the future he had seen so clearly was beginning to fade.

In the fall of 1957, Sonny returned to Hollywood and recorded three more pop-type songs: "Uh-Huh-Mm," "Climb the Ladder of Love" that was never issued, and "Why Can't They Remember." "Uh-Huh-Mm" would be the next to the last song that would chart for

Sonny on Capitol hitting #8 on the country and #92 on the pop charts.

In January 1958 Capitol changed direction with Sonny. They cut twelve songs with Bob Bain and His Orchestra, releasing all twelve on the album "Honey." Sonny was presented as a crooner in this attempt, and once again, not one song in the album featured Sonny's later identifiable guitar licks. Those guitar moves, one year removed from "Young Love," had become a distant memory on his sessions.

A week after finishing the album "Honey," they returned to the studio in Hollywood with Bob Bain and His Orchestra and recorded four more songs but not in the crooner style.

Six months later in June 1958, Sonny was back in Nashville to again try something different, this time without the Jordanaires, and he recorded three songs—again without those out-front famous guitar runs. Nothing charted.

Starting in September 1958 and continuing for seven recording sessions over the next nine months, Sonny was again back at Capitol Studios in Hollywood, recording seventeen songs with a different approach but again without much of any of Sonny's identifiable moves on his Martin D-28. Nothing charted.

On October 20, 1959, they tried using a big orchestra and chorus (The Jack Halloran Singers) and cut three songs at Capitol Studios in Hollywood. One of the songs they recorded was a new version of "I Forgot More Than You'll Ever Know," the song from his third session way back in March 1953 that got beat out by the Davis sisters. This was the third time Sonny was to cut the song. He had also recorded it in April 1957 in Nashville with the Jordanaires providing the background vocals. This third time showed a smidge of potential as the song charted at #80 on Billboard's pop charts.

Following the release of "I Forgot More" in 1959, seven-plus years after Ken Nelson had signed Sonny James to a recording contract and just two and a half years after "Young Love," Capitol and Ken Nelson were forced to make a choice—a choice that had to be a very difficult one for Nelson and very disappointing to Sonny.

This was Nelson's third failure with three artists cutting "pop" material. Gene Vincent was just too difficult to deal with. Tommy Sands was "very insistent" on recording with a big orchestra and a large singing group, and Ken, as he wrote, "foolishly consented." Sonny James— well, that was a very different kind of story. Sonny wasn't very confrontational. Go back to "Young Love" after the third cut with Sonny wanting to do one more take, and Ken saying, "That's it. Period!" Ken got his way, and following the success of "Young Love" in 1957, Ken, in Sonny's case, was "in complete control" and was in a position to "approve every song" that Sonny recorded. Stein's Law was correct, "If something cannot go on forever, it will stop." All Ken Nelson did, and looking back, thank goodness he did, was speed up the process.

On the other hand, Sonny tried; my how he tried, to satisfy Ken Nelson's insistence that he be a pop artist. Sonny even wrote and published the song "Yo-Yo," recording it in early 1959, which was the B side of "Dream Big." Dare I type the words for you to see — at this point—why not:

> Up and down like a Yo-Yo
> Well you got me on a string like a Yo-Yo
> You got me like you just wanna let go
> I'm going up and down like a Yo-Yo Yo-Yo
> To my baby I'm a yo ho Yo-Yo, baby
> I'm a yo oh Yo-Yo, baby
> I'm a yo oh Yo-Yo, baby
> Up and down like a Yo-Yo

Oh, no; that's enough. If you really want to see how far Sonny was willing to go for Ken, the song is on YouTube. Keep in mind—it's not the Sonny James we all remember.

It had gone so far away from who he was that it was going to be nigh unto impossible to get folks to again think country when they thought of Sonny James. Capitol and Ken and Sonny had found it impossible to slow the music carousel down.

Ken Nelson was country music's Mr. Capitol Records. From Ken's autobiography *My First 90 Years Plus 3* published in 2007, Ken gives us loads of information in the section titled "1951-1960." "In 1951, Capitol decided that Lee [Gillette] should produce the popular artists exclusively, and I should take over the artists who at that time were called 'Hillbillies.'" As we have seen, along the way Ken Nelson got distracted big time. Ken's "Hillbilly" roster at that time included Tex Ritter, Hank Thompson, Merle Travis, Tex Williams, Leon Payne, Leon Chappell, Big Bill Lister, Martha Carson and the gospel quartet The Statesmen. Not only was Ken's job to produce these country artists but also to contract new ones. In 1951 he signed Eddie Dean and Jimmy Heap. In 1952, on page 104 of his book, Ken wrote, "Of the artists I signed that year [1952] four would become popular and well known. Faron Young, Sonny James, The Louvin Brothers [Ira and Charley], and Merrill Moore." In the seventy-seven page section titled "1951-1960" Ken wrote about Sonny five different times.

Nelson was at the forefront of all that Sonny did, in fact he was at the forefront of all that all of his artists did. As he wrote on page 99 of the 1951-1960 section, "I was now an artist and repertoire producer (A&R man). My responsibilities were to find new artists and negotiate their contracts. If they didn't write their own songs or bring me suitable ones, I would find songs for them. **I approved all songs to be recorded.**" (bold print and underlining are mine).

That's a line we should not soon forget. That statement nearly established Sonny James as a permanent resident of One-Hit City. On the other hand, Sonny never brought up to me or anyone I know the fact that Capitol and Ken Nelson had released him, and Ken himself never wrote a negative thing about it in his book. The music business is an impersonal Big-Boy Game, and the bottom line is all that seems to matter. As a human being, all any of want to know is that someone, anyone, really cares. It is obvious that Ken and Sonny cared — neither one of them left a burning bridge behind. The question is, would they ever get to care again, and if they did, would their combined approach be the same?

And now, five years and nearly 2000 days and nights since "Young

Love," there was about to be some unknown magic going on, electricity in the air and magnetism on the ground, drawing pieces toward each other, pieces that had no idea that any of the others existed, but pieces destined to turn a solo "Hillbilly" act and then a solo "Rockabilly" act into a team effort - except in early 1962 that exact moment was still two and one-half years away. Sonny was completely in the dark when it came down to all the woulda's and coulda's and shoulda's that were behind him, but that was the unusual strength of the man — he could, and I mean this sincerely, easily put yesterday behind him with the uncanny ability to plod ahead and around the next bend. Sonny was prepared to stay the course — he was prepared to be patient, prepared to keep alive that little spark of celestial fire called determination and prepared to leave deliberate consideration behind and act. As George Washington is quoted as saying, *"Perseverance and spirit have done wonders in all ages."*

We should never, never make the grave mistake of overlooking the power of time. And no problem is too big when you have a team. But before this would happen again, it would be another time and another place a thousand overcast days away.

So while one man's dreams are being dashed, another man's dreams are taking flight. For Milo Liggett in 1959, his dream hadn't quite gotten off the runway yet. He had just graduated from ACC (Abilene Christian College) and was fixing (a good southern term) to spend eighteen months in the army. More about Milo and all of that later.

For two young men just entering college at ENC (Eastern Nazarene College) in Quincy, Massachusetts, their dream was about to become reality. It was September 1959, and life was about to take a simple but dramatic turn.

For years, the college had sent out acapella male quartets and ladies trios representing the school during the year on weekends and for ten weeks during the summer. During those summer months the groups would represent the church-related college all across the northeast. If you were fortunate enough to get into one of these groups the school would pay half of your tuition. As you might expect, after ten weeks in the summer, some of them would have graduated, and others would not have any interest in doing the routine for another year — so in September you might find totally new groups or a couple of partial groups looking to replace a member or two and sometimes three. Such was the case in the fall of 1959.

Ken Kern (bass) decided to stay on, and he picked up three new members — Claude Diehl (1st tenor), Duane West (2nd tenor), and Bill Wilhoyte (baritone). A few weeks or so into the fall term, Wilhoyte decided he didn't want to travel for another year, so the remaining three were looking for a baritone — enter, how do I say it — eighteen-year-old me. And so the beginning of a long-term yet unrecognized dream began to take shape for two of us in the group — Duane West and myself. During the next school year, Ken and Claude decided to move on, and we replaced them with Glenn Huggins (bass) and Lin Bown (1st tenor) — and that was when the magic really began. The four of us had this natural blend, something we didn't have to work at, so natural that it was like we were born to sing together.

On the other hand, for Sonny James in 1959, uncertain drifting times began.

> Life is a storm, my young friend.
> You will bask in the sunlight one moment,
> be shattered on the rocks the next.
> What makes you a man is what you do when that storm comes.
> You must look into that storm and shout, as you did in Rome
> "Do your worst for I will do mine."
> Then the fates will know you as we know you.
> —Lines from the 2002 movie *The Count of Monte Cristo*

Recognizing that Ken Nelson was, as his book indicates, in complete control, it had to be an onerous moment when the gavel was in the hand and the vote was being cast. In Ken and Sonny's seven-year association, Ken Nelson had produced all thirty-seven of their recording sessions which included 115 songs, and they had recorded in Dallas (six), Nashville (thirteen), and Hollywood (eighteen). But in spite of the personal attachment and even the questionable choice of songs or direction or control, the handwriting seemed to be clearly on the wall in 1959 — and when the votes were tallied and the gavel fell, Capitol Records informed thirty-one-year-old Sonny James that he had been released. Such are the arbitrary but totally business-oriented ways of record companies.

It was not quite as Sonny had recalled some thirty-three years later in 2002 in his interview with Samuelson. Of the ninety-three songs he had recorded since "Young Love" and through the end of 1962, his guitar runs were barely on seven songs, and from the session records of those recording dates, those licks were played (as Sonny alluded to in his bio) by other guitar players Bob Bain (one), Howard Roberts (two), Hubbard Atwood (two), and Howard Heitmeyer (two).

So here we are in the closing months of 1959 — Nelson didn't find those follow-up songs and all of the best-laid plans of mice and men stuff didn't happen, and Sonny James career had been sacrificed for Ken Nelson's beautiful dream.

The next number of years would find Sonny floating around to three different labels in three years with only one touch of success — "Jenny Lou" that charted on the NRC label in 1960, reaching #22 country and #67 pop. Following "Jenny Lou," not one of Sonny's next eight singles would even make the country charts, let alone the pop ones. By that time Sonny was hardly considered a country artist and the tag The Southern Gentleman lay dormant in some file cabinet folder somewhere, along with his great-grandfather's fiddle that had been stuck away in the back corner of a closet.

By 1960 Sonny's music style was quite a long way away from the uncomplicated sounds that had put him on the map in 1956, and a longer way from the sounds the tall, lanky boy born in Hackleburg had grown up enjoying.

From NRC, where he recorded seven songs in 1960, Sonny moved to the label that his old friend Chet Atkins was producing records for — RCA. Surely some magic had to be just around the corner with all the well-known musicians RCA would contract to play on Sonny's songs — Floyd Cramer (piano), Bob Moore (bass), Jerry Reed (guitar), Grady Martin (guitar), Hank Garland (guitar), The Anita Kerr Singers, and The Jordanaires (session back ground vocalists).

But out of the twelve songs Sonny would record and Chet Atkins would produce for RCA in 1961, one of those songs was probably the new low-point of his career. Before getting into that song we might stop and see what else Chet was producing/recording for RCA in '61. For himself - Chet recorded a John D. Loudermilk song that was a staple for Chet and his guitar for the rest of his life — "Windy and Warm." Look it up on YouTube — you will instantly recognize it. In 1961, Chet was also producing George Hamilton IV, who from 1961 through 1963 was constantly charting country (#9, #13, #22, #6, #21), and then a classic #1 country and #15 pop song "Abilene," written by Bob Gibson, Albert Stanton, Lester Brown, and John D. Loudermilk.

According to Wikipedia, "Atkins spent most of his career at RCA Victor and produced records for The Browns, Hank Snow, Porter Wagoner, Norma Jean, Dolly Parton, Dottie West, Perry Como, Floyd Cramer, Elvis Presley, the Everly Brothers, Eddy Arnold, Don Gibson, Jim Reeves, Jerry Reed, Skeeter Davis, Waylon Jennings, and many others."

It's human nature, as time goes by, to remember only the successes, but if we get right down to brass tacks, for everyone in the music business from the labels and producers and the artists, there is failure after failure that history kindly redacts. One of those failures for Chet, as hard as it is to believe now — would be his old friend Sonny James.

Here's a story lost in the haystack of time. Rick Hall, the genius behind Fame Recording Studio in Muscle Shoals, Alabama, passed this along to me in a lengthy and wonderfully informative phone conversation in July 2016. Rick was invited by Chet Atkins to sit in on a recording session on October 11, 1961 at RCA Studio B in Nashville. It was the third of what would be five sessions Sonny would do for RCA, with the last two being in January 1962. The songs they would end up recording that day were "Young Love" and "Broken Wings." It seemed like on every label change Sonny would make since his release from Capitol in 1959 that the record companies wanted to capitalize again on the prior success of Sonny's only major hit.

For Rick, this was the first time he had sat in on a session in Nashville, and it just so happened to be with a recording artist that he knew and respected and had even spent time fishing with in Alabama. The session featured the cream of the crop studio musicians: Bob Moore (bass), Buddy Harmon (drums), Floyd Cramer (piano), the Anita Kerr Singers (vocal background) and Sonny not only singing but also playing his Martin D-28. The recording engineer was studio icon Bill Porter. Chet was not hearing what Sonny wanted to hear, and Sonny kindly asked the engineer to turn up his guitar. Relating the story to me Rick said Bill Porter looked at Chet, and Chet told him to turn Sonny's guitar up a bit. They tried another take or two and according to Rick, in a moment of uncustomary frustration, Sonny went as far out of character as Rick said he had ever heard with Sonny blaring out, "If *you* don't mind, turn *me* up."

It had to have been exasperation to the max. Here was Sonny's Alabama friend Rick Hall sitting unannounced in an RCA recording session, produced by none other than Chet Atkins, and all RCA could come up with was a re-recording of "Young Love" and a song titled "Broken Wings." Looking back these many years later, the words to "Broken Wings" wrapped up perfectly where Sonny was in his career in 1961.

With broken wings no bird can fly
And broken promises mean love must fade and die
I trusted you
You can't be true
My heart no longer sings
Its wings are broken too
Written by Bernard Crum and John Jerome

At this point Sonny had survived a number of music genres — country, pop, crooner, and orchestral arrangements with only one success—his unexpected country-flavored cross-over to pop hit "Young

Love." And the previous session, just before the one Rick Hall had sat in on, RCA and Chet crossed their fingers and stepped way out there into "just maybe land."

I have a real interest in the spoken lines in movie scripts, and I was watching the 2007 movie *Argo* starring Ben Affleck. The dialogue in one spot went like this:

"You think this is more plausible…?
Yes, we do.
There are only bad options.
It's about finding the best one.
You don't have a better idea than this?
This is the best bad idea we have, sir. By far."

And RCA did. The best bad idea they could come up with in 1961 was for Sonny to cut a novelty song. There had been some big novelty hits in the prior three years with these types of songs. Here are a few examples:

1958 Sheb Wooley - *Purple People Eater* #1 pop
1958 Bobby Darin - *Splish Splash (I Was Takin' a Bath)* #3 pop
1958 David Seville - *Witch Doctor* #1 pop
1959 The Coasters - *Charlie Brown* #2 pop
1960 Larry Verne - *Mr. Custer* #1 pop
1960 The Hollywood Argyles - *Alley-Oop* #1 pop
1961 Lonnie Donegan - *Does Your Chewing Gum Lose Its Flavour (On the Bedpost Overnight?)* #5 pop

In addition Alvin and the Chipmunks had been around since 1958, and starting in 1961, the Chipmunks were featured in prime time on CBS on *The Alvin Show* that ran for two seasons.

So after four years of un-success, what's to lose and maybe, just maybe, the time was ripe for Sonny James to cut something unconventional—and here's the proof. The teen pop novelty song that they found for Sonny to record in 1961 was titled "Hey Little Ducky."

It had been recorded four months before, and I feel sure Sonny's level of contained chagrin was still high on that particular day when Chet had invited Sonny's friend Rick Hall to sit in. The Ducky song was written by Lamar Jacobs and produced by Chet — it's a duck talking, and Sonny singing to it. I first became aware of the song in about 2002 and innocently brought it to Sonny's attention. All he did was shake his head and groan. I am as sure as I can be that simply being reminded of it was all he could stand. I never brought it up again. Sometimes artists look back and wonder what they were thinking at the time. Personally, I wonder what Chet was thinking.

I saw Bobby Lord commenting on one of those Country Reunion Shows about his Columbia Records groaner "Pie Peachie Pie Pie" and his reaction, though he was laughing at the time, was similarly reminiscent of Sonny's reaction. When I was eleven years old, my parents had purchased a 78 rpm of Frankie Laine and Doris Day singing the catchy tune "Sugar Bush." The flip side was "How Lovely Cooks the Meat," which is still my number one "what was I thinking at the time" groaner song - out distancing "Pie Peachie Pie Pie," and "Hey Little Ducky" by a long way.

Since "Young Love" Sonny had now recorded a total of eighty songs with three different record companies (Capitol, NRC and RCA) in a number of different styles with nothing much to show for it. "Hey Little Ducky" recorded in June 1961 was, as it would have been for any artist, nearly the bottom of the last barrel. Of all the songs Sonny had recorded since "Young Love" in 1956 Chet Atkins had played guitar on fourteen, Buck Owens played on four, The Jordanaires sang on eighteen, The Anita Kerr Singers vocal sounds were on five, Hank Garland had played guitar on five, Al DeLory was the pianist on two, and trumpeter Herb Alpert of Herb Alpert and the Tijuana Brass fame had also played on two songs. No magic resulted from any of those magical musicians and magical singers and those magical producers.

Even though they are all exceptionally talented individuals — the small handful of ones that were used on Sonny's Nashville sessions were not able to take the songs that Sonny recorded after "Young Love" and give them the "whatever else it needs" to make the songs chart worthy. Sonny tried, the musicians tried, the producers tried and it was just not to be.

As the last of Sonny's five RCA sessions wound down in January 1962; it became obvious once again that even **all of Chet's choruses and all of Chet's men couldn't put Sonny together again.** It was going to take something else, something different and new. In early 1962 nobody had any idea what that "new something else" might be.

But "Hey Little Ducky" laid probably the biggest egg of all and even though it was going to be a hard egg to break, Sonny, as was his way, stepped over the egg shells with a new determination — this dream can work — he just needed to find the right combination. By this time in his career it was plain to see — record labels couldn't force-feed song soup platters to folks who had no interest in digesting them.

But here's where Sonny was at the beginning of 1962 — released from RCA and once again without a record label. And what did he find that was interested in him — of all things it was Dot Records. That's right—Dot, the same label that had covered Sonny's "Young Love" with Tab Hunter's version in early 1957. Dot would record thirteen songs with him in California in 1962 and release an album titled, you guessed it, *Young Love*. It was five years after the song had hit, and all the label had to offer was another "Young Love." In October of 1962, Sonny did his last recordings for Dot and found he was once again, and maybe for the final time, a man without a label.

And the "now what do I do?" question resurfaced. The decisions are not easy. There are many conflicting ways to go. I've always enjoyed laughing at those contradicting statements. One says "do" and the other says "don't." They both make sense, and when looked at in total it's no wonder decisions are hard to make. Here are a few examples:

• Two heads are better than one. / Paddle your own canoe.

• Haste makes waste. / Time waits for no man.

• You're never too old to learn. / You can't teach an old dog new tricks.

- A word to the wise is sufficient. / Talk is cheap.
- It's better to be safe than sorry. / Nothing ventured, nothing gained.
- Don't look a gift horse in the mouth. / Beware of Greeks bearing gifts.
- Do unto others as you would have others do unto you. / Nice guys finish last.
- Hitch your wagon to a star. / Don't bite off more that you can chew.
- Many hands make light work. / Too many cooks spoil the broth.
- Don't judge a book by its cover. / Clothes make the man.
- The squeaking wheel gets the grease. / Silence is golden.
- A stitch in time saves nine / If it ain't broke, don't fix it.
- Seek and ye shall find. / Curiosity killed the cat.

It's the end of 1962 — a long way from Hackleburg, and Jimmie H. Loden, and Sonny Boy and the Loden Family, a long way from Korea and the 252nd Truck Company, a long way from Hamilton, Alabama, a long way from 1952 and Chet Atkins introducing him to Ken Nelson and a Capitol Records contract, and a long five years since "Young Love" had exploded onto the music scene. Sonny, at the end of 1962, wasn't a kid anymore and would never again be packaged up to the public as a pop singer — he was now halfway through his thirty-fourth year.

Through all of these experiences, Sonny had a distinct advantage over many others in the music business and even in life in general. At some point in his youth, he had determined what life was really about, and he resolutely followed that guiding star. He didn't let the disappointments along the path defeat his spirit. Somewhere along the way, he had learned to accept a major disappointment as a nondefeat.

When you've got what you consider unfinished business here and the music is still in your head — you keep on keeping on. For Sonny

James, the failures didn't give him pause. In my opinion, that is what set him apart — at 11:59 p.m., today was about to be history. At 12:01 a.m., today turned into tomorrow, and tomorrow was all about promise. Look — midnight straight up is a "magic moment" we all get to observe once every twenty-four hours, and at that moment, we get to choose between either yesterday or tomorrow. The dilemma is, all of us are forced to pick one. It does a body no good to look back and fret — and it served Sonny well - he didn't. The moment to Sonny never seemed bigger than he was.

So by late 1962 — following six years, four different record labels and ninety-three recorded songs after "Young Love"—it was beginning to look like Sonny James was destined to be anchored to his signature song as long as he decided to stay in the music business. The writing on the wall was a bit clearer as the final hours of the year wound down. Sonny James, no matter how much get up and go was still left in him, was pretty well into stacking the blocks of a foundation that would forever keep him residing in that neighborhood where all those well-known one-hit wonders resided, living out their musical dreams by singing just one memorable song along with performing other people's hits and a bunch of mediocre filler songs in order to put on a show and make a living.

All of the deductive reasoning in the world indicated that he would never see that "Young Love" type of success again. His legacy would, at this point, most likely be chained to one mammoth hit song in 1957. But rather than caving to that line of thinking, he kept at it. In spite of what the sages of wisdom would suggest, he kept at it. He never gave up—*never*! Giving up just wasn't in him.

In 2003, a made for TV movie titled *Open Range* debuted. It starred Robert Duvall as Boss Spearman, Kevin Costner as Charley Waite, and Annette Bening as Sue Barlow. Charley Waite had been a disappointment in this life but Sue knew there could be some magic between them if Charley could just come to the realization that the answer for them was possibly right around the next corner.

I've been holding back my love a long time Charley. I know you feel something for me. I don't have the answers, Charley, but I know people get confused in this life about what they want and what they've done and what they think they should've because of it.

Everything they think they are or did takes hold so hard that it won't let 'em see what they can be. I've got a big idea about us Charley and I'm not going to wait forever, but I am gonna wait. And when you're far away I want you to think about that — and come back to me.

Yes, the past can take hold of us and never let go. The failure of the past can so overwhelm that we start to believe there is no light at the end of the snaking tunnel — in fact, we start to believe that it's only a tunnel to another tunnel which finally leads to nowhere. But then when we get far enough away from our fifteen minutes of fame, there is this familiar voice calling out that says, "I want you to think about it — come back to me. Come back to what got you here in the first place. Come on — get up and go get it."

CONNIE ENGLISH SNIPPET

I became a Sonny James fan at a very early age. One of my most memorable Christmases ever was when Santa brought a Sonny James album that contained "Young Love." In the summer of 1970 at age thirteen, I met him at the grand opening of the second Southern Gentleman Furniture Store in Ensley, Alabama. I shook his hand and got his autograph—about five times. On May 23, 1971, I saw him in concert at the Boutwell Auditorium in Birmingham. I still have my $2.50 ticket stub.

I began writing letters to him in 1985 because I really I wanted to meet him. I wrote two letters that year and two more letters in 1987. I also drove 100 miles to Hackleburg and spoke with his brother-in-law in hopes of getting Sonny to write back. He gave me his post office box in Nashville. In May, 1988, I wrote to him about some of his memorabilia (three autographed albums, an autographed picture, and a shirt he had worn on TV) that I had bought at an Alabama Music Hall of Fame auction, and he sent me a "thank you" note.

Shortly thereafter, I had a new brilliant idea and began sending postcards each week. The first postcard stated that I was going to send one postcard a week until he agreed to meet me or told me to leave him alone. After the seventh postcard in 1988 he agreed to meet me "sometime later this year." I wrote back to acknowledge receipt of this letter and to let him know that I would be looking forward to hearing from him.

Few people are ever lucky enough to have their hero call them. On Saturday morning, October 14, 1988, my phone rang. A woman's voice said, "I have a person-to-person call for Connie English." "This is she." "Hello Connie. This is Sonny James." My knees got weak as I blurted out these brilliant words: "Oh, my goodness! Let me sit down."

He and Doris were going to be in Birmingham the next day. I met them at the Holiday Inn near the airport for lunch. His wife was as beautiful as I had always heard she was. And he was every bit the gentleman I thought he would be.

Long and short of it—I fought him for the bill—and yes I got both of them to sign it. Sweetly, Doris wrote, "Connie, you're special." Sonny signed with his famous "My Best, Sonny James."

Yes dreams do come true—I got to meet him, and those postcards from me quit showing up at his post office box every week, which was probably also a dream come true for him.

Connie English—*Fultondale, Alabama*

CHAPTER 8

WHEN THE DREAM BECOMES NOISE

When all of your dreams have been reduced to just noise inside you
— that's when the battle really begins — that lonely struggle
to make the noise become music again.

—LEE ROBERTS

The music recorded by Sonny and presented to radio stations following the success of "Young Love" was very random, what you might expect from someone searching left and right for something rather than sprinting ahead toward the next marker.

Sometimes success explodes on the scene with such a brilliant flash that it leaves one utterly dazed with no idea of what to do next. As regional sportscaster Charlie Mack, a recent new acquaintance of mine from Stan Smoot's Golfing Center, said to me recently when discussing all of this: "It would have been better to have had a few songs that reached #20 on the charts instead of the shock of an unanticipated monster hit that brands you as something you were not."

Suddenly the song identifies the artist rather than the artist identifying the song. A hit of that enormity can easily, and usually does, turn the artist into it. It grabs ahold of the artist and the song morphs the songster into the song rather than pointing the song toward the performer — and you are, as in Sonny's case — "Young Love" and not Sonny James, the country boy from Hackleburg, Alabama. It is the situation of putting the buggy before the horse — and that's where Sonny's career was headed: the song ahead of the artist, the artist spending the rest of their life being harnessed to the past.

Just, for a moment, think of some of the big songs you like and try and remember who recorded them. Now let's pick a few songs from the "Young Love" year of 1957 to simply make the point that the song outlives and so often overshadows the artist.

Here are the songs listed alphabetically — who is the artist?
- Gonna Find Me a Bluebird
- Green Door
- Happy, Happy Birthday Baby
- I'm Gonna Sit Right Down and Write Myself a Letter
- Little Bitty Pretty One
- Marianne

The artists below are listed alphabetically by first name
- Thurston Harris
- The Hilltoppers
- Jim Lowe
- Marvin Rainwater
- The Tune Weavers
- Billy Williams

Match them up if you can. All the artists have Wikipedia pages.
Here's some Billboard chart data on the songs:
- Gonna Find Me a Bluebird - peaked at #3
- Green Door — the artist's only #1
- Happy, Happy Birthday Baby — reached #5
- I'm Gonna Sit Right Down and Write Myself a Letter — got to #3

- Little Bitty Pretty One — charted at #6
- Marianne — made it to #3

Here's another example, the #2 song from 1981 (it should have been a #1) — the song is *Just the Two of Us*. The artist released twenty singles in twenty-two years. Seventeen of the singles didn't even make it to Billboard's top 100 pop charts. Two others did going to #54 and #92. Do you know who the recording artist was? Let me help you out on this one. Here's the opening line of the verse and the chorus:

[Verse]
I see the crystal raindrops fall
[Chorus]
Just the two of us
Songwriters: BILL WITHERS, WILLIAM SALTER, RALPH MACDONALD
© BMG RIGHTS MANAGEMENT US, LLC, BLEUNIG MUSIC

The point, to say it again, is that so often *the song lives on and the artist who recorded it just disappears into a bottom of the page footnote in music history.*

And there's one other fact that should be mentioned here. It wasn't as if "Young Love" was Sonny's song alone — Tab Hunter, and also the Crew Cuts had chart success with it in early 1957. Sonny's record reached the Billboard charts on January 5, 1957, and reached #1 pop and stayed at #1 country for nine weeks. Tab Hunter's record reached the Billboard charts on January 19, 1957, and when it hit #1, it stayed there for six weeks. The Crew Cuts record charted on January 26, 1957 and reached #24. It's quite obvious that the song was not linked to one artist and one artist alone. The difference here, though, is that Tab Hunter was not into a music career and Sonny was. Sonny would come out on top as the singer most identified with the song, but the song was about to take over and once again be on its way to turn the artist into a music trivia question.

Trivia answer to who recorded "Just the Two of Us" — Grover Washington Jr. — remember him?

As for the other six songs previously mentioned, see how you did in matching them up: "Gonna Find Me a Bluebird" — Marvin Rainwater; "Green Door" — Jim Lowe; "Happy Happy Birthday Baby" — The Dream Weavers; "I'm Gonna Sit Right Down and Write Myself a Letter" — Billy Williams; "Little Bitty Pretty One" — Thurston Harris; "Marianne" — The Hilltoppers. The artists have been long forgotten, but their songs live on in music history.

This was a bit similar to what happened to Sonny at the beginning of his recording career in 1952. His second release, "That's Me Without You," was legitimately squashed by Webb Pierce who quickly covered it, charting at #4 — a move that the industry accepted and Sonny never complained about. Webb did what was looked upon in the industry at the time as fair and square. As someone who wasn't around the music business then, I can't help but scratch my head on that one. Sonny's third release was destroyed by a slightly-less-than-honest man (my words, not Sonny's), a man who sat in on that third session and took one of the songs to another label, and without their knowledge of what he had done, got the Davis Sisters to record it. Right after both of their records were released, the Davis Sisters were in a terrible automobile accident in which one of them lost her life. Their record soared to #1 on the country charts, sinking Sonny's release, and there he was — stung again. Yet, he still didn't complain.

So went the first eight months of recording, a very disappointing eight months for sure, eight months that might have discouraged a less-determined man right out of the business. But somehow in 1953, Sonny knew what he had to do — just keep on breathing in and breathing out because tomorrow was always a brand new day and wait for the winds of time to change.

It was now 1957, five years since Sonny had signed with Capitol Records in 1952. "Young Love" had thundered onto the music scene with the distinctive guitar sound that would identify him in later years. The success of "Young Love," which had been Sonny's first session at what would later be named the Quonset Hut in Nashville, also became the first million seller recorded there. His follow-up release,

"First Date, First Kiss, First Love," settled at #9 on the pop charts, also included his famous guitar licks and was recorded at the Capitol Recording Studio in Hollywood.

Then for the reasons presented in the previous chapter, Sonny's promising career wandered off course into other musical worlds. After those first two simple acoustic guitar-driven songs, Sonny's music became, as our first tenor Lin Bown later described it, quite "poppy."

This section, taken from the official biography written by Dave Samuelson and Sonny in 2002, explains what we are alluding to:

"He [Sonny] readily admits mistakes were made regarding his recordings. 'I should have set aside more time for writing and screening demos publishers were sending me—I'm sure I overlooked some good songs and settled for mediocre because I was runnin' all the time, thinking I had to be everywhere for everybody to keep my career at that level. Also by now, there were several records of mine out there. I figured my fans would want me to do something different once in a while. So I'd leave my guitar off a record now and then, change the background, and feature other players and other folk's arrangements for a change. That was a mistake on my part; I was wrong.'"

Let's pause here for a moment. Sunday October 16, 2016, was the annual Medallion Ceremony at The Country Music Hall of Fame where Fred Foster, Charlie Daniels, and Randy Travis were inducted. Milo and I were in attendance, representing Sonny and Doris. As was always the case, the inductees had chosen three songs to be presented by artists of their choice. Singing were Dolly Parton, Kris Kristofferson, Brandy Clark, Trace Adkins, Trisha Yearwood, Jamey Johnson, Garth Brooks, Alan Jackson, and Brad Paisley.

As prerecorded segments were played, and as the guest artists commented before singing, it was clear that there is no single formula that unlocks the door to success. As of 2018, there have only been 133 artists elected into The Country Music Hall of Fame since the first inductions fifty-five years earlier in 1961. Of the thousands upon thousands who have tried over the years, only a very small percentage find that small crack in the door that gets them in and allows them to build a career and then to be so honored. Some of the stories from that night had a number of names to thank for their success. Others just happened to be in the right place at the right time. Others had to just dig it out by sheer determination. It was really fascinating to hear.

For Sonny James, well, his story is just plain and simple. It's just the way it was. I have found that it takes a lot of research and then a lot of time to make heads or tails of it all. I find at this point that I am able to say things about Sonny's career that Sonny would not have felt comfortable saying about himself, and I am sure that applies to so many of the stories that Milo and I heard that night.

In Sonny's case, the ship was sinking and he knew it. All the record labels, songwriters, producers, and studio musicians had carried him he knew not where. It was his ship to save or scuttle. He was alone at the end of 1962 as the captain and crew of a damaged vessel that was taking on water. There's a saying, *"When the ship's in trouble you look to the bridge."*

At this point Sonny's story would be different from the rest — so different he would never find a way to express it properly.

Quite suddenly in 1962, the music industry would start to lean another way, and all that one-hit wonder stuff twirling around in his mind since 1957 would be challenged because the musical wind chimes would start carrying its frequencies in another direction. And when all of that happens, you have to put yourself at a place where when the gale hits you head-on, you are wise enough to turn the ship around and put the wind at your back. That's when you jump off the lunar excursion module and state, *"One small step for man, one giant leap for ..."* But I'm one year and one giant leap ahead of myself. Let's back up for a moment to a year earlier — to 1961, remembering — the challenge is never over — it just changes shape.

*Born on May 1, 1928 -
Sonny as a child.*

Playing a different stringed instrument.

*His first instrument (before age
four). Made by his Pop from
the bottom half of a molasses
bucket.*

*Boyhood home. Six miles south of
Hackleburg, Alabama.*

*Sonny, Pop Loden, Mom, and
Sis Thelma.*

Sonny's Scrapbook from his teenage years.

*Sis Thelma as Arta Vee Horsefeathers.
She was the comedian on their shows.*

*Sonny Boy and the Loden Family —
Sonny around age fifteen. Little Ruby
Palmer on the left — unknown in the
middle and on the right.*

1948 Hackleburg H.S. basketball team.
Sonny—2nd row from top,
last player on right

The Loden's store 2018

1950 - The 252nd Truck Company
from Hamilton, Alabama ready to
be deployed to Korea.

Picture taken and originally captioned
"Sonny Loden." After "Young Love" hit
in 1957, "Loden" was crossed out and
replaced by "James."

1952 — with Chet Atkins in Nashville.

*1953 — Poster for WFAA Shindig
out of Fort Worth, Texas.*

*1954 — The house Sonny
originally rented in Dallas,
Texas, on Capitol Street.*

*1954/55 Elvis on WFAA Shindig. To the
left of the reflection on the mike stand is
Sonny watching and smiling.*

1954/55 Elvis on WFAA Shindig. He borrowed Sonny's guitar. The letters "S-O-N-N-Y" are on the upper left hand corner of the Martin D-28.

1957—Sonny on stage after Young Love. L–R Dude Kahn, Sonny, Harland Powell, and Gene Stewart. Harland was with Sonny from 1954–1957 and played steel guitar before "Young Love" hit.

May 5, 1957. Sonny standing on the street eating a sandwich. The marquee to his left is where he would be appearing on The Bob Hope Show. Sonny stayed overnight with Bob and Delores Hope in their home.

Late 1957. Sonny in what has been called the "snazzy jacket" picture. Poster behind him includes not only Sonny's name but also the Everly Brothers. The jacket still survives.

The Brothers Gibb in the late 1950s, wearing Southern Gentleman ties.

1961 — Sonny's star on the Hollywood Walk of Fame.

Sonny and Doris' home in Hackleburg, Alabama. Completed in 1962.

December 1966 — All of us kneeling around the star.

CHAPTER 9

HELLO, CAROLE, IT'S SONNY

"In life we all need three things: Someone to love, something to do,
and something to look forward to."
— RUSS FOX, PGA TEACHING PROFESSIONAL
STAN SMOOT'S HARPETH VALLEY GOLF FACILITY
NASHVILLE, TENNESSEE

It was the start of 1961. Of the three things Russ said we all need in life, Sonny only had one left — he had Doris. Something to do and something to look forward to had collapsed in on him like the darkest hours on the darkest night. On professional matters Sonny had very few people with whom he felt he could talk frankly; however, that trait that kept him anchored also kept his disappointments closely guarded secrets.

There are very few plaques or medallions hung in prominent places recognizing the amazing contributions made by the many support players in the music business — individuals and groups whose talents should earn them a place of honor alongside the stars they supported. Some of them were obvious, out front where their extraordinary talents were known to their contemporaries. But others, just as important but unknown by name, rolled along behind the scenes in the shadows of other's careers. They would ultimately become the hazy silhouettes in someone else's walk of life.

For Sonny James, so to speak, old things were where he always put them which meant they were never in the way as new things were getting ready to start lining up. Already in place was Sonny's publishing company Marson Music which he had started in 1959. The second part in line was a thirty-four-year old lyricist from East Tennessee who had been under contract since 1956 to Capitol Records country producer Ken Nelson and his publishing company Central Songs. Her name was Carole Smith, but as Ken was wont to do, he had changed it for writing purposes to Billie Carrol.

As I was preparing this section I was able to secure Carole and her husband Lyman's phone number, and on July 26, 2016, I gave them a call. It was the very first time I had ever spoken to Carole and Lyman, and it was an absolute thrill to hear their voices.

When Central Songs signed Carole as a lyricist to a five-year contract in 1956, the very first song of hers that Central Songs got recorded was released by the Jordanaires in April of that same year. The Jordanaires were on Capitol Records and were also in Ken's stable of artists, so he was also producing them at the time. This happened just a few months after Elvis had slipped through Ken's fingers and had signed with RCA. The kids were boppin' to the Elvis beat and Ken came up with this thoroughly novel idea — get the Jordanaires to do a religious-flavored Elvis-rockin' type song. It was an exciting moment for Carole Smith — the first song of hers to be recorded would be cut by The Jordanaires on Capitol Records and was unhymnally titled "Rock & Roll Religion."

We'd probably chuckle about it today, but in 1956 with Elvis just coming into his shakin' own, the fundamental churches balked, in fact they wanted nothing to do with this "Rock & Roll Religion" song, as the lyrics say, "You ask me why I'm happy, why I wanna sing and shout, but I've found a new religion that I couldn't do without, The Rock & Roll Religion — makes me feel just grand…" With Carole and

Lyman on the line, I found the song on YouTube and played it for them over the phone. As unbelievable as this sounds, they told me that this was the first time they had ever heard the recorded version. When it was released both as a promotional and then as a for-sale record, they never received a copy from Capitol, and in disappointment mode they never even went out and bought one. Reason being —it rocked, in fact it rocked so much that Lyman said it was banned, literally rocking itself off the air.

But Carole wasn't alone in having a banned song from that era. We laugh about it now but in 1957, "Wake Up, Little Susie" by the Everly Brothers; 1958—"Splish Splash" by Bobby Darin; 1960—"Tell Laura I Love Her" by Ray Peterson; and in 1962—"Puff The Magic Dragon" by Peter, Paul, and Mary were also banned. But probably the topper of all was the song "I Go Ape" by Neil Sedaka on RCA Victor Records in 1959 that was banned in the South because some felt it was embracing Darwinism. (Thanks to songwriter and music historian Brian Jasper for this long-forgotten bit of information).

In late 1957 the flip side of Sonny's single "Uh-Huh-Mm" was a song co-written by Bobbie Carroll (Carole Smith) and Sonny. In late spring 1959, Sonny released a single written by Bobbie titled "Talk of the School" with the vocal background supplied by The Eligibles. This was eerily similar to a song released by Ricky Nelson a year earlier in 1958 titled "Poor Little Fool." Trying to cut Sonny along the lines of Elvis didn't work: why not chance a shot at recording a song written by Bobbie patterned along the style of Ricky Nelson. It also didn't work, as the clock kept ticking down on Sonny and Capitol. And until Sonny was released from Capitol at the end of 1959, that was the extent of the Sonny James and the Bobbie Carrol connection. During that five-year time period Ken Nelson recorded Bobbie's songs with Capitol artists Jean Shepard, Wanda Jackson, and Tommy Sands who did Bobbie's "Teenage Doll" in May 1958.

Near the end of 1961, two years after Sonny's contract had been canceled by Capitol, Ken Nelson's writing contract with Carole ran out and he felt Carole and Sonny might try and combine their efforts

— Carole as the lyricist with Sonny adding the melodies to her lines. Seeing Sonny already had Marson Music, the move for Carole from Central Songs to Marson was a simple transition. At this point in 1961 Sonny and Carole had never met; in fact they had never even spoken to each other. Their combined efforts had been with Ken Nelson as the go-between. So one day, out of the blue, the phone rang at the Smith residence in Chattanooga, Tennessee, and when she answered it, the male voice on the other end said, "Hello, Carole, it's Sonny." And thus, with just a four-word introduction, began a most incredible writing combination.

As Sonny was known to do over the years, he added Lyman and Carole to his constantly expanding Christmas mailing list, and with the arrival of that first unique Christmas card, Lyman got to see for the first time what Sonny and Doris actually looked like. As Lyman told me, he wasn't into the music business even though Carole loved to write; if it hadn't been for the card, he wouldn't have known Sonny James from Ernest Tubb, or Doris from Kitty Wells.

There's a great story surrounding that first card. Lyman had a very responsible job that required him to travel a lot, and on one occasion in 1962, he was staying at a Howard Johnson's in Atlanta, Georgia. Lyman had finished eating and headed toward the cashier to pay for it. Because the Christmas card always included a picture of Sonny and Doris, he recognized them off in a corner of the restaurant enjoying a meal together. Lyman hesitated before walking over to them, giving himself some time to figure out just what approach to use. Then it hit him. He casually made his way over to their table, and ignoring Sonny, turned to Doris and said, "Excuse me, but aren't you Doris James?" The official first meeting was a perfect story to begin a relationship they could smilingly look back on for the rest of their lives.

In 1962, Sonny and Carole co-wrote two songs that Sonny cut on RCA and two more songs that he recorded on Dot. Sonny and Carole were like two shoestrings ready to have a knot tied into them to form the Sonny James and Carole Smith song-writing team, but the real success of the combination was still over a year away.

I know this part of the story sounds simple and small and explainable in just a few short paragraphs, but it would be the seeds of the first major piece of a puzzle that was just around the corner.

Over the next number of years, the combination would develop into arguably one of the best below-the-radar songwriting teams in Nashville—and it would develop in such a personal way that the phone calls would eventually change to, as Lyman told me, "Hello Sis, it's Son."

CHAPTER 10

THE PIVOTAL YEAR — 1962

"Success is not final. Failure is not fatal.
It is the courage to continue that counts."
—WINSTON CHURCHILL

In September 1981, a man was referred to me for insurance. His name
was James A. Gilmer; he worked for United Artists here in Nashville
in artist management and record production. Going back to 1963,
Gilmer was the lead singer in a group that had a really big hit, "Sugar
Shack," a song that they recorded at the Norman Petty Studios in
Clovis, New Mexico. The group was Jimmy Gilmer and The Fireballs
and their song "Sugar Shack" stayed #1 on Billboard's pop charts for
five weeks from October 12 to November 9. Of the next ten singles
for Jimmy Gilmer and The Fireballs, only one charted, and that was
a year later. So what happened? Did they just choose bad songs to
record, or was it some unseen thing in the music industry that did
them in? Again, as Paul Harvey used to say, *"Now for the rest of the
story."*

What happened was the musical turn-around of the 60s — the
British invasion. The Beatles recorded "I Want to Hold Your Hand" in

October 1963. In mid-December, "I Want to Hold Your Hand" went to #1 on the UK charts and stayed there for five weeks. It was released in the US in mid-January 1964, and went to #1 on February 1, staying there for seven weeks. The purpose for telling this is that when the Beatles songs hit the charts the pop music business totally changed, and ended the whole shebang for many artists. When the business changes its shape and you find you are not in vogue any longer — if you can't find a way to adapt and change with it — then you will be forever known by your past hits. On the other hand, when you become known for a particular style, varying from that style can quickly make you lose your faithful following, halting an advancing career.

Back in the mid-1980s, my oldest son Greg and I contracted for one year with a well-known gospel group to supply major sound reinforcement for their concerts. The group, which will remain unnamed, had already won four Grammy's and thirteen Dove Awards and, as you might imagine, had a very loyal and mature audience. They were in constant demand and could have ridden their career well into their sunset years.

But, at that time, the gospel music scene was dramatically changing — it was being directed at the younger audiences. The main group leading the charge into that new direction was Petra, and they were good at it (we even bought a few pieces of equipment from them). The type of songs and all that came along with this new trend was overwhelming to say the least. Rather than sticking to what they had carefully tailored into an extremely successful venture, the group we were working with wanted the "big powerful speakers to knock your socks off" sound system that the up-and-coming generation was demanding and the lighting system that had to accompany it. That sound would be supplied by us — monstrous EAW speakers with throw horns and 1500 watt amps and monitors and anything else you could imagine. Greg traveled with them as their sound engineer, mixing all their live performances.

You can see it coming, can't you? The long slide from grace for a group like this, if the change is not accepted by their crowd, can be summed up in a one cruel word—disastrous. The members of the group were not young anymore. The driving force behind them was one of their founding singers from back in the 1960s, a man who in the mid-1980s was over fifty years old. It was a very sad mistake by what had been a very popular group.

It's a powerful force that's in the DNA code of the music business, that powerfully attractive and fascinatingly magnetic pull that reaches out to players, singers, and writers alike. It grips the heart and tantalizes the soul with its beguiling promise — "this is simple, and anyone can do it if they really want to." Simple, in that writing and playing and singing a few lines in a 2:30 song are all it takes. What's so difficult to understand about that? Well, the hidden deception is that the music business itself is an optimistically complicated game of chance. It requires a certain amount of wisdom and passion, which for most folks is cultivated slowly over time.

As Maxine Brown, one of The Browns (Jim Ed, Maxine, and Bonnie), wrote on page 47 in her 2005 memoir titled *Looking Back to See,* "The music industry, whether it's country, pop, or punk, has some fine, upstanding people in it. However, it also crawls with shysters, crooks. and con artists."

Not every executive angel that you meet sitting behind a Grand Palais dark walnut desk with a well-rehearsed smile, promising you an eternal career if you'll just sign on the dotted line, is a divine messenger from heaven.

The dream of making it in the music business is far from the reality of the end result. The point is that it takes even more than talent, more than a masterful touch on a guitar, more than feeling you were gifted by the Almighty to do this, and more than a song that seems destined to become an evergreen — sung forever by everyone. To be good, and lots and lots of people are really good at it, takes diligence, grit, and determination. On the other hand, to be genuinely successful takes great imagination, great endurance, a very discerning eye, and something else no one can seem to define, because when it really comes down to it, as undignified as it may sound, most dreamers make it on luck — you just happen to meet the right person or be in the right place at the right time, regardless of your talent.

And while Jimmy Gilmer and the Fireballs were about to be overrun by the British boys, and while Sonny James was looking for another new direction to his career as he was being released from his latest record label, there were four young men attending a college in Quincy Massachusetts busily looking forward to harmonizing for their third consecutive year and performing in their small way as much as any professional act. There was nothing standing in their way, no Beatles, no record label, only what the college they represented would expect as ambassadors of a religious institution.

While thirty-four-year-old Sonny James and twenty-two-year-old Jimmy Gilmer were concerned about their future in the music business, these four young men known as The Parsons, average age right at twenty, well, they were only thinking about their next singing engagement. A music career was not something they thought or even talked about. They loved to harmonize, others recognized they were good at it and, to top it all off, they were too young to think about much of anything else. There were no Billboard charts or record sales to worry about because they never recorded songs to be released, and there were no record producers or radio disc jockeys to impress — what they really had was what every quartet would long for — a great natural blended sound. But probably, as important as anything else, they shared the same values and the same prankish sense of humor.

Seeing as I was the keeper of the journals, I thought this thirty-four- day period from the early part of 1962 might be interesting to include. By the way — John DeBrine was the head of Youth for Christ in the northeast. At the time he was also the pastor of Ruggles Street Baptist Church in Boston and we were still, supposedly, full-time college students. So in addition to representing Eastern Nazarene College (ENC), we were also tied into The Youth for Christ organization (and probably as important as anything, YFC didn't ask about grades).

PARSONS SCHEDULE FOR 34 DAYS IN 1962	MILES	ROUND TRIP
Jan '62		
27 Sat. Youthtime w/John Debrine Boston, MA	22	
28 Sun. a.m. Ruggles St. Baptist w/Debrine - Boston, MA	22	
28 Sun. 5 p.m. Covenant Congregational N Easton, MA	38	
31 Wed. p.m. Youthtime w/Debrine	22	
Feb '62		
03 Sat. p.m. Grace Baptist Worcester, MA w/Debrine	112	
04 Sun. Norwood, MA (all day)	27	
06 Tue. Woodward School for Girls Quincy, MA	2	
09 Fri. Everett, MA	30	
10 Sat. Norwich, CT. w/ DeBrine	184	
11 Sun. p.m. ENC Quincy, MA College Church Service	0	
12 Mon. 6:30 p.m. Chicopee Falls, MA	196	
14 Wed. Youthtime w/ DeBrine	22	
16 Fri. Bloomfield, NJ w/ DeBrine	235	one way
17 Sat. Pennsville, NJ New Jersey NYPS Zone Rally	114	one way
18 Sun. Collingdale, PA (all day)	27	one way
19 Mon. Arrive back at ENC — Quincy, MA	327	one way
20 Tue. Boston Men's meeting w/ DeBrine	22	
21 Wed. Boston Youthtime w/ DeBrine	22	
22 Thu. Springfield Gardens (no notes on it)		
24 Sat. Boston, MA Youthtime w/ DeBrine	22	
25 Sun. New Bedford, MA (all day)	68	
26 Mon. Boston, MA Mens Meeting / DeBrine	22	
28 Wed. Boston, MA Youthtime	22	
Mar '62		
03 Sat. Newark, NJ YFC w/DeBrine	462	round trip

In that thirty-four day period we performed twenty-four times and traveled just over 2,000 miles. It doesn't take much imagination to determine what our GPA was and that was part and parcel of our undoing — but that academic misadventure would blindly lead us to what so many strive for but never attain.

We continued to sing for the college and YFC through March, April, and May of 1962, anticipating our third summer representing ENC for ten weeks across New York State, Pennsylvania, Eastern Ohio, and West Virginia (in the winter months and during the school year, our travels were almost exclusively in the New England area). In late May of 1962, and completely out of the blue, the school informed us that our academic problems had become a big issue in the minds of the administration. The powers that be at the college had determined, regardless of the good-will we had spread representing them, and maybe rightly so at the time, that our poor grades made us unacceptable representatives of the institution. They gave us their verbal pink slip, indicating they were not going to let us travel for them during the summer of 1962.

Looking back, that termination notice should have ended it for the Parsons. It would be the first time in three years that we would be a ship without a sail, and even if we had a sail and the wind blew, there was nowhere to go. I mean, what future was there in singing as an acapella quartet for a church college? We weren't into joining The Blackwood Brothers and The Statesmen Quartet in the Southern Gospel circles. In fact, we didn't know any of these guys, and as an acapella quartet that had never sung with a piano player or a live band, what were our options? We had never even considered that harmonizing and blending might not hold a future for us.

Without question, we would look back upon 1962 as a turning point for Sonny James and this northern church college vocal quartet. Nearly midway through 1962, these four "Parsons" would be denied another year singing for the college (that pesky college demand for good grades had done them in), and in late fall of 1962, Sonny James, after recording 147 songs over a ten-year period, would be released by his fourth record company without having had a song with them that charted (that pesky record company demand for a hit record would do him in). And so it was—both Sonny and the Parsons would find themselves floundering about in a musical sea of rip currents with everything clearly pulling them down.

Sonny and Doris would pack up their stuff and move back to Hackleburg to take up residence in their newly completed house while the Parsons would pack up their stuff and move back home with their parents for the summer.

Hope is probably the most difficult burden to carry because *hope never dies.* Even the great writer Studs Terkel wrote about it in 2003 when he penned the book, *Hope Dies Last: Keeping the Faith in Difficult Times.*

In 2015, journalist Judith Miller released the fifth book of her writing career — a book titled simply *The Story.* The opening line of the second chapter begins with these words, "I was lucky. Being in the right place at the right time for a journalist has always been important." I am sure in journalism, being in that place at the right time could give you another great story to write about, another "scoop" if you will. However, in the music business, being in the right place at the right time could deliver more than a story — it could give birth to a career. And that's where we find ourselves in the lives of Sonny James and the Parsons, just weeks away from the beginning of another chance.

Suddenly in the middle of the summer, a light went on for the four of us, and we thought we had found a new beginning. ENC didn't want us — OK. So we applied for a transfer to a sister college in of all places, Nashville, Tennessee — Trevecca Nazarene College (TNC)—and surprise of all surprises, they accepted us, bad grades and all. And in that move, it was obvious to us that our harmonizing would continue. Get to Nashville, and with our ENC and YFC resumes leading the way, we could easily become one of Trevecca's traveling quartets and be off on a southern musical journey. What could be better than that? So at the end of the summer, the four of us, two of us with our new brides at our sides (both of us had married at the end of August), we packed up our stuff, and on Monday, September 3, 1962, our three-car caravan left Endicott, New York, and headed off on a 900-mile, two-lane road trip to our new college adventure in Nashville, Tennessee. Leading the way was our quartet's 1952 Chrysler Crown Imperial limousine that we had driven 25,000 miles during our last year at ENC, singing for the school and for YFC.

The musical events of 1962 were to offer up a potential kindling of hope for anyone brave enough to strike a match to them; while for four hapless young guys heading south across the Mason-Dixon Line in the fall of 1962, Trevecca Nazarene College would be the spark that would help keep their flame flickering for another year.

GREG PARKER SNIPPET

To the greatest singer and entertainer the world has ever known. Ever since I heard you sing "My Love" on *The Ed Sullivan Show* at the age of twelve, I have been passionately hooked on you and your music. Thank you for all the great music you've given me in your lifetime. Your songs have left an imprint on my heart forever; you'll always be my favorite singer. Thank you for your signed autographed picture. I pray you'll have God's comfort and strength, and I thank you for being a man of principle and integrity.

GREG PARKER — *Lakeland, Florida*
(Written by Greg in a note to Sonny on December 2, 2015)

RAMONA POWELL SNIPPET

My husband Harland Powell worked for Sonny on two separate occasions—in the middle 1950s for three years and for a couple of years in the early 1970s. Harland was a great musician and singer, and from 1954 to 1956, recorded thirty-nine songs with Sonny, including being one of the singers on "Young Love." During their time together, Sonny was always looking for a Church of Christ to attend. One Sunday, there was one just down the street from where they were staying. As Harland told it, they put on their Sunday clothes and walked down the road to the church. When they got to the front door, they heard not only singing but instruments playing. Sonny turned around, and they headed back to the motel. His conscience just wouldn't let him walk in. I think that story tells a lot about Sonny—he had a set of standards that he lived by.

RAMONA POWELL — *Dallas, Texas*

MY SNIPPET

Our son Dale is a pastor of a church in the Nashville area with a contemporary form of worship music (live instrumentation). Sonny had known our son since birth, and when both Sonny and Doris were going through health issues, Dale would go by and visit with them as if he was their pastor. On a number of occasions, Sonny and Doris indicated they would love to hear our son speak, and I thought they might drop in one Sunday in spite of our live band. It never happened, and it took me some months to make sense of it. Would I rather have them ignore their consciences, or would I rather have them stick by their core beliefs in spite of our friendship? I chose the latter, and I came up with a solution. We made a CD of a couple of his messages, minus the music, and took it by their home. They told us how much they enjoyed hearing him. Looking back, we felt so good that we had friends like them that never compromised what they believed — even for one of their very good friends.

GARY ROBBLE — *one of The Southern Gentlemen*

CHAPTER 11

THE "COLE"ABORATION

"The fact that in history events happen simultaneously, while in a narrative account the historian can only tell of one event at a time, creates a problem for which there is no solution"
—PAGE SMITH

Every singer has their own favorite singer, and Sonny and Archie (Pop) Loden were no exception. They were lifelong fans of Nat King Cole.

Beginning in the late 1940s, Cole began recording and performing pop-oriented material for mainstream audiences, in which he was often accompanied by a string orchestra. His stature as a popular icon was cemented during this period by hits such as "(Get Your Kicks on) Route 66" (1946), "Nature Boy" (1948), "Mona Lisa" (1950), "Too Young" (the #1 song in 1951), his signature tune "Unforgettable" (1951), and "The Christmas Song" (1963) — opening lyrics, "Chestnuts roasting on an open fire, Jack Frost nipping at your nose."

In August 1962, Nat, then forty-three years old, recorded the country-flavored hit "Ramblin' Rose." Cole's recording of the song was released by Capitol Records, reaching #2 on both the *Billboard* and *Cash Box* charts and sold over a million copies as a single. In 1962, the song spent five weeks at #1 on the *Billboard* Easy Listening chart and the Australian charts, while on the R&B chart, the song reached number seven. It was released as a single from Cole's album of the same name, which also was a million seller.

The Back Story

In the spring of 2014, my son Greg and I were sitting down with Sonny for one of our regular visits to go over some new updates for sonnyjames.com. As Sonny and I shared some old stories, Greg found himself smack-dab in the middle of some laughs. Near the end of the session and out of the blue, Sonny casually gifted Greg with a photo of himself and Nat King Cole and stated it was a picture from a time the two had spent together at Capitol Studios in Hollywood.

When lifelong friend Sonny James gives anyone, especially your son, a photo of himself with Nat King Cole sitting at a piano in the Capitol Recording Studios in Hollywood, having never before mentioned this, you certainly take notice. With follow-up research, Greg and I began to learn more and more about the influence Cole's meeting would contribute to Sonny's search for a second career.

As we would learn over time, every now and then, like Sonny did with the picture of himself and Nat, he would say something or, as in this case, just show you something that had real history behind it, but that was about all you came away with — just the knowing. Sonny had this very private understated side that said without saying it — you want to know what this means — go do some digging for yourself. It was like he didn't want to be quoted on things.

It's important to realize Capitol Records, which began in 1942, relied on the success of Nat King Cole to such an extent that the Capitol Records Tower in Los Angeles is commonly known as "The House That Nat Built." Cole was literally and figuratively the heart and soul of Capitol's established brand throughout the 1950s as they became one of the preeminent record labels across a wide variety of genres.

From Hollywood to Back Home

In 1959 Sonny had purchased some land in Hackleburg and plans were being made to build their first home there. For a period of time beginning around 1960, Sonny and Doris had moved west and were living in Hollywood. Sonny spent his time writing, fishing for songs, and recording, as well as building other industry relationships. Yet for the sacrifices being made to try and create a new, more sustainable music career for himself, his work was relatively unproductive. Finding a second career was beginning to look like an impossible task.

But while their house was being completed in 1962, some brand-spanking new music-magma had been building up in the business — something entirely unanticipated and potentially career changing for the right person in the right place at the right time.

On February 15, 1962, the Don Gibson song "I Can't Stop Loving You" was recorded by Ray Charles and hit the #1 slot on Billboard's pop charts. The album that followed was called *Modern Sounds in Country and Western Music* and was also a huge hit. A few months later in August 1962, "Ramblin' Rose" was recorded by Nat King Cole in a contemporary country-flavored style and as previously mentioned topped out at #2. But it wasn't that those two songs were simply country-styled. No, it was much more than that. Anybody can record a countryish song. It was so obvious going back and listening to them; both of their songs kicked off with this full multi-vocal sound surrounding the artist's voice—country flavored, absolutely, but presented in a brand-spanking new fresh way—and both of these men and their record companies had absolutely no interest, let me state it again, *no interest* in turning them into country recording artists. And that should have been the end of that. But there was to be another couple of twists to the story.

Capitol's noncountry division apparently saw some potential in this new sound, and in the early fall they signed twenty-six year old Bobby Darin away from Atlantic Records subsidiary Atco. Quite immediately, Bobby was in the studio and recorded country flavored "You're the Reason I'm Living," a song he had written featuring the same big vocal background sound that had been so successful for Ray Charles and Nat.

And while that was going on Sonny was back in the studio, recording what would turn out to be his last release on DOT Records. A song written by Sonny and interestingly titled "The Only Cure" was recorded on October 25, 1962, at the Gold Star Recording Studios in Hollywood.

At this point, Sonny was thirty-four years old, had invested ten years of his life chasing a dream, had recorded 147 songs since 1952, and had but one #1 song from 1957 to lean on, and a #22 country and #67 pop hit "Jenny Lou" from 1960. All of that means very little in the music business. Dot records released Sonny, and for the fourth time in four years, he was once again floundering without a label.

It had to be in Sonny's mind at the time — the incident with the autograph seeker from ten years earlier who had approached George Morgan and said, "Mr. Morgan, I just knew you were going to be a big star after 'Candy Kisses'," followed by the question, "What happened?" At least in 1952, George still had a label — Sonny at this point didn't. He had no place to record, and no one who believed in him enough to give him a chance to release song #148, with the hope for a continuing career. Without a label in 1962, you were flirting with a downhill slide to the end of the line.

Not certain of what the future held, Sonny and Doris up and left Hollywood in late 1962 for the solemn 2,000 mile drive back to the quiet and friendly confines of Hackleburg, where their newly completed home awaited them. It was the first time in their five-year marriage they would live in a place they could call their own - a modest 2,029 square foot house located on Cedar Tree St. They settled in preparing for their first Christmas together in their new place with the folks in his hometown, with no expectation that anything extraordinary would catch up with them there.

On the other hand, the new young Capitol Records star carrying that unique 1962 sound forward just might turn out to be Bobby Darin; and after the song's release it was obvious he would to be.

"You're the Reason I'm Living" hit the charts on January 19, 1963 at #87 and started its climb. In a consecutive sequence it went like this: #56, #30, #20, and by February 16, it was at #12 on the Billboard pop charts. While the song was climbing, Darin was back in the studio recording follow-up songs, but there was nothing much country about them and for good reason. Bobby Darin recorded whatever he felt like recording. His Wikipedia page indicated his genres as: jazz, rock and roll, traditional pop, blues, swing, folk, and country. Like Ray and Nat before him, Bobby Darin was not going to allow himself to be labeled as a country singer, and his follow-up releases made sure of that.

Reenter Ken Nelson who, as Capitol's head A&R Country Music exec, saw the potential in this new sound in the country market. Long and short of it — Bobby Darin would turn out to be Ken's new Tommy Sands; a young man with his own ideas about his career. On the other hand, Ken and Sonny hadn't burned any bridges when Capitol released him at the end of 1959, and to top it all off, Sonny was free to be picked up and signed to a contract. But it wasn't to be as simple this time as getting Sonny to sign on the dotted line — Capitol would see to that.

Flash ahead fifty-five years with me as I was writing this section, to a goosebump moment when the 1963 picture of Sonny and Nat, and a Billboard list of popular songs recorded in 1962 struck me like a lightning bolt. I quickly went to YouTube and pulled up the three songs to hear them one after another — something I had never done before. And *bang*, like a million volts of electricity from above, it hit me. I couldn't push the numbers fast enough as I phoned my son Greg and said, "I've found it. I've found what the picture has been trying to tell us." The facts had been sitting there since 1962 just waiting to be uncovered.

It reminded me of a similar incident that occurred ten years before the picture had been snapped. It occurred on February 28, 1953, when James Watson and Francis Crick uncovered what is now accepted as the first correct double-helix model of DNA structure. Crick was out of his mind with excitement and barged into the patron's lunch at a pub in Cambridge, England, and excitedly announced that he and

Watson had "discovered the secret of life."

We found that the photo had most likely been taken in early 1963. After Bobby Darin's "You're the Reason I'm Living," the third of those three country-flavored songs that had climbed the charts, Capitol's Ken Nelson saw the handwritings all over the wall. I wanted to go to the rooftop of the tallest building around and shout, "I've found it — I've discovered the secret of the picture." Of course, nobody would have known what I was hollering about. So what did these three songs have to do with Sonny James? It can be explained very simply with one ten-letter word — *everything*.

And so for Sonny, the right time had started to roll itself out like a red carpet in anticipation of just the right moment to be walked on — but there was one catch, one major catch for sure. Sonny would be required to find the right song before Capitol would re-sign him.

During the early months of 1963, Capitol and Ken Nelson eagerly flew Sonny back to Hollywood in order to have him collaborate directly with Nat King Cole and work out a deeper musical approach and production understanding of how Cole had arranged and recorded "Ramblin Rose." They let Sonny know that if he could find an original song and record it with the same qualities for country music, that new opportunities awaited him at Capitol. Out of that meeting came the picture of Sonny and Nat seated in front of a piano. Ken Nelson realized that this big vocal sound would die on the vine with noncountry artists Ray, Nat, and Bobby, but he saw its potential in the country market. It was a new idea they would be introducing into country music. It was as fresh to the ears as the aroma of a honeysuckle bloom was to the nose, and it was right there in front of them, and ready for the picking.

Both Cole and Capitol certainly felt the "Ramblin Rose" approach to the right song was a potential formula for making hit country records at that time, but it seems they also knew it was a formula Cole himself could not fully adopt because it would redefine him as an artist, a country artist if you will. Nobody was going to try and redefine the style of Nat King Cole. Nobody.

Because Nat and Sonny were both born and raised in Alabama, their kinship was natural. Energized by this collaborative effort, Sonny and Doris, along with the photograph, quickly returned to Nashville and rented an apartment to begin his frantic search for the song. It was obvious that Sonny James would have to do what many of us have to do sometimes in our lives — we have to start a certain amount of demolition before we start rebuilding. By early 1963, Sonny James had been roughed up but he hadn't been licked. He was alone and without a label, but as was the personality and determination of the man, he could see the oak tree in the acorn in his hand. All he needed to do was find the right song, the right soil if you will, in which to plant the seed. Where was it? Who had it? Who would write it? Would it fall into his hands?

Search for the Song and the Sound

It is in moments like this that time is of the essence. Windows of opportunity in the music business can close shut just as quickly as they can open wide. Every artist, every record label, and every record producer is looking for the next new thing; the competition at this point can be enormous and usually is. The question at the moment was — was anybody other than Capitol Records aware of what was going on? In looking over the musical arrangements being released during this period of time, there was no competition. Sonny's only competition would be the man staring back at him in the mirror.

Back in Nashville, Sonny began quietly reaching out to others he trusted to aid in his search for the song. He had to be careful at this moment not to let the cat get too far out of the bag. We can talk about cats and bags all we want, but the music business inherently, regardless of what we think it is, is a competitive business. When Jimmy Gateley's "The Minute You're Gone" came to his attention, Sonny felt it might not only be the song Capitol was hoping he would come up with, but that the song would also hold the second-career potential he had been determined to find.

The first question I had was how Sonny had come across the song. Songs just don't float down from out of the blue; well, maybe sometimes they do. It was a question I had never asked, and it was a fact Sonny had never revealed to anyone — and once again, that private below-the-radar side of Sonny would raise its head. In fact, I had never even thought about where the song came from until Rick Hall's six-word comment: *"I pray history recognizes the legacy"* had stirred me, which left me struggling to reach out to anyone, anyone at all, to find that answer.

One thing led to another, and in the spring of 2016 I was finally able to secure the phone number of Jimmie Gateley's son, Robert (Jimmie had passed away in March 1985 at the age of fifty-three). Robert and I had a couple of conversations, and between our chats he had spoken to his mom, and neither of them had a clue as to how "The Minute You're Gone" had found its way to Sonny, which was a shame for all of us. How the song came to be written more than made up for that unfortunate gap in the facts, a hole in the story that will probably never be filled.

According to Robert Gateley, the song took root during the DJ (Disc Jockey) convention held in Nashville in 1962. Jimmie and some other musician friends had made their way to a local restaurant during a break in the activities. At that time, Jimmie had been living in Springfield, Missouri, working on radio and television with Red Foley on the Ozark Jubilee. He had already had some songwriting success with the song "Alla My Love" that country singer Webb Pierce had released earlier in the year, charting at #5. A few years later in 1965, he would co-write the song "Bright Lights and Country Music" which would reach #11 on the country charts.

Jimmie had made the trip from Springfield to make some new contacts with music people. He was sitting at a table in a restaurant with musician friends, ordering a meal. Life can seem so ordinary, but it is at times like these that some of the most important things can happen. They had all ordered, and their meal was taking a bit longer than expected to make its way from the kitchen to their table. One of the guys at the table excused himself to tend to some personal needs, disappearing around the corner where the facility was. No sooner was he out of sight, than here came their waitress with their order. One of the guys at the table commented, *"Wouldn't you know it — as soon as you're gone they bring out the food."*

Song ideas come out of the strangest things at the strangest moments in the strangest places. Marty Robbins' idea for the song "A White Sport Coat" is a great example. Marty said the idea came to him while riding in a car heading to do a show in Ohio. At some point they passed a high school where he saw students all dressed up getting ready to attend a prom. According to Marty he wrote the song in twenty minutes as the car rolled along toward their destination. That's just the way it happens sometimes.

Jimmie couldn't wait for the meal to end as the phrase "as soon as you're gone" began to develop in his mind. Heading quickly back to his room; the song floated down from out of the blue, and within an hour, according to Jimmie's son Robert, "The Minute You're Gone" was written. As all songwriters know — some songs are a struggle to write, others take years, others are never completed, and some just make their way down from somewhere up above. The writer is just the scribe, whose part in the transition from up there to down here is simply to write down the words as fast as humanly possible.

A short time after talking with Robert Gateley, I was visiting Doris and told her I was looking into how "The Minute You're Gone" had come about and how the song had ended up in Sonny's hands. I was hoping she might have some long-forgotten piece of information that she could share with me. At that request she beamed and said, *"I still can see it happening just like I saw it back then."* What she told me was way more than I had bargained for. It's all so simple — if you don't ask the questions you most likely will never get the answers.

Doris recalled that early in 1963 they were living in an apartment in Nashville, and Sonny was sitting at the kitchen table working on an arrangement for "The Minute You're Gone." Doris said she didn't know how Sonny came by the song, but he had called in an acquaintance of his to work with him on it. Doris said she would never forget watching the two of them at the table—Sonny, and artist and arranger Ray Stevens working out the arrangement to Sonny's satisfaction.

Without much delay, on March 15, 1963, Sonny was, for the first time since October 20, 1959, back in a studio recording for Capitol Records. This time the approach was to be totally different. His producer at the Quonset Hut in Nashville was Marvin Hughes. Ken Nelson, who produced every song Sonny had recorded in his first stint with Capitol, stayed away. Capitol and Ken would never again push Sonny toward the pop market. This time they agreed on a Nat King Cole "Ramblin' Rose" contemporary country-flavored style approach. It would be a new and different Sonny James sound, but a style Sonny could easily identify with. It was also obvious Capitol and Ken were not going to spend a lot of their resources on this second, and chancy, go-around. In that first comeback session they only cut three songs. They weren't going to go back into the studio until "The Minute You're Gone" proved they were on the right track. The thought most likely was — let's see if the country crowd will buy into this new Sonny James sound before jumping in with both feet.

1963 - The Hopeful Beginning of an Era

With the finding and arranging of Gateley's song, 1963 quickly ushered the return of Sonny James back home to his first love - Capitol Records. Having found the song they were looking for, Sonny, for the second time in his career, officially signed with Capitol. Back in 1952, his first release on Capitol was "Short Cut." His initial release back on Capitol eleven years later would be the song we have been talking about, "The Minute You're Gone," and it immediately found significant success. It was as if the public was saying, "We've been waitin' for you Sonny—find the song and the sound that's really you, and you've got us back"—and with one song he had.

One of my favorite singers is Alison Krauss. The simplicity of the arrangements and the meaning of the words to the songs she records have always spoken to me. In 1999 Alison released a CD on Rounder Records titled *Forget About It*. The last song on the CD was written by Allen Reynolds and published by Universal Music Publishing Group and was titled "Dreaming My Dreams with You." I've often thought how fitting the words would have been right at this moment in 1963 for Sonny. The first verse says all that needs to be said right here:

I hope that I won't be that wrong anymore
I hope that I've learned this time
I hope that I find what I'm reaching for
The way that it is in my mind

The three songs Sonny recorded on that March 15, 1963 day were interestingly, in order, "Gold and Silver" (written by Sonny's future band member and bass player Milo (Shurl) Legate, "The Minute You're Gone" (written by Jimmie Gateley), and "She's in 411" (written by Sonny and Carole Smith). The songs were recorded in the same studio in Nashville where Sonny had recorded "Young Love" some six-plus years earlier.

Coincidentally on the following day, March 16, Bobby Darin's "You're the Reason I'm Living" would reach #3 on Billboard's pop charts and stay there for two weeks. The baton for carrying this full multivocal sound forward for Capitol Records was now securely in the hands of Sonny James. It seemed like this was the moment when all the tumblers were finally starting to click into place.

From those original three songs Capitol pulled Milo's "Gold and Silver" along with "The Minute You're Gone" as the two sides of Sonny's next single record. Upon its release "The Minute You're Gone" was promoted as "Sonny James Returns to Capitol" and in September, the song would reach #9 on the country singles chart and incredibly #95 on the American pop charts. It had taken a long time and a lot of strange bends and turns and potholes in the road to get there, but the success let Sonny know that what he and Capitol were looking for was locked up in that song, and in that Cole-influenced arrangement.

Four months later, starting on July 17, 1963, and continuing on the twenty-fourth through the twenty-sixth, Sonny and producer Marvin Hughes were in the studio again, laying down a total of thirteen songs in four sessions as they prepared for an album release. It looked like Capitol and Sonny had learned their lesson this time around and were determined not to be wrong again.

Within a month, and with "The Minute You're Gone" riding high on the charts, Sonny was faced with a decision he had steered away from for years, save for those few months after "Young Love." Could he make it work long-term this time as a solo act or would it take a team effort? He seemed to have been averse to that. If it was the latter, he would need to start mixing the mortar of his dream with the solid stones of reality and do it now. In August 1963, he took on his first full-time team member since mid-1957 — twenty-eight-year-old bass player and songwriting friend, Milo.

On August 16, the two of them did their first show as a team in the state of Virginia. Also on that first show was Johnny Cash and The Tennessee Three, June Carter, and Gordon Terry. (The chapter "The Fork in the Road — 1965" goes into much greater detail about August 16).

It wasn't crazy like the "Young Love" days at this moment, but for Sonny and Milo, it was a different kind of new crazy — the beginning of a new beginning — and if fate and luck and the hand of Providence had anything to do with it - it was potentially something Sonny would ever be thankful for.

At the same time, Sonny was taking on Milo, our quartet was in its eleventh month as residents of Nashville. My wife Thelma and I were living in our small mobile home, and we had settled into a church across town. My folks decided to make their first trip to Nashville from Endicott, New York, for a visit. It was August in Nashville, almost unbearably hot and humid. Our trailer had no air conditioning, but fortunately it was shaded under a very large and leafy tree, which offered some relief. We had attended services on Sunday at McClurkan Church of the Nazarene with my mom and dad and for some reason our wonderful pastor, Rev. Ed Cox, decided to drop by for a visit a few days later. Rev. Cox and my mom hit it off admirably. Mom was a reader, and dad was a sportsman — the good parson picked the right one of my parents to direct his questions to.

Somewhere along in the conversation our pastor asked my mom if he might offer a bit of advice as to her son's future. In my presence he told my mom that she should encourage me to give up on the dream built around three other guys. My mom very kindly replied that if I believed in what I was doing, she would continue to support me in that dream. If my mother had agreed with him, that might have been the end of the quartet. I have thought about that conversation many times in my life. In a moment, in a blink of an eye, anything can come to an end. The dream endured, and my mom, bless her memory, saw to it that it did.

CHAPTER 12

FINDING MILO - 1963

"He wasn't the best ... but the best wanted him."
—DON MCKAY

"Why?" That one word cuts through the superficial and requires a much deeper response than just stating what happened. There are reasons why things happen, an inner drive that leads us to do, a small voice that tells us why we should quit doing, why we should keep on, or why we should apply a dose of patience for a bit. "What" gets us started; "why" gets us to the heart of the matter. Something inside each one of us says that the facts of the matter are not the end of the matter. That personal spokesperson inside pushes us to the ultimate answer by asking the ultimate question — "Why?"

It's as simple as a phrase we have heard all of our lives, that is, when someone does something that seems totally off the wall, people tend to ask, "What were they thinking?" There's another question that folks ask at times like this: "Why?" Why did that happen?"

* * * * *

Milo was born just eight miles south of Detroit—Detroit, Texas that is—a bump-in-the-dusty-road town of Possum Trot in southwestern Red River County in northeast Texas, a settlement that was originally established in the 1870s until it was given its high-dollar name Fulbright in 1882 when its population had mushroomed to all of twenty five. Fifty-two years later, Milo (not his birth name) was one of those responsible for bringing its population up to just over 300. With a more-than-humble beginning in a shotgun house on a prairie cotton farm on Tuesday, September 4, 1934, Shirley Wilson (his birth name) joined his sister Beryl Jean as the second child of Roy and Myrtie Legate. His father labored in the fields as a share cropper, with Shirley Wilson growing up understanding that life was hard work at best. At an early age, the soles of his feet were already calloused by the dirt of the field, and his hands were sensitive to the sting of cotton burrs.

After laboring for six days to earn what would be their family's percentage share of the cotton crop, Sunday was the time they could kick back and share with each other. But the evening before the Sabbath was the jewel night of the week — the family would sit near their battery operated Zenith radio set (they had no electricity in their home at the time) and listen to The Grand Ole Opry on clear channel WSM out of Nashville.

They were hard-working, plain-spoken folks who made their living from the soil. Existing from day-to-day offered not much in the way of amenities; and livin' and dyin' were as much a part of their everyday routine as the hot sun beating down on their heads by day and the coyotes on the prairie howling by night. There were lessons to be learned from hands-on, real-life experiences, and those lessons never ceased.

When Milo was around three years old, his father took him by the church house to pay his respects to a cotton farmer from Fulbright, who had passed away. It was his father's way, maybe in the same way his father before him had taught him a lesson, but in his father's mind it was the right time for the child to experience a real piece of that real life. As they approached the casket, Roy picked up his young son, so he could see the man laid out before them and said, "There's Mr. Tan Massey … you'll never see him again." It was a real-life, never-to-be-forgotten moment for young Shirley Wilson.

A touch of what his young mind thought was real-world adventure came to him through that radio. Shirley Wilson fell in love with the fifteen-minute radio program, *Jack Armstrong, the All American Boy.* The broadcast opened and closed with an acapella quartet singing the theme song followed by an adventure waxed lyrical with sound effects, enough to stir the soul of any youngster. There were other radio adventures that sent this receptive mind into an unfamiliar world but none like Jack Armstrong. Some of the programs they listened to had more music than others, music with unknown instruments playing behind the words, which was really hard for this young mind to envision.

Roy saw that music was a natural passion for his son, and when Shirley was five years old, his dad encouraged him to do some song leading at church. In the Fulbright Church of Christ, all the hymns were sung acapella, and the first song he led was "To the Work." The first verse and chorus seemed to reflect what a sharecropper's life was really all about:

> To the work! To the work! We are servants of God;
> Let us follow the path that our Master has trod;
> With the balm of His counsel our strength to renew,
> Let us do with our might what our hands find to do.
> *Refrain:*
> Toiling on, toiling on,
> Toiling on, toiling on;
> Let us hope, let us pray,
> And labor till the Master comes

Another vivid memory of the prairie life was the weekly bath. Every Saturday night, little Shirley Wilson would splash around in a #2 washtub in the "heater room" (AKA the living room) where the woodstove was located. Following his bath, his mom and dad took their turns in the tub, using the same water (Beryl Jean had married young and, by that time, was out of the household).

When he was about six, on a cold Saturday night after taking his bath, his parents sent him to the unheated bedroom in the back of the house. Now that the house had been electrified, the radio was kept up front in the heater room. Shirley, being in the back room, could barely hear the Opry music from Nashville coming out of the radio's speaker. He hollered, "Daddy." No answer. So a little louder, "Daddy." Again no answer. Then yelling, "Daddy," finally the answer came, *"What?"* "Turn it up, Daddy, I can't hear the words." Shirley Wilson found himself listening to Roy Acuff on the Opry that night singing, "They Can Only Fill One Grave" — a song that stirred something inside this young boy — a song that struck him and stuck with him for the rest of his life. Coming out of those speakers was Mr. Acuff's voice singing:

> No matter how high in society they go
> Or how much money they save
> When they close their eyes in death
> They can only fill one grave

(Somewhere along in this section we need to stop and explain a thing or two about Shirley Wilson Legate — and this is as good a time as any. We never knew him as Shirley or as Shirley Wilson — he was only Milo. Oh, he was born Shirley sure enough, and that came from their Scottish heritage. Much like boys and girls could both be named Pat or Dana or Dale or Kelly, so it was with Milo. Shirley was an acceptable Scottish name for a boy or a girl, and his parents wanted a name in advance of their second child's birth that would be acceptable for either one — so Shirley it was. Like Jimmie Loden became Sonny James, Shirley Legate would later become Milo Liggett at about the same age. So from here on out in this narrative Shirley Wilson will be referred to, as we all knew him, as "Milo.")

In Fulbright, your life was an open book — the town was so tee-ny-tiny that not much stayed hidden, so there was this overriding something or other that let you know that if you did it, the whole town would eventually know about it. So, just be careful because your life would be out there for everyone to see.

His name was Mr. A. V. Price, a teacher at the Fulbright school and someone Milo looked up to. When Milo was about fifteen, Mr. Price took the school's baseball team, the Fulbright Indians, the unbelievable distance of sixty miles away to see a preseason major league baseball game in Texarkana, Texas. The Cleveland Indians pitcher that day was the ageless Satchel Paige. Those firsts in life stick with you forever, like your first kiss or the first time you had to stand in front of a crowd or, as in this case, the first time you laid your eyes on somebody who was really important. Those moments tower over your life like the tallest building you ever saw, whether you grew up rich or poor, and they loom larger than life over a lifetime. Aside from our parents, we all need an early mentor, and Milo's teacher, Mr. Price, filled the bill precisely.

Life in Fulbright was quite predictable, and so was schooling. A couple of years after seeing Satchel Paige, Milo graduated from high school with honors as the class valedictorian - #1 in a graduating class of twelve (that's right — twelve). Mr. Price, without ever saying so, raised Milo's grades enough, so he could become the valedictorian, winning over another boy, Milo's cousin Paul Reynolds, whose parents could afford to send their son to college. Being the valedictorian enabled Milo to get a scholarship, whatever that was, which took care of tuition for the full year at Paris Junior College in Paris, Texas. Years later, Milo came to an understanding of what Mr. Price had really done for him. Paul Reynolds was smarter, but his family's "richness" was their downfall, and Mr. Price found a way to allow "fairness" to play its part.

The following year Milo was looking forward to a second term. That valedictorian scholarship thing he won simply meant he went to school for free — he didn't know it had a dollar value attached to it. When Milo found out it amounted to all of $40 to go back for a second year, he was shocked. The shock was from the realization that it was now up to him to come up with those forty big bucks himself. As luck would have it, he had a cow that had a calf at that time so he sold the calf, giving him enough to pay that $40 tuition. In that second year he would also be able to live on campus because he accepted a gardening job, tending the flower beds at the school.

Milo's roommate during that second year was Wilbur "Whit" Whittington. One day late in the afternoon, Whit barged in and said, "Shirley, let's go to the country show tonight." To which Milo replied, "What's that?" He had never heard the term *country show*. What Whit was trying to tell him was that there was going to be a country music show that evening promoted by local KPLT radio DJ Jim Lefan. Appearing on the show, which was going to be held in the college auditorium, would be a group from the Louisiana Hayride. Milo and Whit got to see Billy Walker, the Carlisles, and Johnny Horton perform on stage. It was a "you've been lassoed moment" for him.

In fact, it was even more than that — it was a "big-eyed" moment for Milo. On stage, Billy and Johnny were outfitted in their sequin-laden Nudie Suits, outfits as foreign to Milo as anything he had ever seen — and they were playing guitars — only the second time in his life Milo had ever seen one. The first time was when he was in high school where his cousin Billy Allen owned one.

This "country show" inspired Milo to go and spend $3.50 for a plastic ukulele, so he could learn to play. However, wanting to play a real guitar, which neither he nor his family could afford, Milo went to his Aunt Agnes, his mother's sister, whose son owned the first guitar Milo had ever seen and asked if he could borrow it. She agreed, and off he went back to school with his cousin Billy's guitar in hand. He realized he didn't have a clue as to how to tune the thing, but he was aware of a football player named Lucas who played a guitar, and Milo got him to tune it. After a day or two Milo realized it needed "touchin up" again because it wasn't sounding right. So he went back to Lucas for the second time, knowing that he just couldn't keep going back time after time to ask this linebacker to fix it — so after the second re-tuning Milo went back to his dorm room and figured out how to do the "touchin' up" on his own. A short time later, he scraped together $1.25 and bought a *Mel Bay Guitar Chords* book which advertised itself as guitar chords in picture and diagram form, and he went to learning some chords.

As life often was for someone whose family existed on such a meager income, Milo couldn't come up with the $40 for his third year at school, so he took a job at a hardware store in Texarkana, making more money than he could ever have imagined — $45 a week. While working there, he wrote his first song, "Walkin' on Air." During his year-and-a-half tenure at the store, he saved up enough money to buy a good Gibson guitar, paying the astronomical sum of $140 for it. While working there he also started collecting *Country Song Roundup*, a fairly new publication recognized as the Who's Who of country music at the time. But more than just articles on the artists — each issue would include fifty or sixty song lyrics that he could play and sing along with.

When you are young and not well-connected, workplace politics can raise its ugly head, becoming an issue as it did at the hardware store. Milo was an outsider, and he began to realize there were some insider things going on. As a result he decided the financial gain wasn't worth all the daily grief, so he up and headed back to the peaceful environs of Fulbright to work for a while with his dad as a sharecropper until something else came along.

The year was 1953, and as he was heading home, he saw a radio tower being built just a bit south of Clarksville, Texas. Knowing there hadn't been a radio station in Clarksville before that time, Milo put one and one together. There was a small 40ft x 40ft building near the base of the tower with a road leading up to it. It was one of those spur-of-the-moment, bells-going-off-in-your-head things as Milo made a right turn, heading toward the tower, thinking, "What's to lose? Maybe there's an opportunity here that would be a bit better than sharecropping." He walked in and was greeted by the man who was in charge of the place. They talked a bit; then the gentleman said that the next day they would be starting three days of preliminary testing but had yet to add a person to speak into the microphone for checking the equipment, so he asked Milo if he was good at reading. Milo told the man he had taken English and speech classes at college, so the fellow tore off some news coming in on the teletype and asked him to read it. He did and on the spot, Milo was hired for $25 a week as a DJ. It was a 500-watt clear-channel station, and Milo signed on with "This is KCAR 1350 on your radio dial, broadcasting from Clarksville, Texas." One of his many responsibilities, in addition to being a disc jockey, was playing guitar and singing on the live thirty-minute Shirley Legate Show. This is where *Country Song Roundup* became really important to him because of all the song lyrics printed in it.

It was quite a special time for Milo. Now he owned a guitar, now he was a DJ, now he had a live half-hour show, and he was receiving *Country Song Roundup,* which inspired him to write his own lyrics to the songs that were in his mind. One song that he wrote during that time tells us a lot about his country upbringing in little homespun Fulbright. He titled the song "When Heaven Was at Chesapeake and Main," even though Fulbright didn't have streets by those names. The opening few lines clearly describe his simple upbringing and his ability to pen lyrics:

> When a spool of thread was a nickel
> And a Coke was too
> And there was no keen awareness
> Of who hates who
> Where the dogs had rubber teeth
> And the neighbors knew your name
> And a handshake was your word
> And love was not a game.

The beauty of being a DJ at KCAR was he got to play the records not only of country artists, but music of every type from every genre. In addition he got to sing some of his original tunes live. Milo remembers that the first time he heard Sonny's voice was at KCAR. The record that he spun in the last few months of his employment at the station was a song Sonny and Jack Morrow had written and Sonny had recorded in 1954: "Oceans of Tears." But more than that, Milo got to hear people's reactions to his own singing, and a dream took root.

As Milo expressed it, "I felt I needed to find someone who sees in me what I felt I could see in myself—I needed to keep my eyes open to sign a recording contract."

After a year and a half, Milo left the radio station, and once again found himself back in the friendly confines of Fulbright, wondering "what's next." Out of the blue, there came a knock at the door. Standing in the doorway was Whit Whittington, his roommate from his second year of junior college. Whit blurted out, "Shirley, let's go to Abilene and go to college again." So with just a handful of words being spoken, Milo's life took another turn, and in September 1955, the two of them headed off for the three-hundred mile trip to Abilene Christian College (ACC), located a world away in Abilene, Texas. Milo and Whit roomed together for one year at college until his friend fell in love and married, which left Milo by himself again.

It was May of 1956, and Milo had secured a summer job working just 130 miles from Fulbright at a warehouse in Dallas, Texas. Upbringing has a lot to do with life's priorities, so after finding an apartment, Milo asked someone where the closest Church of Christ was. He was told that the one at Peak and Eastside was just a few blocks away.

On church day, Milo made his way to Eastside. When he walked in, his first greeting was from this tall, handsome man with a crop of curly dark hair, who stepped up to him and initiated the conversation with "My name is James ..." What a coincidence.

Ever understated as he would be throughout his life, even though this was six months from "Young Love" being recorded and released, Sonny was just trying to be Jimmie Loden from Hackleburg. Because of Milo's subscription to *Country Song Roundup,* he recognized Sonny from a picture or two he had seen in the magazine. Sonny wasn't a national figure yet, but there in Dallas he was already a star, having appeared on the Shindig out of Fort Worth, from 1952 until its demise in 1955, and then on the Big D Jamboree.

The "what" happened is obvious, Milo met Sonny the first time he walked into Eastside Church. The coincidental "why" of it all will forever remain a mystery, but if a coincidence is a "miracle where God decides to remain anonymous," then this is a perfect example of that.

For the remainder of that summer, and again the following summer, Milo would live in Dallas, working to earn enough for his next year's college expenses while also attending Eastside. Also during these two years, Milo's songwriting was flowering, and he was presenting some of them to Sonny.

In late October 1958, Milo decided to make a 260-mile trip to Clovis, New Mexico, hoping to fulfill a long standing dream — get a recording contract with Norman Petty. It wasn't a prearranged thing — Milo's intention was to show up at Norman's studio, hoping that Petty, when he heard his songs and his voice, would be interested in signing him. Milo didn't write "country," and Milo didn't sound "country," though from head to toe he was anything but big city. Milo was just what he was, and his thought was that if Norman Petty could hear what Buddy Holly and Buddy Knox were recording in his studio, then there was a good chance he would hear what Milo was all about. Unknown to Milo at the time was that Petty had returned from New York City where he had recorded Buddy Holly just two weeks earlier, singing a song written by Paul Anka titled, "Well I Guess [It Doesn't Matter Anymore"]. (Buddy died in a plane crash two and a half months later on February 3, 1959, and the song became a posthumous hit on the Billboard Hot 100, going to #13 in the US and #1 in the UK.)

When Milo arrived at Petty's place unannounced, he was greeted by Norman's wife Vi. It was lunch time, and Milo was surprised when she told him her husband was still in bed. Clovis at that time was a booming oil town, and Norman's recording studio was not soundproofed, but more detrimental than that was the fact it was located on a road where the oil trucks ran up and down all day long. So for that reason, if you recorded anything worth keeping you recorded at night. So, as the sun made it way down in the west Milo showed up at the studio, and Norman Petty called in four musicians: a piano player, a guitarist, a bass player, and a drummer, and the recording machine started turning. Petty recorded one of Milo's songs over and over and over all night long. It was an original tune titled "Anchor Your Heart."

After recording until the sun was about to come up, and not even letting Milo hear a playback of the song, Norman Petty placed a pre-signed contract and pen in front of the hopeful twenty-four-year-old. After looking over the document and realizing that Petty wanted 50 percent of the writing credit on his song in addition to 100 percent of the publishing rights, Milo said, "Mr. Petty isn't this is a little irregular?" The irregularity was Milo expected the publisher to get 100 percent—that seemed normal, but to get half of the royalties as a songwriter for a song he had almost nothing to do with—what was right about that? Norman responded, "Yeah, but I changed a word that made the song, and that's just the way we do things here." You see, Petty gave himself songwriting credits on some of Buddy Holly's songs in addition to songs written by other artists. This had been a common practice for decades, especially among managers and label owners. Interestingly, Petty discontinued this practice within a few years.

It's a fact worth noting — if Milo had gone to Clovis, say in 1960, and Petty wasn't asking for 50 percent of the writer's royalties, Milo might have put his signature on the contract and been on the Brunswick label, the same label Buddy Holly was on. At this point that's all speculation, which is what makes the entire story so intriguing.

There's more to Buddy Holly than the hits we know about. Originally, Buddy had signed with Decca records. His first session was on January 26, 1956, and was produced by a Nashville icon, Owen Bradley. In 1956 alone, Decca released four singles on Buddy without any success. Holly became increasingly frustrated by his lack of creative control as Bradley selected the session musicians and arrangements. On January 22, 1957, Decca informed Holly that his contract would not be renewed, insisting he could not record the same songs for anyone else for five years.

Unhappy with Decca and Bradley, and inspired by the success of Buddy Knox's "Party Doll" and Jimmy Bowen's "I'm Sticking with You," Holly turned to Norman Petty who had produced and promoted both of those records.

On February 25, 1957, Buddy Holly was in Petty's studio, and in addition to some other songs, he recorded a demo of "That'll Be the Day." Petty became the band's manager and sent the demo to Brunswick Records, which released it as a single in May 1957, charting at #1 on the US Hot 100 charts (the writers were listed as Jerry Allison, Buddy Holly, and you guessed it—Norman Petty). Its success was followed in October by another major hit, "Peggy Sue" (once again the writers were Jerry Allison, Buddy Holly, and Norman Petty). It was released in September 1957, on a Decca Records subsidiary, Coral Records, charting at #1.

So let's pick up a piece of the story left out when we first introduced Milo and Norman Petty. The reason Petty had recorded Buddy Holly in the Big Apple was simple — Norman wanted strings on one of the songs, and it wasn't until the very early '60s that Nashville started to get serious about using a string section on records with a sound that was worthy of recording. The first song I have found is a late 1959 release with strings by Roy Orbison on Monument Records titled "Uptown."

The lesson in this 520-mile round trip to Clovis was that Milo found there were folks who didn't deserve a penny of his earnings, but who were more than willing to help themselves to half of it. Milo's conscience wouldn't let him give away part of the song he had written regardless of Norman Petty saying, "That's just the way we do things here." Long and short of it was that Milo didn't sign the contract. He put his guitar back in its case, climbed into his car, and headed back to college. It was the first time Milo had seriously reached out with his talents, and the biggest thing he got was a new life-lesson: it wasn't as simple as being talented, and there were people who would use you if you didn't know better.

Following Milo's graduation from ACC some six months later in May 1959, he once again headed back to Fulbright, but this time to help with his mother's care during the last struggling months of her life. She passed from this world at age fifty-three on October 12, 1959.

Having stayed in touch with Sonny all this time, Milo now picked up pencil and paper and penned a few new songs—ones he felt had some real merit. Sonny thought Pat Boone might be interested in some of them. Sonny and Pat were both Church of Christ men and, at the time, good friends. Pat was Sonny's junior by six years and those links brought forward an opportunity for Sonny to help Milo.

Pat had attended Columbia University school of General Studies in New York City and graduated *magna cum laude* in 1958. By that time Sonny had hit it big with "Young Love," and Pat had had a #1 single some months earlier in 1956 with an Ivory Joe Hunter tune, "I Almost Lost My Mind." A year later in October 1957, and while still attending college in New York City, Pat started hosting a half-hour variety show on ABC-TV, *The Pat Boone—Chevy Showroom,* which ran until mid-1960.

It was a brainstorm idea, and Sonny felt his friendship with Pat would be enough to get Milo to him with some songs. Milo was used to doing things face-to-face, the Fulbright, Texas way, so he and his good friend Bud Smith jumped in a car and anxiously headed off to New York to meet with Pat in the early spring of 1960, even though an official meeting had not been set up.

When they got there, the city was way too big and way too much. Milo and Bud found a publishing company near the ABC facility, and without knowing how things worked, went in and asked to see someone because they had some songs for Pat Boone. A seedy-looking character invited them to follow him upstairs. That's when Bud took over, whispering to Milo that they ought to get out of that place pronto. They did, and that was the end of the song-pitching trip to New York City to see Pat Boone. They got back in their car to make the 1,450 mile two-lane trip back to Fulbright. Rack it up to another one of life's little lessons.

Back in Fulbright again, Milo remained at home with his father and worked with him on the farm until June 1960, when he decided to join the Army. While Milo was in the military, Sonny had signed on with RCA; in February 1961 in Nashville he recorded a song Milo had written titled "Magnetism." Milo served his country for eighteen months with stops in Fort Carson in Colorado, Fort Hood in Texas, and Fort Benjamin Harrison in Indiana. Following his military service, Milo found himself back in Fulbright in December of 1961 at twenty-seven years old. Creeping up on thirty years of age woke Milo up to the real reality of life. That magic number started shouting out loud to him— "Life goes by fast, doesn't it? You'd better hurry up and find yourself."

Early in the year of 1962 Sonny left RCA and moved to California to record for Dot Records. In June, Sonny stepped into the studio and recorded another of Milo's songs, "Just One More Lie." Sonny at that time still had an open line with Capitol Records and Ken Nelson in Hollywood, and for that reason Milo decided to make the 1,500 mile trip by himself to California to pitch songs. It was in the early summer of '62, and Sonny had made an appointment for Milo to see Ken Nelson and Lew Chudd at Capitol Records, but again, nothing came out of that scheduled meeting. Stymied once more by another one of life's lessons, it was back to the safe confines of Fulbright.

Then 1963 rolled around. Light was beginning to flicker at the end of his dark music tunnel.

Without warning, Milo up and left Fulbright and made his way to Nashville in early March to give a music career another shot. This time, it wasn't solely about songwriting, it was about getting a recording contract. The first thing he did when he got there was to give Sonny a call. Sonny asked him where he was staying, and when Milo told him, they realized they were just less than a mile from each other. The next question from Sonny was: "What are you looking to do in Nashville?" "Well, I came here to get to somebody at Monument Records. I think that anybody that can hear Roy Orbison would hear me."

So Sonny made a call and set up the appointment, and Milo headed over to Monument Records for another one of those hopes-set-high meetings. (Orbison had been on Monument Records since 1959 and was already riding a three-song success: "Only the Lonely," a #2 hit in 1960; "Running Scared" a #1 and "Crying" #2—both hits in 1961). 1962 for Orbison started off with a bang with the song "Dream Baby" reaching #4. The next three releases in 1962 didn't fare very well, and at this timely moment, in walks Milo with a folder full of songs and a unique recording voice to match.

Milo sang a couple of songs just playing along with his guitar. It's as if things at Monument had built up over time and were ready to explode as Monument's CEO asked Milo if he had enough songs for an album. Milo said he did, and the CEO said, *"I'm going to offer you a deal that will warp the heads of the industry."* As quick as that, Milo was told that they were going to cut twelve songs, recording each one as if it were a single release. They picked the twelve, and Monument spent the next couple of weeks arranging the songs, assuring him that he would be recording before the month was over.

A few days later on March 15, 1963, Sonny cut "Gold and Silver," the third song of Milo's he would record in just two years, and the very first song he would record after re-signing with Capitol. The second song Sonny recorded on that day was "The Minute You're Gone," which would be his first major charting release since "Young Love" six years earlier. The light at the tunnel's end suddenly stopped flickering —not only for Milo, but also for Sonny. The end of the tunnel was just ahead, and the light now seemed bright as day. Life's new lesson was clear— perseverance really does pay off.

Before month's end, twenty-eight year old Shirley Wilson Legate was about to be christened anew. Charles Hardin Holley had become Buddy Holly, Harold Jenkins became Conway Twitty, and Shirley Wilson Legate was about walk into RCA Studio B as Monument Records' new artist Milo Liggett for the first real recording session in his life. He was greeted by seventeen musicians, four background singers, and an entire string section. In two days, in three recording sessions, they would cut a total of twelve original songs. It was an explosive month for Milo—hard for any of us in today's music environment to imagine.

As Milo was waiting for Monument to release his first single, Sonny's new Capitol release, "The Minute You're Gone," had reached #9 on the country charts and #95 on the pop charts. It was time for Sonny to go from being a solo artist with a guitar to a whole lot more if he wanted to sustain this second career opportunity. In August, Milo, who had never played the bass guitar before, somewhat reluctantly joined Sonny as his bass player. Even though Milo would never be the best bass player that ever was, Sonny wanted him. Also, Sonny and Milo had an understanding; that is, if Milo's Monument release caught on, he would perform it, along with Sonny on his shows. Sonny and Milo even went to the expense of having a promotional picture made up of the two of them together. In addition Sonny still had that private picture of him and Nat King Cole sitting at the piano—a promotional photograph Sonny couldn't wait to release publicly.

Sonny soon began a string of touring engagements following the success of "The Minute You're Gone." Just a month after taking on Milo as his bass player, an incident occurred that changed not only one of Sonny's plans, but so much of everything in America. On Sunday morning September 15th, 1963, Sonny and Milo were preparing to leave Birmingham, Alabama, following a show they had performed the prior evening at a race track on the southern outskirts of town. Downtown Birmingham on that Sunday morning was in turmoil. Sonny and Milo soon learned the source of the activity was that the historic Sixteenth Street Baptist Church had been bombed during their morning service.

Sonny had, for nearly half a year, been holding that picture he had been planning to use as a promotional piece to show the connection between himself and fellow Alabamian Nat King Cole—the picture of the two of them sitting at a piano in the Capitol recording studio in Hollywood. But that September 15 occurrence would change it all. As has been mentioned before, Sonny was always understated about himself. His approach to how he had determined to live out his life, including his political views was a very private matter to him.

How Sonny seemingly internalized these American struggles was in no way about an interest in changing country music or being drawn into a national unravelling because of that innocent picture—that wasn't his style. So the photograph of Sonny and Nat King Cole was put in the back of a folder and delicately silenced.

Instead, Sonny's approach in 1963 was simply about creating a fresh appeal in his music which would hopefully expand the country audience beyond current boundaries, and find new musical ground in country music between the rural country life he knew growing up, and the urban city life he was adapting to. If he could perform and record holding to the standards of life he had developed for himself and be appreciated by country folks and city folks alike, then that would be the measure of his professional and personal success while contributing something positive to the American fabric.

To pull that off, Sonny would require of himself that measure of grit that makes a man stay the course no matter what the future outcome. When you got to know him up close and personal, you eventually understood and appreciated two of his most admirable traits—his immense dignity and his solemn restraint.

Sonny believed he had the ability to turn what Nat King Cole and Capitol had provided into an identifiable country top ten hit, but he also knew that a crucial piece to the puzzle going forward would be finding the right backing vocals that would not only complement this new style and identity but fill up the sound and provide additional energy on stage.

A unique assembly of singers had been the mixed vocal group on the recording for "The Minute You're Gone" (both the single and the album), but they were studio singers and did not tour. The dilemma at that point for Sonny was simple but complicated—how to duplicate that full background vocal sound on his personal performances that they were able to capture in the recording studio. One thing was for certain—Sonny and his guitar along with Milo playing bass were far from capable of pulling that one off.

And while Sonny was taking on Milo Liggett as his first team member in August 1963, in a small trailer located just four miles away from Sonny's apartment, a well-intentioned pastor, kindly trying to advise a young man and his visiting parents, failed to convince them that their son's quartet dream was not worth devoting his life to. They were just four short miles away, yet they had never heard of one another. Might a situation occur that would shorten the distance and put them at the same place at the same time? What would fate and time and coincidence have to say about it as 1963 would slowly turn itself into 1964?

CHAPTER 13

FINDING THE SOUTHERN GENTLEMEN — 1964

"It's hard to beat a person who never gives up."
—BABE RUTH

As far as our vocal group was concerned, Lin was the best blending first tenor you could find anywhere; our baritone Duane had this expansive, rich voice that sounded one and one-half times wider than it actually was; and our bass singer Glenn had a natural depth that rounded the entire four voices into one smooth sound. Our unique blend and close harmonies identified us as a tightly-knit group rather than as four distinct individuals. There was really nothing special to say about Lin Bown, Gary Robble, Duane West and Glenn Huggins other than when we put our voices together something magical happened.

The four of us had so many similarities that led us to this point that to explain all of what was happening from four different perspectives would distract from the story we have set out to tell. Using my wife Thelma and myself as the overall example will give you in a smaller way the bigger picture of what we all went through.

It had been only fifteen months since we had pulled into Nashville in September 1962, but the route we had taken in that year and quarter made it seem so much longer. Our quartet had anticipated, wrongly as it turned out, that the sister college in Nashville would welcome us with open arms as those churches in Maine and Vermont and New Hampshire and Massachusetts and Pennsylvania and New York and Rhode Island and Ohio and Maryland and Delaware that we had so faithfully served up north—but oh my, how we were fooled, and we were too young to understand why. So any thought of paying for our new college adventure by singing was thwarted before it ever got started. The Nazarene College in Nashville showed no interest in us, and the eighty-five Nazarene churches in the Tennessee district fell in line with the college's thinking. Years later, it made a little bit of sense, but it was disheartening nonetheless.

By the beginning of 1963, three of us had purchased mobile homes (they were called trailers back then), and we were living in the same place — Elm Hill Trailer Park that was just down the road from where we had enrolled in college. Thelma and I were debt free when we first arrived in Nashville — all of the singing our group had done had enabled us to leave ENC without any financial obligations hanging over our heads. We had taken $300, nearly all the money we had, and put it down on a trailer — 288 square feet in a 36 x 8 foot place that we would call home for three years. By the end of 1963, Thelma and I refinanced the trailer and got the payments down to $34 a month plus $5 a week for the space in the trailer park. Looking back, in fact you didn't need to look back to see it — it wasn't a very nice place. Best I can calculate it had about fifteen trailers in it, and in the three years Thelma and I ended up living there we came to find out that it had its own population of scurrying little critters.

Soon after arriving in Nashville, Thelma secured a job at RL Polk Company for the magnificent wage of $1 an hour. It kept us alive — that's all that mattered. Sadly, the four of us guys had to secure non-singing jobs to stay afloat. My first job while I attended TNC for the one quarter was as a delivery boy for Robert J. Young printing company. My interview went like this: "Are you a good driver?" "Yes, sir." "Do you know anything about Nashville?" "No, sir." "Can you read a map?" "Oh, yes, sir." "When can you start?" "Anytime." "You've got the job." And so every day I would drive the 1952 Chrysler Crown Imperial limo to work, park it in the parking lot, jump in a delivery truck along with a map, and make delivery stops all over Nashville.

I then floated through a succession of jobs I wasn't fit for — outside sales that took me through selling sewing machines to encyclope-dias—work I wasn't very good at, but it taught me how to communicate, how to carry on conversations with strangers. But learning how to talk didn't pay the bills. There were way too many days during this time where the evening meal for Thelma and me was a nineteen-cent package of Kraft's Macaroni and Cheese. And it was even worse than that—at times we would walk along Murfreesboro Road, looking for discarded Coke bottles that we could take to the store and get back the five-cent deposit in order to pay for the mac and cheese. Charles Dickens' opening words in one of his novels was, *"It was the best of times — it was the worst of times."* When it came to our quartet at that moment — Dickens was only half right.

In the meantime, Thelma and I had found a little church in west Nashville where we met some of the best folks in the world. They didn't know, or maybe they did, just how we were struggling to make ends meet. There was one older couple who had never had children of their own and who took an interest in us. On occasion they would invite us to their home to eat (do I hear an amen?). Ernest and Ira Woodside remained our faithful friends for years. They eventually became Woody and Nanny Woody to our boys. They'll never know how much they meant to us. I wish they were still around so they could see their names in this book.

Just as a matter of fact — our quartet went our separate ways when we weren't singing together. The other guys found friends and a place of worship in Nashville that was right for them. In spite of being a team, you had to have a life of your own — it was a lesson we had learned over time.

One Sunday night we went to the evening service, and as the offering plate came by, I reached into my wallet and took out something I had carried with me for some time. It was all the money Thelma and I had to our names at that moment — a silver dollar — and I dropped it in the plate. I have often wondered who counted the offering that evening and what they thought when they saw that silver dollar. The immediate thought was that I had been faithful since I was sixteen to what I believed, and this was no time to pull back from that.

I had felt since I was in my mid-teens there was more to life than "just sticking to it." Everything I had come to understand told me if I "stuck to my guns" while I was awake, that the One who was watching knew more people that I ever even thought about, and while I was sleeping, He would be working on those folks on my behalf.

The most gregarious, the most outgoing, the one of our group with the most chutzpah was our first tenor Lin Bown. He could sell a mouse trap to a mouse, a monkey wrench to a monkey, and even sell ice to an Eskimo. While I was bouncing around between selling sewing machines and encyclopedias, Lin had gone to work for a used-car lot across the street from the college, and just a couple of hundred yards from the trailer park where we lived, so you would find the other three of us occasionally wandering in on him during the middle of the day. We all had jobs that were anything but eight-to-fivers — if one of those recording sessions came along, we didn't need to be begging a boss for a three-hour break to record with someone nobody ever heard of.

To our everlasting benefit, the word had got around town about us at the low-rung level, and we were happy to be doing some custom sessions in egg-crate studios (an inexpensive but eye-sore way of sound-proofing a room)—but there were never enough sessions. I guess the low point was when we recorded with an older man from Michigan named George Shilthroat, and they gave us vocal background credit on his single as The Michigan Playboys.

In early December, Lin and I applied for work with American National Life Insurance Company, collecting insurance payments door-to-door. They told us we could start the first week of 1964 with a guaranteed salary of $75 a week to collect insurance payments from clients, plus commissions on any life insurance we sold. The beauty was we could set our own hours as long as the route got collected by the end of the week. It was an opportunity with a guaranteed salary to keep the dream alive a little longer — those early tough days were just that — early and tough. I could tell this same story from Lin or Duane or Huggins' perspective, but our stories were all about the same; we were in survival mode as the jobs we secured enabled us to keep doing those custom background vocal sessions in those little egg-crated garages around town. Somehow we never lost sight of our crazy love and desire to blend and harmonize — and in spite of it all there was this natural drive that burned inside us. While we were waiting on a decision from the insurance company, we didn't have any idea that our lives were about to turn on a dime — or maybe on a silver dollar.

Completely out of the blue, Lin's boss at the car lot had set up a meeting for us with his friend Archie. (His boss is the one name I wish we knew; unfortunately, we don't.) So there we were in late December 1963, in an apartment on Hillside Avenue in the Melrose section of Nashville being questioned by a man named Archie, some-one we knew nothing about. After a good bit, and I really have no idea how long, and after singing one acapella song after another—Archie said rather matter-of-factly, "You boys are good enough to be on The Grand Ole Opry."

Archie turned out to be country singer and comedian Archie Campbell, and five years later would become known all across America as the barber on *Hee Haw*. Archie was working for a publish-ing company in Nashville, and started using our group to do the vocal background on demos, and for the first time we found ourselves in some really nice recording studios — egg-crateless of course.

As Maxine Brown wrote in her book *Looking Back to See,* "We pretty much knew that you had to have a record out to get near that famous place (The Grand Ole Opry)." Well, our quartet not only didn't know that, the fact of the matter was, we didn't even suspect it. Oh, the innocent ignorance of it all. Now here's what I know—whether it was the hand of fate, or the Hand of all Hands guiding things I have no clue — but that's exactly the way we replaced the Jordanaires as The Grand Ole Opry quartet. In the space of just a couple of weeks we rechristened ourselves and retired the name Parsons.

I can still hear it as if it was yesterday; in reality it was the first Saturday night of 1964, "And now ladies and gentlemen let's put our hands together and make welcome to The Grand Ole Opry — The Chordsmen."

JAY WEST SNIPPET

It's a long way (2,632 miles) and many years from the early 1940s where the four of us kids grew up in an 1,800 square foot (we occupied half of it) two-story stone house with a full basement on 109 Brooklyn Ave, Salisbury, Maryland, to where I live now, in Pahrump, Nevada.

The West family came pretty close to never being. As a single lady Mom was a pretty firm religious task master, living and preaching stern rules of discipline to herself and others. On the other hand, our dad, not yet having met our mother to be, was a bare fisted boxer (no kidding). It was 1939, and Ernest West and some buddies of his had made up their minds to disrupt a religious tent meeting that our mom-to-be was singing in by standing outside the canvas structure and heckling. If there ever was a combination of two people that should never have been attracted to each other, these were the two.

As we were to become aware some years later, Dad ended up being smitten twice at that tent meeting, once from a vertical source and once from a horizontal source that was sitting right there up front on the platform. In the space of three weeks, Ernest proposed to Marie, and she accepted on the promise that he quit boxing. He promised, he did, and they married. A year later they lost their first child at birth. A year after that on April 28, 1941, their next child was born, and they named him Ernest Duane West.

Out of that most unlikely combination came three more children, another boy and two girls named Leah Mae, Howard Jay, and Verna Ann.

The Southern Gentlemen, still at that time the Parson's Quartet, tell a story that clearly identifies our parents. The boys had sung in our church that Sunday, and two of them were staying at our house, Gary and, of course, my older brother Duane. Mom had strict rules about no work no play on Sunday with the ping-pong table in the basement being totally off limits.

I guess Gary thought he would challenge my mom on that issue with what he considered a good plan.

The day rolled around until the clock hit midnight. The plan was, as everybody knew, Sunday ended at that time, and 12:01 a.m. was Monday—everybody, that is, except my mother. Ping, pong, ping, pong was coming from the basement just after midnight and the hurried sound of my mother rushing downstairs from the bedroom. "Put those paddles down and get in bed" came her terse warning. "Duane, you know there's no ping pong in my house on Sunday!" "But Mrs. West" came Gary's reply, "It's after midnight, and it's now Monday." "Not in my house" came her response, "It is Sunday in this house until the sun comes up." And through the commotion, as usual, Dad slept on through all of it.

JAY WEST - *Pahrump, Nevada (brother of Southern Gentlemen baritone Duane West)*

CHAPTER 14

ONE GIANT LEAP

"Who knows what fortune will do for us. Great things have been affected by a few men well conducted"
—GEORGE ROGERS CLARK

It's 1964, and the waterwheel of life had been turning since Milo joined Sonny in August 1963, and fresh water was flowing under the bridge. In the last months of 1963, Sonny also started using a duo, the Light Brothers, to occasionally sing backup with him up on stage.

For Sonny, 1963 started a sequence similar to what he had been through seven years earlier. In 1956, and for the first time in his career, Sonny had back-to-back records that charted. He had a #7 country record, a #11, and a #12 before "Young Love" hit and went to #1. In 1963 following the success of "The Minute You're Gone," which reached #9 on the country charts in August, Sonny's next four releases would go to #17, #6, #27, and #19. The last two of those singles were released on one 45rpm record (Capitol #5197) on January 6, 1964. One side, "Sugar Lump," went to #27 and the other side, "Ask Marie," peaked at #19.

At the same time, #5197 was being released, and we were hitting

the stage of The Grand Ole Opry as The Chordsmen, Milo was returning from a working Christmas vacation in Fulbright. By working, I
mean Sonny and Milo had come up with an idea — a unique bass
that would attract attention on stage for their basic two-man show.
Being an all-around handyman, Milo spent those weeks back home
designing and making what would become his one-of-a-kind bass —
an instrument that absolutely attracted all sorts of attention.

On January 21, 1964, Sonny went back into the studio and cut
remakes of songs that had previously hit for other artists: "The End of
the World" by Skeeter Davis, "Burning Bridges" by Jack Scott, "Love
Letters in the Sand" by Pat Boone, and "Are You Lonesome Tonight"
by Elvis. All four would end up being released on albums.

As January turned into February and then into March, our vocal
group had been doing spirituals like "Swing Down Sweet Chariot" and
one of our favorites, "This Old House". Sometime along the way we got
this feeling we ought to learn something, as we called it, "a little more
worldly." We had heard a song we really liked and put together a good
arrangement on it. We showed up one night in March determined to
do it if the Opry band could pick it up. We rehearsed it with them;
they got it in no time, which was really impressive because we thought
the song might be new to them. That night we stood before the WSM
microphone on the stage of The Grand Ole Opry, and before it was
over, we had received eleven encores. We had no idea that the song we
did that night, "Kaw-Liga," had been a hit for Hank Williams eleven
years earlier, staying at #1 on the country charts for fourteen weeks. In
fact, it's worse than that — we didn't even know who Hank Williams
was. You must never forget — we were an acapella quartet from a
church college in Quincy, Massachusetts — not exactly a hot bed of
country music in early '60s.

It was late March 1964, and the unexpected benefits of being
the Opry Quartet started to show themselves. Nugget Studios in
Goodlettsville, a fairly new recording facility was owned by the comedy duo Lonzo and Oscar, the Homer and Jethro of The Grand Ole
Opry, and they started using us on many recording sessions. One of

the singers on Nugget Records was Dolores Smiley. She worked as a secretary for a music publishing company in Nashville, and hers were some of the earliest sessions we did there. In fact, her song "Near Me" was the first song we had done the background vocals on that I ever heard played on the radio — I heard it on WENO as I was driving down Gallatin Road.

As that was happening, Milo and Sonny had an idea for a trick fiddle — a break-away instrument that would add a comedic routine to their road show. Milo went to a pawn shop, found a cheap one for $3.00, took it by Sonny and Doris' apartment, and let it soak in the bathtub long enough so Milo could easily take it apart. With a bit of Milo ingenuity, he put it back together using an oil dipstick he got from some car in a junk yard, and made the idea work. Now the Sonny and Milo team had two new members — a strange-looking custom bass and a break-away trick fiddle. Even so, Sonny still knew he needed more energy and sound on stage: with the Light Brothers duo having gone their separate ways, the challenge was before him.

We need to pause right here to set up the back story. There are two parts to it: first is Sonny's discography, and second is Ray Walker. Years before I even thought about writing this book, I was fortunate to come across a detailed list of every song Sonny had ever recorded over his career. The discography included the date, the musicians on the session, the songs recorded, and so forth. It was in great detail. So much of what is in this book would not have been possible without that detailed discography. So let's start with the second item—Ray Walker.

As I was putting the pieces together for this chapter, Milo and I were having a cup of coffee, and as usual babbling on for hours about the good old days, when he mentioned what he had understood to be how Sonny came to hear about us. In bringing it up, I somewhat remembered hearing Duane speak about the same thing, so I decided to give the source of the story a call to see what he would have to say about it. There was just one problem—I didn't have a number for Ray. A few days later in a phone conversation with Alabama native

Giles Hollingsworth, who along with his brother Richard had written some great songs that Sonny had recorded (one of my favorites that we did was "Red Mud"), Giles completely out of the blue brought up Ray Walker's name. That opened the door for me to ask if he had Ray's phone number — incredibly he did.

So I picked up the phone and gave Ray Walker, the bass singer of the Jordanaires for fifty-five years, a call. I got his deep, resonant voice message, identified myself, and hung up, really hoping I might hear back from a man I hadn't spoken to in over forty years. In a matter of minutes my phone rang; it was Ray. That was the first of two revealing conversations Ray and I would have in less than one hour. So let's pick up the story with my filling in the dates and songs for Ray from the discography, and Ray Walker filling in the conversational blanks.

On April 10, Sonny was back in the studio, with the Jordanaires doing the vocal background for the first time since using them two years before on January 23, 1962. They did three songs: "Every Step of the Way," "Sugar Lump," and a Paul Anka song, "I Guess It Doesn't Matter Anymore." Sonny, at this session, asked the Jordanaires' spokesman, Gordon Stoker, if they could join him on some road shows, but Gordon said their busy session work would keep them from doing that. A bit later and off to the side Sonny spoke to his fellow Church of Christ friend Ray Walker, "I need a group like the Jordanaires to join me on my road shows." According to Ray (and I quote him here), "You need to get the boys from the Nazarene college who took our spot on the Opry—and don't argue with me about it, Sonny; just hire them." Ray first gave me a quote a little bit different, and just a few minutes after we had hung up he called me back, and requoted the last statement as it is above.

On April 28, Sonny was back in the studio again with a mixed group of singers, and they spent the entire three hours recording only one song, "Ask Marie," which ended up being rejected for release.

On May 16 and 17 the first major country music extravaganza featuring country artists was held at the old Madison Square Garden in New York City, complete with closed circuit TV coverage. Produced by Vic Lewis, the National Country Music Cavalcade of Stars, as it was promoted, was a huge leap for country music. As a result of our recording session with Delores Smiley, she was instrumental in getting Vic to contract with our quartet to do all the vocal background on the two dates. They were the biggest shows we had ever been on.

In June, we decided to learn another "worldly" song. This time we picked "Good Luck Charm." It fit us perfectly with our bass singer Huggins doing the "uhh huh huh" as Ray Walker did on the original with Elvis. Once again, ignorance can be bliss — but this time ignorance failed us. We didn't know that Elvis appeared on the Opry only once, on October 3, 1954, and had vowed to never come back (which he never did). In 1964, as we would come to understand, The Grand Ole Opry was not an Elvis fan — not by a long shot. When we finished what we considered a good rendition of "Good Luck Charm," we expected the applause to be what it usually was for one of our numbers. To those of you that don't know, when an artist finished singing a song on the Opry, the announcer would put his arms in the air and shake his hands around vigorously to get the audience to applaud — not much different than having an applause sign for TV programs. I assume that the Opry announcer was told to keep his hands in his pockets when our clueless vocal group finished singing because the applause was, surprisingly, on a scale of ten about a three at the very most. Yes — ignorance can be advantageous or detrimental — that's the price you pay for not knowing.

Just one month following the "Good Luck Charm" fiasco, on July 18, we were standing back stage at the Ryman when one of the Opry's stars approached, and without much in the way of small talk said, "I really like your sound, and tell you what - I'll give you a station wagon to travel in, and all you have to do is show up at my performances. The only thing I need to know is what it would take for you guys to go to work for me."

Not knowing that he was twelve years older than us and was one of the Opry's most successful and colorful stars, as the spokesman for our group I responded with, "Well, I'm not all that familiar with you

—where would we be playing?" He informed us that we would be appearing in auditoriums, in theaters, at fairs, and in clubs and the like. Not meaning to be unkind in the least, I informed him that we had never been in a club, and that was an opportunity we would be uncomfortable stepping into. I guess he wasn't used to being turned down, but I will never, ever forget his immediate reaction as he took a step forward, jammed his finger into the center of my chest, and said, "Well, I'll tell you what, son — you boys will never make it in this business," and he impolitely wheeled around and walked away. I suppose ego always seems to find a way to play its part.

"No." In simple terms that's what I said to him. Not "*No*" with emphasis — just "no." We walked away from that moment thinking, if that's what it takes to ply our trade in the country music business, then maybe he was right. For a few days, that finger in my chest became a jab in one of the values the four of us held, and it brought us all slap to the floor. On the other hand, maybe we were just too rolled up in our innocence to realize we were dealing with the wrong person at the right time. Be that as it may, there was a second part to it — by this time we were in excellent singing trim, and by saying "no," we were sticking to the standards we had set for ourselves, and the politely worded "no" was the only answer we could honestly give him without stepping on his values. Some thirty-two years later, that same man, at a low point in his life, sadly cashed in his chips with a single puff of smoke.

On August 1, 113 days after Ray Walker had told Sonny about us, from out of the shadows, this tall, dark-haired man approached us backstage at the Opry saying he'd been listening to our singing, and would like to talk with us. In the short few moments we had before jumping back out there to open the next segment doing the Coke commercial, he spoke to us quite openly. "I'm trying to put a second career together, and I feel like a combination of your harmonies along with my bass player Milo, I think this might have some real potential." I spoke up," We'll be right back" as we hurried onto the Opry Stage.

The band did the opening two measures, then the four of us sang:

—

> Coca-Cola Coca-Cola
> Things go better with Coca-Cola
> Things go better with Coke
> Life is much more fun when you're refreshed
> And Coke refreshes you best
> It's the refreshingest.

And as we made our way back off stage, my first thought was, "Well, here we go again." So here we were right after doing the Coke commercial with this new tall stranger standing in front of us. Being the spokesman for our group, I said as I had said just a couple of weeks before, "Well, Sir, I'm not familiar with you." His respectful response was, "Well, I'm Sonny James, and back in 1957, my big song was 'Young Love.'" Now I guess that was supposed to make my head fall off and spin around on the oak floor, but he wasn't fooling me. I was from the southern tier of New York State—Endicott, New York, to be exact—and I knew about the song "Young Love," so my honest response back to him was, "No, that wasn't you—that was Tab Hunter." You see—in my hometown we didn't have a country station so Tab Hunter's version of "Young Love" is what they played—I had never heard of Sonny James. As you might expect, Mr. James went on to politely explain that after he had released "Young Love," Dot Records immediately got movie star Tab Hunter to record it, and both he and Tab had hits on it at the same time. (This incident was always reason for a big laugh when we brought it up—that is, that the first time we met Sonny James, I called him a liar).

The conversation went on from there, and as unreal as it might sound, this is exactly what happened next — I, that's correct, I interviewed Mr. James. I don't recall him asking us anything much about ourselves. (Years later, it became quite evident in conversations with Ray Walker that Sonny had done some homework before approaching us.) So I asked him just as I had asked the other man a few weeks earlier: if we joined him, in what kind of places would we be expected to appear? He made this promise right then and there: "You'll never be embarrassed to have your family, your best friends, or even your pastor to come and see us perform. I don't play places where there is drinking or dancing." It was obvious in just those few words that he had stayed true to his values, and said "no" to some things in his life long before that August night.

August 15, 1964

When you come to the fork in the road, take it.
—YOGI BERRA

At every fork in the road, you make a choice.
And it is those decisions that shape our lives.
—MIKE DEWINE

Two weeks later on August 15, we joined Sonny James and changed our names from The Chordsmen to The Southern Gentlemen. It was how we grew up believing it was supposed to work — first you pass the test, and then you receive the reward. It's not an easy notion to accept, but as days and weeks and months turn into years and years, you come to understand that life is not just about success or failure — it's about right or wrong. Sometimes what seems like a failure is a test. Two weeks after saying "no" to the wrong man, the right person at the right time came along. It doesn't matter who you are — things that happen to you like that are hard to explain with words.

Like Easy Company in the HBO movie *Band of Brothers*, the first group of paratroopers to ever jump out of a plane and into combat happened on June 5, 1945, after two long years of intensive training. Our group had been in in Nashville for just short of two years, and we had no idea we were training for just this moment. Before arriving in Nashville in September 1962, we had never done any vocal background work with anyone, anywhere, at any time. Since then, most of those early recording sessions we did were with singers whose names never lit up a marquee at a country show or got national recognition. Probably the most recognition they had was on the local country station in their hometown area, playing their record. But all of them had afforded us the training we had to have in order to develop the confidence to know that we were ready to make the big jump if and when that day should ever arrive. And more than that — it was now up to us to prove ourselves equal to the challenge we had chosen.

Those names still stand out to me as bold as the training and parachute jumps of Easy Company: Clarence Tudor, Charlie Rife, Patsy Penn, Howard Rhoten, Barbara Dale, George Schilthroat, Allen Dorral, Carol Stevens, Dolores Smiley, Arthur Thomas, Teddy Bart, Archie Campbell, Demetrius Tapp, Lonzo and Oscar, and many more — you get the picture. To them we owe a great debt of gratitude.

It had taken us a good while to learn a lot of the Opry singers' names; to us they were just ordinary people who sang and played guitars — men like Hank Snow who dressed in sparkly outfits and women like Kitty Wells who wore tasteful long dresses. This scene for a number of months had become the fairly regular story of our lives at the Ryman Auditorium — the Mother Church of Country Music as we were told it was called. But for some reason we had not appeared on any segments Sonny was on since we had replaced the Jordanaires, nor even in the months before then when we were the Jordanaires' Opry guests, so Sonny James was completely unknown to us.

But I'm getting a bit ahead of myself here. To understand the sequence that led up to this out-of-the-blue moment we really need to go back about eighteen months to February 1963.

There was one thing, and only one thing that attracted us to The Grand Ole Opry — the Jordanaires. We had no dreams of being stars, or even trying to get a recording contract. We never talked to record companies or looked for songs to record or anything like that. The four of us hadn't dreamed about moving to Nashville to sing on the Opry. For us, I guess, it was more about the adventure of it all. We came here to sing for a church college, but that Jordanaires gospel album we had in college drew us toward them like a magnet, especially since that southern church college, as my Alabama friend Don McKay reminded me years later — wasn't interested in a bunch of "harmonizing carpetbaggers." I guess none of us really knows what can happen after a dream kicks in.

In early 1963 our baritone Duane had made the first contact with Ray Walker, the Jordanaires' bass singer, and one thing quickly led to another (we learned later that Ray was also the worship leader at Madison Church of Christ). Before we knew it Ray introduced us to their first tenor Gordon Stoker, but Ray was always the main one to us. Ray invited us to be their backstage guests, and after their spots we would go out with Ray to The Flaming Steer restaurant just a dozen or so blocks down on West End Avenue. It became a bit comical to us in later years, but when we'd go to the Opry as their guests, we would occasionally wear the suits we wore as a college quartet. On other occasions we would spread ourselves out in the balcony, cheering and whistling to get the Jordanaires's encores. That was really a hoot for us at the time.

We got to see Patsy Cline backed up by the Jordanaires in late February 1963. I also remember like it was yesterday, standing backstage near six-foot-five-inch Hawkshaw Hawkins who, surrounded by fans and admirers, took out his wallet and thumbed through a bunch of hundred-dollar bills, to the gasps of all observers.

Little did we know that just a few weeks later, on March 5, Patsy, Hawkshaw, Cowboy Copas, and Randy Hughes would die in a plane crash one-hundred miles west of Nashville in Camden, Tennessee. On Wednesday, March 6, my wife Thelma and I were visiting her folks in Toronto, Canada. I was at a station on the corner of Eglinton Avenue and Keele Street, filling up my car with gas when the radio flashed out the news that Patsy Cline's plane had crashed, and all on board had been killed. Years later, while traveling through Camden, I got off I-40 and drove the few miles to where the plane had come down. It was a sobering moment.

As spring 1963 rolled around, Lin and Glenn started doing work for Ray and Gordon at their homes and on their rental properties. Gordon's house was at an elevated point on Benton Smith Road, and being the Jordanaires first tenor, he had a sign out front, having christened it "High Note." Along with being invited into his home office and seeing all the pictures on the wall of the Jordanaires with Elvis, Tennessee Ernie Ford, Patsy Cline, and a bunch of others we didn't know, Gordon even invited the four of us to join him one afternoon at Percy Priest Lake on his houseboat. How neat was that — Lin and Glenn diving off the boat into the water and Duane and I, a bit more reserved, just watching in amazement as Huggins and Lin took one giant leap after another off of Gordon's boat into the lake. We even signed a log book he had, I guess for tax deduction purposes, indicating that we were music business guests of his that day.

Years later, it became quite clear that the Jordanaires just wanted to remain in our loop — that is, to know what we were up to, who we were recording with, and at what studios. I am sure, after being in the business for years, the Jordanaires were aware of the old adage, "Keep your friends close, but your competition closer." Proud as young peacocks, I think we puffed up a bit and strutted about, telling them everything. Looking back — we must have had harmonies that caused them some angst, but we were oblivious to all of it. It is well to remember here that in early 1963, Duane and I were just twenty-one, Glenn was twenty, and Lin was only nineteen. We were really still just kids, completely in the dark when it came to the fact that the music business had a lot more to do with business than with music.

One piece of business Sonny chose to pursue was to make sure an official announcement was released that we had joined him as The Southern Gentlemen, but he only agreed to take three of us on the road with him. I feel quite secure in saying that it had a lot to do with comfort. Six of us in a four-door car would have been cramped, especially with Sonny and his long legs. In any case, we looked forward to the time when all four of us would be on stage with him, but until then it was to be three. As a result, an announcement would appear in the September 5 issue of *Billboard* Magazine.

On Wednesday August 19, just four days after we had joined him, Sonny was back in the studio with his usual mixed group of background singers that he had been using up to this time. They spent the entire three hours recording "Behind the Tear," but they never got a good take. The song was rejected, which meant it would not be released.

"You know, everybody thinks we found
this broken-down horse and fixed him,
but we didn't.
He fixed us - Every one of us.
And I guess, in a way, we kind of fixed each other too."
(*SEABISCUIT* — the last lines in the 2003 movie)

No, this part of the story is not about a race horse — it's much more than that — but the stories are so similar. At this point, Sonny wasn't broken down, but he was in need of some serious fixin'. And no, our quartet wasn't ready to be put out to pasture yet, but there were signs pointing that way. It is well to remember, Sonny approached the four of us and Milo, not the reverse.

By mid-1964 Milo was thinking—I will be turning thirty in September. He had noticed that quite a few traveling road musicians like him, guys around thirty years old, suddenly weren't in bands any longer. He remembered asking someone in Hank Snow's band what had happened to one of Hank's road musicians—a fellow named Scotty who was Milo's age. Milo was told that Scotty had left and was now selling used cars.

It was during the disc jockey convention at the Hermitage Hotel in downtown Nashville where it really hit him. Milo's record company had set up a hospitality room promoting their artists, and anybody could drop by to meet them and hob-nob for a bit. The record company had a jukebox set up that was playing all of their artists' songs. Milo went over to it, and not one of his records was on it.

By the first week in August 1964, even after our eleven-encore performance, The Grand Ole Opry had cut back on our quartet's appearances to the point that it started to look like the end of the road for us. We didn't have a manager, not a single soul to stand up for us. All we had was a pitch pipe. Pink-slipped by the college we had so faithfully represented for three years because of academics, outlawed by its sister college in Nashville, and slighted at the Opry by a flurried high-profile Opry member because our encores just happened to be on his thirty-minute segment, there was nowhere left for our quartet to go. We didn't want to be stars. We weren't wishing to be penalized for having been raised above the Mason-Dixon line, and we didn't do "Kaw-liga" to take away from anybody's time. Stating the fact again—we didn't have a clue as to who Hank Williams was, and for sure we didn't know that he had even written the tune. All we wanted, the only thing we were looking to do at the time was to blend and harmonize—was that asking too much? Maybe we just needed to let it go. Really, and I mean really, what hope was there for a quartet like us? The way it was going we figured we probably only had another month or so before the Opry simply cut us off.

Oh, we didn't talk about it, nor did we fret and whine about the spin-down, we just felt it was happening. We hadn't gone out of our way to solicit possibilities from artists or the like. I guess we just accepted the fact that this might be the end of the trail for four young men who really enjoyed and were good at what they were doing. After all, what could be better that leaving on a high note — that is, doing something that you really love to do until it ended.

So there we were — at that moment a bass player with a fading dream and some guys who could harmonize like nobody's business with nowhere left to go. There was Milo — all he wanted to do was to write songs and record them. And there were the Chordsmen, and all we wanted to do was to be singing full-time somewhere so we could continue blending our voices like we had for five years.

But then there was Sonny. Six and a half years after "Young Love" had sent him to the top of his profession, his long-awaited second hit, "The Minute You're Gone," revived his slumbering career. At the same time the dreams of Milo and the four of us seemed to be hopelessly slipping away. In an uncertain business where legendary careers are sometimes the result of a relatively unknown artist luckily stumbling across or being pitched a perfect song; this, however, was the case of an established artist finding the perfect sound along with the men who could help provide it. Perhaps we were strangers, but we were kindred spirits who were blessed with the ability to harmonize, and Sonny recognized and respected that. What he saw and heard in us allowed him to pursue and accomplish, both personally and professionally, what he perceived his future musical career to be.

And in that moment everything got fixed. We got to be, as Rick Hall wrote, the turtle wax on the '57 Chevy that would be the shine on one of the great comeback stories in the history of country music. Right then and there, starting on that hot, steamy August night — Sonny James fixed it; he fixed all of us, including himself.

But during that two-week period of August 19 to September 2, a melody and a song idea had developed in Sonny's mind—a song featuring a vocal group chanting in the background through the entire song — something he couldn't have pulled off on stage before taking us on. The following is verbatim from a radio interview Sonny did years later:

"Well the string of hits really began with a song 'You're the Only World I Know' that I had written with Bob Tubert. That came about kind of as an unusual kind of writing. I was having breakfast one morning with my wife here in Nashville, and I had an idea for a song. I called Bob Tubert, and he was doing the same thing — he was having breakfast. I said Bob I've got an idea that I would like for you to work on the lyric. I have the melody already in my mind. It just hit me. He said, 'What's that?' I said 'you're the only' - at that time I didn't have the title. I said I want each phrase to begin with the word 'you're'. Like [Sonny says 'you're', then hums the tune and repeats the process two more times]. Anyway it was a very personal song, and I said I want it real simple, nothing complicated, just statements, each phrase just a statement. And he (Tubert) said that would be unusual, and you don't want it to get deep? I said no no. Just very simple. I want it to be talking to your girlfriend or your wife, someone you love. He said alright, I'll work on it. So he came up with the lyric and the title. Incidentally, he got the title when he was just working on, I suppose, certain phrases, and it just came across, and I never will forget him calling (mimics Tubert,) 'I've got it, Sonny; it was in the shower! I've got it, I've got it!' And he was all excited and he said, 'You're the Only World I Know.' I said sure."

"You're the Only World I Know" would become Sonny's first #1 hit in eight years.

September 5, 1964 — Sonny's announcement appeared in *Billboard* Magazine

James Holds Trio

NASHVILLE -Capitol's country singer Sonny James, after two successful appearances on the "Grand Ole Opry" with a new group known as The Southern Gentlemen, has decided to retain the trio as a permanent fixture of his act. The Southern Gentlemen, comprised of Milo Liggett and Gary and Lin Down will appear with Sonny on all "Opry" engagements and on most of the personals arranged for James by his manager, Bob Neal, of the Bob Neal Agency.

The piece had a number of noticeable errors. It's quite evident the Bob Neal Agency put out the release in a rush and didn't take the time to do a little fact checking. We weren't a new group; by this time we had been together for five years. Also it should have read, "The Southern Gentlemen, comprised of bass player Milo Liggett, and background singers Gary Robble, Lin Bown, and Duane West ..."

In either case — the starter pistol had been fired.

On January 18 and 21, 1965, we were in the studio recording what would be Sonny's one and only religious album, "'Til the Last Leaf Shall Fall."

On January 23, 1965, "You're the Only World I Know" reached #1 on the country charts and stayed there for four consecutive weeks. In addition, it went to #91 pop. During that same week, we were in New York City, doing *The Jimmy Dean Show*, our first network television show as Sonny James and The Southern Gentlemen.

And so for Sonny James, the two-horse race was on — the mixed vocal group or us.

CHAPTER 15

THE FORK IN THE ROAD — 1965

"There are known knowns — things we know we know. There are unknown knowns — things we don't know we know. There are unknown unknowns — things we don't know we don't know."
—Donald Rumsfeld

Forks in the road are fine, but as we all know, actual forks for eating have three or four prongs with just enough space between the prongs for stuff to slip through. Rumsfeld had it right — known knowns, unknown knowns, and unknown unknowns. When we made the two changes in our vocal group's personnel during our early college years, it took six months before the new additions actually felt like members of the team — it takes time to jell. When Huggins and Lin took their places — they took our already good sound to another level.

When we started with Sonny, there was a lot we didn't know about a lot of things. We didn't know very much about the country music business, and we certainly didn't know anything about Sonny. How much he actually knew about us we will never know. With so many unknowns floating about, jelling was bound to take longer or even

194

find itself in jeopardy.

Three years before Sonny's passing, my son Greg and I took a real interest in knowing more about him, things that interviewers would never have thought to ask (this was before the idea had even crossed my mind about writing a book). It had reached the point where we had set up a time and place for Greg to interview him, allowing us to get below the surface in his career. At the last moment, Sonny, for whatever reason, decided he didn't want to do it, and sadly, those personal experiences of his would end up being lost forever.

Greg and I were not aware at that time about Sonny's propensity to keep his professional side fairly well shaded from view. As the book's title indicates — **it was a life of willfully shadowing nearly everything from nearly everybody nearly all the time.** As the book started to take shape, and with the aid of people who were helping us to dig into all things Sonny James, it became clearer than clear; nobody, I mean nobody, seemed to be aware of this sequestered side of him. The fork in the road had prongs, and so much about him had unknowingly already slipped through.

This is not a criticism but in our research, we began to realize that this was most certainly one of his "Rules of Civility," one of those predetermined standards he had set up for himself as a youngster, an axiom he would remain loyal to throughout his life.

With that in mind, let's start with an example we used in the last chapter — the September 5, 1964, Billboard announcement that we would be joining him. That was willfully kept from us. Not that it mattered, but it did matter. I would have loved to have had it just for the sake of having it or would have loved to have sent a copy to my folks. On the other hand, because it was unknown to us, our group was totally under the assumption when we joined him that we would be doing his personal appearances and recording sessions — we had paid our dues so to speak in those garage-type studios. I guess we thought he knew that. When Don McKay came across the Billboard announcement some forty-five years later, there was no mention of our recording with him. All the seventy-five-word piece said was that we would be "a permanent fixture of his act."

On January 18 and 21, five months after joining Sonny on August 15, we were in the studio recording the religious album, "'Til The Last Leaf Shall Fall." That was what we expected when we signed on—it wasn't said in so many words, yet we just assumed as much. But it wasn't until we came across Sonny's complete discography that this willfully private side of Sonny that had escaped the light of day started to surface. In between the eighteenth and the twenty-first, on the twentieth to be exact, Sonny was back in that same studio recording with the same mixed group of background singers he was using before we came on board. He never told us he would be recording with them, and he never told us that he had recorded with them. With this rule he had set for himself, it was his and his alone to know—to us it was an unknown unknown.

There was nothing moral or immoral about this intentionally private side, and as much as it would be part of him throughout our time with him, it nearly came back to haunt him before the year's end. The lesson to be learned here is — if the rule you have set for your life has nothing to do with morality, don't be afraid to bend it every now and then if needs be. The lesson from the next eleven months would make that clear.

You can follow the sequence of events in Chapter 16, "The Itinerary '65 and '66." We did the Porter Wagoner TV show on February 16, and a week later we were in New York City filming the *Jimmy Dean Show,* the same time "You're the Only World I Know" went to #1.

Between March 15 and the 18 The Southern Gentlemen had been contracted to do all the vocal background on-screen singing in the country music movie, *Second Fiddle to a Steel Guitar,* which was produced by Vic Lewis and filmed in Nashville, the same man that in May 1964 produced the big two-day country music extravaganza in the old Madison Square Garden, where we did all the vocal background work. In total, we appeared with nine different artists, doing fourteen songs, which included doing three songs with Sonny and one with Dottie West (it was more of a hello, take 1, take 2, take 3, and goodbye moment). Our part with Sonny was filmed on the sixteenth, with Sonny coming back on the eighteenth to lead the finale.

Unknown to us was that while we were filming, Sonny was back in the studio recording on the fifteenth and the seventeenth. The detailed discography indicated Sonny cut nine songs in those two sessions, again using a mixed group of background singers. We didn't know anything about it, and as was Sonny's way, he never brought it to our attention.

On May 29, we appeared on the Opry without Sonny; Roy Acuff introduced us as "Sonny's Boys," and we did "Kaw-Liga."

June 1965 was busy as the itinerary shows; on the twenty-fifth, we were back in town, and once again, unknown to us, Sonny was back in the studio. The next day we were on the Opry with Sonny—again no mention from him that he had recorded the day before. This is not a complaint all these years later—it's just a reminder as to how really private he was about things. Remember, we didn't have reason to complain because we didn't know at the time that he was recording, and we were also in the dark as to that private side of him.

But then came an incident thirty-seven years later, revealing the date that had challenged, as you will see, the loosely-tied knot holding Sonny James and The Southern Gentlemen together. It had all started with our meeting Dottie West on a show date sometime in 1965 - none of us guys (that always means excluding Sonny) could remember where and when we first met her.

In 2002, I had begun searching the internet to find anything about us—records, tapes, magazine articles—just anything at all. I had given away all of our albums save one—that beat up Astrodome album that was scratched to nearly unplayable death. It was near the beginning of spring in 2002 when I came across an item for sale on eBay. The seller was promoting it simply as, "Sonny James and Milo Liggett autographs." My interest piqued, and back then you could contact the seller for additional information—which I did.

It happened that the seller named Darren was from California; he had purchased an autograph book on eBay that had originally belonged to a lady from Roanoke, Virginia. What Darren had set his mind to do was tear out individual autographed pages and put them up for sale on eBay. The first page he was fixin' to tear out was a page that Sonny had signed on one side and Milo had signed on the other.

I jumped at this and informed Darren that I was one of The Southern Gentlemen with Sonny, which led him to telling me that he had an autograph book full of the signatures of the Who's Who of country music. A Vivian Barton had apparently attended a good number of country music shows and had secured autographs of only country music artists, and Darren thought he could make some money by selling off the autographs one torn-out page at a time. He went on to tell me that Sonny and Milo's autographs were in the book two different times and that Vivian had dated each autographed page.

The first page of Sonny and Milo autographs that he was offering up for sale was dated in August 1963, and the second was dated two years later, in July 1965. That second date included the autographs not only of Sonny and Milo, but also the autographs of the rest of us Southern Gentlemen. It also just so happened at that time in 2002 that our baritone Duane was going through some serious health problems, and that page, with not only ours, but especially Duane's autograph, was something I really wanted.

Putting my mind to work, I came up with an offer that I thought Darren might not be able to refuse. I told him that if he would be so kind as to consider a trade I would get him a one-of-a-kind autographed picture of all of us — I promised him that I would get all of us to sign a photo and that would mean that he would have the last picture ever signed by Sonny James and The Southern Gentlemen, but I asked if he would just give me some time to get it done. Lin and Huggins (Glenn) both lived in Colorado, and after getting them to sign the picture, I would need to get with Sonny and Milo, who lived in Nashville, and then go by to see Duane, who lived in Shelbyville, Tennessee. What I asked for was his trust and patience, which he gave me. So the process started.

Before the actual final swap of the book for the signed photo took place, Duane West, our baritone since 1959, passed away on June 23, 2002. Six days later on June 29, with the book now in hand, I sent the signed photo along with a letter to Darren, as I wanted him to have a certificate of authenticity-type document.

With the autograph book finally in my possession, I opened it and couldn't believe my eyes. Darren was right—Vivian did have an autograph book full of the Who's Who of country music. The first name in this book, which included 106 signatures in total, was Tex Ritter and was dated August 1, 1963. The first autograph of Sonny and Milo was two weeks later and was dated August 16, 1963, and that date also included the autograph of Johnny Cash.

Even though Milo had known Sonny since 1956, this was the first show that he had done as Sonny's bass player, which just by itself was mind-boggling, and here we had signed and dated proof of it — but the names went on from there.

The book included autographs of not only of Sonny and Milo, but of Tex Ritter, Loretta Lynn, Jim and Jesse (McReynolds), Ray Price, Kitty Wells, Roy Drusky, Buddy Emmons (who would eventually become one of the A-Team steel guitar players), Johnny Cash, June Carter, Luther Perkins, W. S. Holland (Johnny's drummer), Marshall Grant (Johnny's bass player), Porter Wagoner, Norma Jean (the female singer for Porter who was replaced by Dolly Parton in 1967), Don Warden (Porter's steel player), Buck Trent (Porter's banjo player), Bobby Lord, Marty Robbins, Sammy Pruett, Ferlin Husky, Tommy Floyd, Ralph Stanley, and a slew of others.

The story wouldn't be as clear as it should be if we didn't pause here to explain a few things about us guys (Lin, Duane, Huggins who wasn't traveling with us at the time, and me). We all were what we were, and our natural personalities complimented one another. Duane was a friend to everyone, and everybody who ever knew him really liked him; he just blended in easily with strangers and friends alike. And while Duane was calmly friendlin' everybody, you'd find Lin out there in the middle of things, working the room—he was a natural point man. As I mentioned in a previous chapter, he was a born salesman, and that's not a stretch by any stretch of the imagination. Huggins—now there was one interesting guy. He quietly had a bit of all of us in him, yet he never asserted himself. On the other hand, with that deep voice leading the way, he had this cool mischievous side about him—you never really knew what he was thinking—and he constantly kept us on our toes. As for me, I guess you could say I was the administrator. When it came to arranging what we did in sessions, or keeping up with our dates (I kept up with all of our scheduling in college), that was the spot I filled in the group.

So here I was — Vivian's book sitting open in front of me while I was staring at the second Sonny and Milo pages from July 4, 1965. The additional autographers on that day were all of us guys, and then I turned one page and *bingo*, Dottie and Bill West autographs dated July 4, 1965 — answering that long-hidden, long-standing question The Southern Gentlemen had asked many times over the years: where and on what date had we really got to meet and know Dottie? I immediately went to my 1965 journal and updated that fourth of July date to read — with Dottie West. And it was right then and there, in that singular moment, with the facts finally in chronological order for the first time when it hit me—that's where the innocent unjelling of Sonny and The Southern Gentlemen began — the unintended consequence of one of his nearly sacred life's rules—*willfull shadowing*.

Now, with that piece of the puzzle finally in place, I am able for the first time, to explain the Dottie West connection correctly—all made possible thanks to my journal, the detailed discography, and last but not at all least, Vivian's autograph book.

Right along about this time Sonny's latest album, "I'll Keep Holding On," made its way into my hands, I was somewhat shocked and confused. I had been expecting the "Til The Last Leaf" album to be released, so I could present my folks with our first recordings with Sonny. But, after ten months with him, here I was holding an album and wondering: when had Sonny recorded these twelve songs? We were sure he hadn't recorded all of these before meeting us. And oh, how disappointingly right we were.

I brought the album to Lin and Duane's attention, knowing we had no interest in only being touring background singers. We had done that touring thing for nearly three years in college, and for six months we had been waiting for our next recording session with Sonny. And right then is when the entire sequence of events clicked into place.

On July 3, we left Nashville for a show in Knoxville, Tennessee, followed by a Sunday performance in Fincastle, Virginia, on July 4. I said that to say this: I had made up my mind to bring up this album without us on it to Sonny as soon as possible. That opportunity would present itself before we arrived back home.

However; here we were on July 4, 1965, in Fincastle, and for the second time in less than three months, as Vivian's autograph book revealed, we were with Dottie West. The first time was during the filming of *Second Fiddle to a Steel Guitar* back in March, when we backed her up on "When Two Worlds Collide."

Being on the road as much as we were at the time, and still being very "green" to the Nashville music industry, we didn't have any idea of the major changes that were taking place in town. In fact, the changes were never even a second thought until I started to do my research of that time period for this book, and then as facts started to surface, it liked to have knocked me over. Unknown to us, we were about to be in the middle of a 16th Avenue hurricane, and because we were out of town so much we didn't even know the wind was blowing.

Two questions came up about the same time period: First—was Dottie aware of the winds of change that were about to take place at RCA within a month—changes that were unknown to us? And second—did she know anything about who Sonny was using on his sessions?

Having just become aware of the *I'll Keep Holding On* album without us on it, Lin, as was his way, decided to go bird-doggin' for potential recording session opportunities. Vivian's autograph book had put it all in perspective because we knew Lin had done what I am about to tell you, but until her book showed up, we didn't know the when and where of it. And now it was clear—it started right then and there in Fincastle. Lin, as you might expect, easily raised the issue. It was a one-on-one conversation with Dottie. I wasn't in on it, and there was no reason to be. Lin was good at it, and that's all that needs to be said. Lin's timing was perfect; so perfect in fact, that Dottie immediately invited us to come to McMinnville, Tennessee, six days later and ride in a parade as The Southern Gentlemen. It was an off day for us, so sure, we accepted the invitation.

Now I was never one to purposely burn bridges behind me, but I always reserved the right to spin my tires in frustration on that same bridge. After six years of "internship," I guess it was my turn, but I talked myself out of that idea, deciding on a more kindly approach.

Before heading back to Nashville, we had a show the next day 118 miles away in Kernersville, North Carolina. I kept my eyes open, hoping for a moment when it would be just the two of us alone. I don't know if it was in Fincastle or Kernersville, but that right moment suddenly presented itself: "You know, Sonny, you need to sound the same on your records as you sound on your personal appearances. You need to use us on your recording sessions." Since we had done the religious album with him, I was kind of surprised when he said, "Do you think the group can cut it?" I remember my response, "Sonny, we've been singing acapella now for six years. It's second nature to us." Maybe Sonny didn't really know all that much about us; maybe he didn't know we had paid our dues doing vocal background work in the minor league studios in town. Or, maybe most of his decision to take us on was as a result of what Ray Walker had said to him. We'll never know. What I do know is, as was my usual way, I did my best to be nonconfrontational. Sonny had to know what I was alluding to without me saying it, so I never brought up the album we weren't on. He told me he wanted to think about it. He didn't let me know that he already had a 10 a.m. to 1 p.m. session lined up for Wednesday morning, the day after we arrived back home. However, before we got to Nashville, he let me know that he had sessions lined up for Thursday and Friday, and he would like for us to come by his place and rehearse on Wednesday afternoon for them. That's all I wanted to hear. The first song we recorded on Thursday was "In Memory of Louisa," written by Sonny and Bob Tubert. We also recorded "All My Love, All My Life," and "There's Always Another Day." The smooth transition into recording with Sonny on those two sessions came about without a hitch—minus bold-type words and spinning tires. However, that was no guarantee that he would continue to use us on future sessions. August would consume twenty-three days to do fifteen shows, traveling 7,700 miles in the car. What did Sonny have planned for the future recording dates? Only time would tell—we didn't press him.

For Sonny, the future looked promising as he already had two #1s, a #2, and a #3 in the twelve short months since we joined him. Harmonizing with Sonny James was now our #1 priority since Sonny and I had our little talk, and we finally had done two of his sessions, but because this was after Lin's one-on-one with Dottie, that would have been an unknown to her.

But the die had been cast with Dottie.

Just from that one day we spent in Fincastle getting to hobnob with Dottie and Bill West, six days later we ended up appearing in a hometown parade, honoring her in McMinnville. On that day, our vocal group packed up some stage clothes and made the 147-mile round-trip to McMinnville. The four of us, Lin, Duane, Huggins, and me, found ourselves riding in an open convertible with a sign "The Southern Gentlemen" attached to it. Before we left for home, Dottie asked us if we could drop off a tape of songs at their house the next week, songs we had done background vocal work on, and while we were at it, she asked if we would mind spending some time with her and Bill in their home. So on the evening of Tuesday the thirteenth, we drove over to their place in East Nashville with the tape. The four of us lounged around on the couch backing up Dottie on whatever she felt like singing. It was a fun evening just doing what we loved to do and enjoying every minute of it.

The tape I put together included a few acapella numbers, two songs we had done with Dolores Smiley, a demo session we had done with local TV personality Teddy Bart — a song titled "Hangman" (when we finished that tune one of the musicians said "Who's your bass singer?" Huggins was outstanding on it). The last number was a demo we had done with Demetrius Tapp a few months before we joined Sonny. We didn't know it at the time, but Demetrius just happened to be the wife of Bob Tubert, the future co-writer with Sonny on "You're the Only World I Know." The strange thing was I had nothing of us with Sonny to drop off — the religious album would not be released for another year. That probably told Dottie everything she wanted to know — we weren't recording with Sonny on his records, so she wouldn't be stepping on any toes by using us. That whole recording thing with Sonny, to us, was still up in the air.

We started this chapter with this thought: there are known knowns, unknown knowns, and unknown unknowns. The long-time Sonny and Chet friendship was something that was an unknown unknown to us. Chet, at that time in 1965, was the head producer for RCA in Nashville and was producing Dottie.

In August, we had twenty-three days filled in on our calendar, doing fifteen show dates and traveling 7,700 miles. August ended with a significant twist to it. We already knew our September schedule — Sonny must have liked our sound in the previous two sessions because he scheduled us to record with him again on the first. The rest of the month was full — twenty-four traveling days to do twelve shows while once again the five of us were crammed into Sonny's four-door 1965 Cadillac. Before that month was over we would log over 7,500 miles.

But here we were, having just arrived home after seven days and looking for some R&R. We pulled into Nashville on the thirtieth at 3 a.m. Before I got enough sleep to satisfy the exhaustion, the phone rang. It was Chet Atkins' office asking us to do a session with Dottie on September 7 from 7 p.m. to 10 p.m. As quickly as I could, I rubbed the sleep out of my eyes, checked our schedule, and saw that was an open day for us, and filled it in—"Record with Dottie at RCA—7 p.m." I called all the guys and then immediately called Dottie to see if she wanted us to come over and run through the songs. She said she would really appreciate that. We didn't know the Jordanaires or the

Kerrs didn't do that—they heard the songs for the first time in the studio session. Rehearse before the session—that's what Sonny had us do for the religious album, and back on July 7 before we did those sessions with him, I think we thought everybody did that. The next day the four of us went by Dottie's and rehearsed with her.

In September 1965, when Chet scheduled Dottie's session with us, we didn't realize it, but Chet was about to become our new friend. Maybe Sonny didn't realize it, maybe Chet did, but for us there were no maybes about it. Chet had helped Sonny get his first record contract with Capitol thirteen years earlier; but at this point in 1965 Chet was at a fork in his own road.

Wednesday found us in the Quonset hut for our third session with Sonny since he and I had chatted. The session ran from 10 a.m. to 1 p.m. (that turned out to be his favorite time to record). The next evening (Thursday) we left Nashville at 8 p.m. on a 805-mile jaunt for a Saturday show in Reading, Pennsylvania, followed by a 172-mile drive for a show in Ocean City, Maryland, leaving right afterwards for the 818-mile trip back to Nashville, arriving home at 3 p.m. on the sixth. That left us just twenty-seven hours to get rested and ready to record with Dottie.

I guess we were young and foolish, and whatever else you might think to call it, but we loved harmonizing. We walked into the studio on that Tuesday and unbelievably cut seven songs in three hours with Dottie. One of the songs she did was Sonny's first #1 hit since "Young Love," "You're The Only World I Know." Chet had to have been impressed.

The following day at twelve noon we left Nashville with Sonny for Texas, playing four towns and logging 2,320 car miles in the six days we were gone. The rest of the month we were busy as beavers appearing in Richmond, Virginia, on Saturday and in Charleston, West Virginia, on Sunday. We would also do shows in Albany, Georgia, Fort Pierce, Florida, and Orlando, Florida, before the month was over.

Sometime during that last stretch of shows, Chet's office contacted us to do another session with Dottie on Tuesday the twenty-eighth at

RCA Studio A. It turned out to be a session arranged and directed by Ray Stevens, with not only players from the A-Team (Floyd Cramer, Grady Martin, Harold Bradley, Ray Edenton, Henry Strzelecki, and Buddy Harmon, along with Dottie's husband Bill on the steel guitar) but also with an entire string section.

The three songs that we recorded were: "Would You Hold It Against Me," "Before the Ring on Your Finger Turns Green," and my absolute favorite of the three songs—"Wear Away" (which unfortunately was never released as a single). It was obvious all three of these songs were cut as potential single releases, where the first session we did with Dottie was album cuts. The last session was a thrill—it was our first time to record with strings. At this point it looked like we were on Chet's friends list.

The next day Chet's office called us again—this time to do a Hank Locklin session two days later on Friday, October 1. Hank was already established in the business because of two monster hits, "Please Help Me, I'm Falling" and "Send Me the Pillow That You Dream On." I know there's no law that says you can't make the most of today, but this seemingly innocent request from Chet's office was about to put too much air in our tires. The reason was that Sonny was contracted to appear for the first three days in October in Rochester and Minneapolis, Minnesota, and Des Moines, Iowa.

Believe you me—that telephone call from RCA had a promising ring to it. We had been traveling stuffed in a car for a year with Sonny while, unknown to us, Chet had been sitting in his office since August up to his eyeballs in need.

As much as we have been led to think that everybody in country music was family and nobody was really competing against anyone else in the business—that's a question you hardly ever heard discussed, but it was always there—just carefully kept from the public eye. The label and the artist were always looking for a way to get a jump on the competition through the next song, the next new twist, and the latest new sound that someone else was using that they might incorporate into their records. It was a never-ending struggle to be at the front edge of the industry. Even old and new friendships were subject to the temptation.

The Anita Kerr Singers, prominent in Nashville recording studios since around 1959, had, unbeknownst to us, disbanded in August. They were a staple background vocal group and even had a recording contract with RCA, but Anita, according to written articles, no longer wanted to just be a background singer or arranger on country songs — so she left for the greener pastures of Los Angeles.

RCA was, without question, looking for a group to replace them. Quoting from page 59 in Travis Stimeling's 2017 book on Charlie McCoy titled *50 Cents and a Box Top,* Stimeling quotes Charlie: "Chet's philosophy seemed to be to hire some of the best musicians he could find—especially the younger ones who needed an opportunity to prove themselves—and give them room to create."

Considering Charlie McCoy's statement that forty-one-year-old Chet Atkins was willing to use the four of us, whose average age at that point was just a tad over twenty-three, as replacements for the three remaining pieces of the Anita Kerr Singers, whose average age was near forty—well then, Chet's call to us really made sense. There we were, organized, harmonized, and "homogenized" by six years of acapella singing, road-tested by the same six years, fire-tested in RCA's Studio A with Chet as Dottie West's producer, and on the average as young as Charlie McCoy, who at that point was twenty-four.

Back then, most road musicians were prone to be on a short string —looking for the next move up—hopefully to become stay-at-home musicians. But there wasn't a single group trying to compete with the Jordanaires and The Anita Kerr Singers to do vocal background session work—they had the town wrapped up. We really hadn't been looking for anything, but Sonny's (willfully private) use of other background vocalists had raised a red flag for us guys, and just like that this Hank Locklin RCA opportunity presented itself.

Let's be clear as clear can be—very quickly The Southern Gentlemen had some far-reaching private discussions at this crossroads twenty-four-hour moment. Chet hadn't called us into his office to have a face-to-face discussion, nor had we heard any scuttlebutt to the contrary, but the handwriting was clearly on the wall — Chet needed a solid and tested vocal background group to fill the vacancy left by Anita Kerr's departure, and with successful Dottie West recording sessions behind us, we were just a phone call and a land-line handshake away from most traveling musicians' biggest dream. Nashville didn't wait on you if they wanted you; in the music business you jumped when called, or you would be pushed off the short list and maybe disappear into oblivion.

One thing we did know, however, was that the window of opportunity with RCA showing an interest would be a brief one. The decision while at the fork in the road was which way to go, what should we do? Decisions like this are not easy, believe me, not easy. But the decision turned out to be already made for us. We had committed ourselves with a verbal handshake agreement, and Sonny had already been contracted for the day in question. To give Sonny one day's notice to try to find replacements for us just didn't seem right. It may have been right for us, absolutely, but right in every respect—not at all. If we could give him a month or two notice, or leave at the end of the year; that would be something we could live with, but not just a day or two. Though we could have justified any move on our part because we weren't under a signed contract with Sonny, we recognized that a handshake and a promise had to, in the short run, be considered as binding. We felt as a group, after some serious discussion, a very personal obligation to fill those dates with Sonny and turn RCA and Chet Atkins down for the moment. (Remember—at that time we didn't know about Sonny and Chet's nearly decade-and-a-half friendship). When we got back in town, I called Chet's office over and over and over and over.

You see, looking back, regardless of the final consequences, we did the proper thing and took the morally-correct fork. The hand of fate always seems to loom large over times like this — a lesson we would come to realize many years later. As time passed, it seemed that there were many private conversations going on all around us at that moment, conversations we would never be privy to. So how did our "*no*" to Chet Atkins turn out for everybody? RCA never returned any of our calls, and never called us again. Following the unreturned phone calls to RCA, on Sunday morning, October 10, Dottie asked us to sing in church with her where she attended—Scottsdale Church here in Nashville. We stood around her on the platform like we did with Sonny and sang as you might have expected—acapella. A month later on Thanksgiving Day, November 25, 1965, Lin and his wife had the Wests over to their house for Thanksgiving dinner.

For Dottie West: "Before the Ring on Your Finger Turns Green" was released in December. It hit the Top 50 charts on December 11 at #47, peaking at #22 on January 15. Her next single release that we recorded with her was "Would You Hold it Against Me" with "You're the Only World I Know" on the back side, and it would become the biggest hit in her career to that point, reaching #5 in late May 1966. In July 1966, RCA released the album *Suffer Time*, a release that included songs we had cut with her, and it became the most successful album in her entire twenty-year career, peaking at #3 on Billboard's annual Top Country Albums list in 1966. Dottie obviously had to be delighted with us, but she was under the control of RCA. Apparently she hadn't been told that the label wouldn't be using our vocal group on her records anymore. We never got to record with Dottie, or anyone else at RCA again.

For Chet Atkins: And as for Sonny's old friend Chet Atkins' need for a newly organized vocal background group, that would be solved, not immediately, but within a year or so The Nashville Edition became the staple for him.

For Sonny James: So how would our "*no*" to Chet turn out for him? Well, the proof is in the pudding as they say. Those #1, #2 and #3 songs for Sonny without us on them were immediately followed with another #1 and a #2, and then in February 1967, starting with the song "Need You," that amazing string of sixteen #1 singles in a row began. You can't predict it, but something inside told us to honor your commitment and "stay put." We did, and we will be ever grateful that we did. It would be an adventure very few, if any, ever get to be part of.

For The Southern Gentlemen: And as if to rub our noses in it a bit, that is, as if to say to us, "are you sure you did the right thing," along came the month of November; where we squeezed into the car again, and in the space of twenty days did shows in seventeen different towns, recorded with Sonny twice, and drove an unbelievable 11,016 miles. I don't want to overdo it here, but being sardined into a vehicle seemed to be part of the price for enjoying the opportunity to harmonize. I bring it up again because I have addressed it in a previous chapter: when we were in college and traveling for the Youth For Christ organization, and for YouthTime with John Debrine, we squashed John, his sound man and driver, Tom "Igmoo" Lang, and the four of us into a four-door Pontiac, and headed out for a 500-mile round-trip one-day Saturday night rally. Being crammed in a car was certainly nothing new to us, but it wasn't priority #1 forever.

And there was one other thing that was not new to us. We were fortunate to have teamed up with two older and experienced terrific men along the way — John DeBrine, who was sixteen years older than we were when we joined him for those marvelous two years back in 1961 and 1962, and Sonny, who was fourteen years our senior. Both men knew the ropes, and both were beyond reproach — a stroke of perfect good fortune for a bunch of young guys who could use an experienced older mentor to usher them along in their early "green" years.

On Saturday, December 11, the five of us shoe-horned ourselves into the car again to do our last out-of-town trip of the year, a 414-mile trek to Jackson, Mississippi. Among others on that show was Charlie Louvin. Following our performance Sonny told us he would be making the trip back to Nashville, riding with Charlie. This was the first time Sonny had ever done anything like that, but the four of us, for the first time, in a long time got to enjoy the comfort of a roomy car. As it turned out, Charlie had graduated from a car to a bus, and we guessed Sonny wanted to stretch out that six-foot-three and one-half-inch-frame dominated by those long legs of his, and who could blame him? The following Friday we had a recording session with Sonny, followed by our last scheduled show of the year—a Saturday slot on

The Grand Ole Opry.

That sounds final, but it was still far from it. Following our performance that night, Milo left in a rush for his 550 mile Christmas vacation trip to Fulbright. Sonny got the remaining three of us together, and hurriedly addressed two issues:

First: He informed us that he would be purchasing a bus with the understanding that we would be the drivers. We agreed.

Second: He looked straight at Lin, Duane, and me, and said, "And you're my sound." Suddenly, with just four words, the events of the previous couple of months would start to make all sorts of sense.

Sonny needed two of us to fly up to Schenectady, New York, and drive the bus back to Nashville. Lin and Huggins volunteered to go and get it. After they arrived at Wade Tours they picked up the 1964 Flxible (that is the real name) with only 80,000 miles on it; and without ever having driven anything like it before, the two of them drove the thing 1,000 miles back to Nashville.

When Milo got back from his vacation he ran into one of the biggest surprises of his life — a beautiful blue and silver thirty-five-foot-long bus that he had no idea Sonny was even thinking of purchasing. Within a month the seats were pulled out and replaced with bunk beds and the like, making it as far from that cramped four-door car as possible.

With just a short burst of words from Sonny, our four-door car was exchanged for a touring bus; the mixed vocal background group Sonny had been using became a thing of the past, as we would do every recording session with him going forward. In addition, as if to prove we were "his sound", for the first time there would be pictures of Sonny, Milo, and The Southern Gentlemen on the cover of *True Love's a Blessing* (album); followed by "Room in Your Heart" (singles jacket), *Need You* (album), and *Born to Be With You* (album cover and singles jacket). In 1968 we were also on the cover of the Astrodome album, and a year later on the singles jacket of "My Love".

It was New Year's Day, January 1, 1966. Sonny was hosting a thirty minute segment on the Opry, and in a somewhat unusual move for them, he was scheduled for three spots. We did "Young Love" and "You're the Only World I Know" and wedged in between he wanted The Southern Gentlemen to do one of our favorite songs, a song we had never done on a show with him, "Swing Down Sweet Chariot." And then it happened. Sonny introduced us in a way he had never introduced us before; and I quote, "I tell you, here are some folks who always sing on key because they happen to be the group that goes with me all over the country, and we hear more reports about them, and I'm real proud of them, and of course you hear them on all of my records and now you'll hear them all by themselves, that is except what little I do to foul them up — The Southern Gentlemen and 'Swing Down Sweet Chariot.'"*

With two statements, one private ("you're my sound") and one public on January 1, the collaboration became a team — a real team — a tight-knit team in every sense of the word. On New Year's Day 1966, a new day arrived. With that public introduction we truly became Sonny James and The Southern Gentlemen. We not only came to the fork in the road and took it — we, all of us, took the right one.

* In 2005 and 2006 The Grand Ole Opry and Cracker Barrel released a total of three CD compilations of live (1964-1967) Opry performances. Sonny introducing us singing "Swing Down Sweet Chariot" is track #3 on the Opry Gospel CD (OM-0610).

JAY HICKMAN SNIPPET

I first became aware of Sonny James when I was about ten years old. I vividly recall my mother listening to a country music station and hearing the upbeat sound of one of Sonny's many number one hits. That song was "Running Bear," and it immediately grabbed my attention. I asked my mom, "Who is that singing that song?" Her reply was Sonny James. Shortly thereafter, I asked my mom if I could have some money to go and buy a record with "Running Bear" on it. She gave me a few dollars, and I marched uptown to a record store in Ann Arbor, Michigan. I purchased the *Live at the Houston Astrodome* album because it had "Running Bear" as one of the selections. Over the next several years, I purchased many of Sonny's records and still have all of them in my collection yet today.

A couple of years later (1971, I believe) my family, with me in tow, was driving past Crisler Arena. This is where the University of Michigan plays its home basketball games. The marquee out front made my heart jump! It said something to the effect of Country Music Special, starring several popular artists. One of those listed was Sonny James! What a great surprise that was to me. Keep in mind that Ann Arbor was not exactly a bastion for country music concerts. Sonny's music meant a lot to me, and I asked my parents if we could go. Well, our family consisted of five people. My parents looked into the ticket prices and gave me the sad news that it was too much money to take the whole family. I was naturally disappointed. However, an elderly couple who lived next door to us did in fact get to go to the show. I recall grilling them over and over, asking what Sonny's part in the show was like. When they told me that he sang "Running Bear," the feeling of disappointment came over me again that I was not able to see him live in person.

Over the years I have often regretted the fact that I never got to see Sonny perform live. This feeling came over me again the day it was announced that Sonny James had passed away. A sadness came over me as if a close friend had died. Sonny was a part of my life growing up. His music made me feel good. I always caught his TV appearances when I could. Though I never met him, I always considered Sonny James a friend of mine. I still listen to his music and watch the videos of Sonny James and the Southern Gentlemen on YouTube. I also have had the good fortune of becoming friends with one of the Southern Gentlemen who traveled and recorded with Sonny. He has recounted to me many of the experiences he enjoyed while being a Southern Gentleman. This has made me feel even closer to the man I consider a friend whom I never met. Sonny and his music will always live on for me and be a part of my life.

JAY HICKMAN - *Saginaw, Michigan*

CHAPTER 16

THE ITINERARY '65 AND '66

Jan '65	MILES
02 Sat. Leave Nashville	415
02 Sat. Jackson, MS	208
03 Sun. Memphis, TN	213
04 Mon. Arrive Nashville 3 a.m.	
09 Sat. Nashville - Opry	
12 Tue. Leave Nashville	758
13 Wed. Wichita Falls, TX	427
14 Thu. Beaumont, TX	283
15 Fri. San Antonio, TX	273
16 Sat. Dallas, TX	196
17 Sun. Austin, TX - head for home	859
18 Mon. - 8 p.m. Record w/Sonny "Til Last Leaf Shall Fall"	
20 Wed. >>> [Sonny Records 10 a.m. unknown to us]	
21 Thu. 10 a.m. Record w/Sonny - Religious Album	
30 Sat. Grand Ole Opry	

Twelve dates, total miles driven, 3,632

Feb '65

06	Sat. Leave Nashville	185
06	Sat. Knoxville, TN	185
13	Sat. Nashville - Opry	213
14	Sun. Memphis, TN	213
16	Tue. Nashville - *Porter Waggoner TV Show*	
19	Fri. Left for New York State	922
20	Sat. Endicott, NY - stopover - my hometown	
21	Sun. *Malcom X* shot in NY City	
22	Mon. 5 a.m. Left for NYC	184
23	Tue. Rehearse for *Jimmy Dean TV Show*	
24	Wed. Rehearse again	
25	Thu. Rehearse again	
26	Fri. Tape Show - leave for Endicott, New York	184
27	Sat. Endicott NY - visit in my hometown (Endicott)	
28	Sun. Leave for Nashville	922
29	Mon. Arrive in Nashville 7 a.m.	

Five dates, total miles driven, 2,795

Mar '65

06	Sat. Nashville - Opry	
13	Sat. Leave Nashville	114
13	Sat. Decatur, AL	114
15	Mon. >>> [Sonny Records 10 a.m. — unknown to us]	
15 - 18	Nashville Filming movie, 2nd Fiddle to Steel Guitar	
17	Wed. >>> [Sonny Records 10 a.m. — unknown to us[	

Two dates, total miles driven, 228

Apr '65

16	Fri. Leave Nashville	569
17	Sat. Beloit, WI	421
18	Sun. Hammond, IN	146
19	Mon. Arrive Nashville	
24	Sat. Leave Nashville	67

24 Sat. Bowling Green, KY	472
25 Sun. Detroit, MI	533
26 Mon. Arrive Nashville - arrive at 11 a.m.	
28 Wed. Leave Nashville	531
29 Thu. New Orlean, LA - leave at 4 a.m.	202
30 Fri. Pensacola, FL	491

Six dates, total miles driven, 3,432

May '65

01 Sat. Clearwater, FL	161
02 Sun. Daytona Beach, FL	680
03 Mon. Nashville - arrived 1 p.m.	
06 Thu. Leave Nashville	408
07 Fri. Charlotte, NC	392
08 Sat . Birmingham, AL - head home	191
09 Sun. Arrive Nashville	
12 Wed. Leave Nashville	420
13 Thu. Hattiesburg, MS	453
14 Fri. Paducah, KY	461
15 Sat. Milwaukee, WI	118
16 Sun. Freeport, IL	68
18 Tue. Madison, WI	619
19 Wed. Nashville - arrived at noon	
20 - 26. Nova Scotia & New Brunswick	3,800

Sonny took Duane & Milo - Lin & Gary didn't go

29 Sat. Opry — Southern Gentlemen without Sonny

Fifteen dates, total miles driven, 7,771

Jun '65

01 Tue. NYC - *Night Life* Network TV show	
04 Fri. Leave Nashville	259
04 Fri. Terre Haute, IN	259
05 Sat. Arrive Nashville	
05 Sat. 1 p.m. Gents Recording Session at G&M	

Opry with Sonny — Gents did Coke commercial

07 Mon.	9 PM Gents Recording w/Joe Rhoten at G&M	
08 Mon.	Leave Nashville	249
08 Tue.	Paragould, AR	249
09 Wed.	Arrive Nashville	
11 Fri.	Leave Nashville	248
11 Fri.	Atlanta, GA	248
12 Sat.	Arrive Nashville	
12 Sat.	Opry	
13 Sun.	Leave Nashville	351
13 Sun.	Decatur, IL	351
14 Mon.	Arrive Nashville	
16 Wed.	Gents Demo session with Milo at Monument	
18 Fri.	Tape Pilot TV show at the Opry	
19 Sat.	Leave Nashville	294
19 Sat.	Asheville, NC	394
20 Sun.	Culpepper, VA	590
21 Mon.	Arrived Nashville 4 p.m.	
25 Fri.	>>> [Sonny Records 10 a.m. — unknown to us]	
26 Sat.	Opry with Sonny	
27 Sun.	Loretto, TN (Terry Town) - round trip	191

Eight dates, total miles driven, 3,683

Jul '65

01 Thu.	Rerun Jimmy Dean Show from 03/04/65	
03 Sat.	Leave Nashville	180
03 Sat.	Knoxville, TN	268
04 Sun.	Fincastle, VA, Dottie West on the show	118
05 Mon.	Kernersville, NC	460
06 Tue.	Arrive Nashville	
07 Tue.	>>> [Sonny Records 10 a.m. — unknown to us]	
07 Wed.	At Sonny's - 3 p.m. rehearse- for recording session	
08 Thu.	10 a.m. Record with Sonny	
09 Fri.	10 a.m. Record with Sonny	

10 Sat. McMinnville TN, Gents in Dottie West parade	147
11 Sun. Leave Nashville 5 a.m.	325
11 Sun. Anderson, IN	325
12 Mon. Arrive Nashville	
13 Tue. Drop tape off at Dottie West's house	
17 Sat. Opry	
18 Sun. Leave Nashville	539
18 Sun. Salem, OH	477
19 Mon. Farmers City, IL	394
20 Tue. Arrived Nashville 6 a.m.	
23 Fri. Leave Nashville	762
24 Sat. Bridgeville, DE	483
25 Sun. Columbus, OH	386
26 Mon. Arrive Nashville	
27 Wed. Gents recording with Bill Ralich at MCR	
28 Thu. Gents recording session at Gower & Moore	
30 Fri. WSM filming at the Ryman Auditorium	
31 Sat. Opry	

Nine dates, total miles driven, 4,864

Aug '65

01 Sun. Leave Nashville midnight	447
01 Sun. Angola, Indiana	447
02 Mon. Arrived Nashville 6 a.m.	
06 Fri. Leave Nashville 7 a.m.	369
06 Fri. Hickory, NC	257
07 Sat. Atlanta, GA	651
08 Sun. Dickerson, MD	280
09 Mon. Endicott, NY (my hometown)	274
10 Tue. Navan, Ontario Canada	585
11 Wed. Ocean City, MD	430
12 Thu. North Attleboro, MA	398
13 Wed. Reistertown, MD	132
14 Sat. Allentown, PA	576

15 Sun. Jackson, MI	512
16 Mon. Arrived Nashville 3 p.m.	
21 Sat. Opry	
24 Tue. Leave Nashville 9 a.m.	763
25 Wed. Toronto, Canada - TV show	302
26 Thu. Malone, NY (two days at a fair)	
27 Fri. Malone, NY	561
28 Sat. Monroe, MI	497
29 Sun. DuQuoin, IL -Fair 33,000 at show	219
30 Mon. Arrived Nashville 3 a.m.	

Fifteen dates, total miles driven, 7,700

Sep '65

01 Wed. 10 a.m. Record with Sonny	
02 Thu. 8 p.m. leave Nashville	780
04 Sat. Reading, PA (fair)	172
05 Sun. Ocean City, MD	809
06 Mon. Arrived Nashville 3 p.m.	
07 Tue. 7-10 p.m. Record w/Dottie seven songs in three hrs	
08 Wed. 12 noon Leave Nashville	818
09 Thu. Kileen, TX	67
10 Fri. Austin, TX	196
11 Sat. Dallas, TX	273
12 Sun. San Antonio, TX	404
13 Mon. Fulbright, TX stay in Milo's hometown through 15th	562
16 Thu. Arrive Nashville 8:30 a.m.	
17 Fri. 2 a.m. Leave Nashville	613
18 Sat. Richmond, VA	317
19 Sun. Charleston, WVA - WVA Jamboree	387
20 Mon. Arrive Nashville 8:30 a.m.	
24 Fri. Leave Nashville 7 a.m.	429
24 Fri. Albany, GA	406
25 Sat. Fort Pierce, FL	119
26 Sun. Orlando, FL	685

27 Mon. Arrive Nashville 4 p.m.

28 Tue. Nashville - Gents record w/Dottie West at RCA

29 Wed. Call from RCA to do Hank Locklin session

30 Thu. Leave Nashville   758

             Twelve dates, total miles driven, 7,515

Oct '65

01 Fri. Rochester, MN   84

02 Sat. Minneapolis, MN   245

03 Sun. Des Moines, IA   612

04 Mon. Travel Day

05-08 Tue. Little Rock, AK for four days   347

09 Sat. Arrive Nashville 6 a.m.

10 Sun. Nashville   Gents w/Dottie - Scottsdale Church

11-13 Mon.-Wed. Rehearse and tape two identical *Jimmy Dean Shows* at Ryman

14 Thu. Leave Nashville at noon   1,111

15 Fri. Boston, MA - Back Bay Theatre   401

16 Sat. Baltimore, MD   483

17 Sun. Finley, OH   429

18 Mon. Arrive Nashville 6 a.m.

22 Fri. Nashville - WSM filming at Ryman

23 Sat. Opry with Sonny

28 Thu. Leave Nashville at 8 a.m.   888

29 Fri. Fort Lauderdale, FL   46

30 Sat. West Palm Beach, FL

        Nine dates, total miles in the 1965 Cadillac, 4,646

Nov '65

01 Mon. Leave West Palm Beach 1 a.m.   2,223

01 Mon. Travel

02 Tue. Minot, North Dakota   342

03 Wed. Winnipeg, Manitoba Canada   404

04 Thu. Regina, Saskatchewan   472

05 Fri. Calgary, Alberta   186

06 Sat. Edmonton, Alberta	612
07 Sun. Spokane, WA	347
08 Mon. Open	
09 Tue. Portland, OR	768
10 Wed. Open	
11 Thu. Salt Lake City, UT	483
12 Fri. Gallup, NM	139
13 Sat. Albuquerque, NM	148
14 Sun. Truth or Consequences, NM	1,368
15 Mon. Heading back to Nashville	
17 Wed. Leave Nashville 8 a.m.	973
18 Thu. Endicott, NY - stayed over w/my parents	74
19 Fri . Syracuse, NY War Memorial Auditorium	585
20 Sat. Winston Salem, NC	263
21 Sun. Norfolk, VA	706
22 Mon. Arrived Nashville 12:30 p.m.	
24 Wed. 10 a.m. Record with Sonny	
25 Thu. Dottie and Bill at Lin's for Thanksgiving Day	
26 Fri. 10 a.m. Record with Sonny	
27 Sat. Nashville - Opry	561
28 Sun. Pittsburg, PA	362

Seventeen dates, total miles in the 1965 Cadillac in November, 11,016

Dec '65

01 Wed. London, Ontario Canada	68
02 Thu. Kitchener, Ontario	390
03 Fri. Columbus, OH	389
04 Sat. Nashville - Opry	
06 Mon. Nashville - Recording Session at Bradley's Barn for Movie	
07 Tue. Nashville - Film at Trafco for movie - Las Vegas Hillbillies	
08 Wed. 10 a.m. Record with Sonny	
09 Thu. Nashville - Benefit show at an orphanage	
10 Fri. 10 a.m. Record with Sonny	

11 Sat. Jackson, MS, Sonny rode back to Nashville
with Charlie Louvin on his bus.   414

12 Sun. Arrive Nashville 11 a.m.   414

17 Fri. 10 a.m. Record with Sonny

18 Sat. Nashville - Opry

Seven dates, total miles driven, 1,673

Christmas vacation until January 1. Endicott, NY. Round trip >   1,946

Jan '66 - Traveling in Our New Bus

01 Sat. Opry 3 spots w/Sonny / Coke commercial   541

02 Sun. Davenport, IA (1st date w/1964 Flxble Bus)   541

03 Mon. Arrive Nashville

08 Sat. 10 a.m. record at Monument w/Rhoten

08 Sat. 09 p.m. Nashville - Opry   469

09 Sun. Chicago, IL   469

10 Mon. Arrive Nashville

12 Wed. Ralph Emery WSM radio show 11:00 p.m. -1:30 a.m.

13 Thu. Leave Nashville   346

14 Fri. Greenville, SC — (Jimmy Dean show rerun)   103

15 Sat. Charlotte, NC   408

16 Sun. Arrive Nashville

19 Wed. Nash, Ralph Emery's Opry Almanac TV 6 a.m.

21 Fri. Leave Nashville   560

22 Sat. Milwaukee, WI

23 Sun. Open day   276

24 Mon. Springfield, IL   373

25 Tue. Arrive Nashville 8 a.m.

26 Wed. Leave Nashville 10 p.m.   1684

28 Fri. Phoenix, AZ   373

29 Sat. Los Angeles, CA   120

30 Sun. San Diego, CA   120

31 Mon. Los Angeles - promo pictures at Capitol Records Tower

31 Mon. 2 p.m. Leave for Nashville   2007

Ten dates, total miles driven, 8,390

Feb '66

02	Wed. Arrive Nashville 9 p.m.	
04	Fri. Leave Nashville	503
05	Sat. Akron, OH	190
06	Sun. Detroit, MI	533
07	Mon. Arrive Nashville	
11	Fri. Leave Nashville	930
12	Sat. Endicott, NY stop over at my folks place	129
13	Sun. Rochester, NY	
15	Tue. Leave Rochester, NY 8 a.m.	333
15	Wed. New York City - Sonny business meetings	
16	Wed. In NYC Broadway play - *Man of La Mancha*	
17	Thu. In NYC Broadway play - *Promises, Promises*	232
18	Fri. Arlington, VA	83
19	Sat. Gettysburg, PA	689
20	Sun. Arrive Nashville 3 p.m.	
25	Fri. Nashville - Opry w/Sonny and our own spot — we did Kawliga	
25	Fri. Leave Nashville	333
26	Sat. Macon, GA	333
27	Sun. Arrive Nashville	

Seven dates, total miles driven, 4,388

Mar '66

02	Wed. Nashville 10 a.m. Record with Sonny	
02	Wed. Nashville 10:30 p.m. Record w/Bill Ralich	
03	Thu. 10 a.m. Record with Sonny	
06	Sun. Leave Nashville 1 a.m.	447
06	Sun. Mobile, AL	447
07	Mon. Arrive Nashville 9 a.m.	
08	Tue. 10 a.m. Record with Sonny	
09	Wed. 10 a.m. Record with Sonny	
10	Thu. 10 a.m. Record with Sonny	
10	Thu. Leave Nashville 11 p.m.	548
11	Fri. Warren, OH	16

12	Sat. Youngstown, OH	
12	Sun. Youngstown, OH	
12	Sun. Leave Youngstown, OH	551
13	Mon. Arrive Nashville 9 a.m.	
16	Wed. Leave Nashville 9 a.m.	1095
17	Thu . Montreal, Quebec Canada	287
18	Fri. Peterborough, Ontario Canada	538
19	Sat. Boston, MA	455
20	Sun. Buffalo, NY	
20	Sun. Leave for Nashville 11 p.m.	703
23	Wed. Leave Nashville at noon	758
24	Thu. Wichita Falls, TX	375
25	Fri. Houston, TX	
26	Sat. Houston, TX	785
27	Sun. Arrive Nashville 5 p.m.	
30	Wed. Leave Nashville	246
30	Wed. Newton, IL	298
31	Thu. Racine, WI	338

Thirteen dates, total miles driven, 7,887

Apr '66

01	Fri. Madison, WI	67
02	Sat. Freeport, IL	
03	Sun. Travel day	1988
04	Mon. Seattle, WA	291
05	Tue. Kamloops, BC, Canada	149
06	Wed. Penticton, BC	458
07	Thu. Prince George, BC	486
08	Fri. Vancouver, BC	70
09	Sat, Victoria, BC	421
10	Sun, Spokane, WA (stayed overnight)	
11	Mon, Travel Day	2173
12	Tue, Arrive Nashville 6 a.m.	
13	Wed, Day off (get some rest)	

14 Thu.	Leave Nashville 11 p.m.	724
15 Fri.	Clearwater, FL	30
16 Sat.	Tampa, FL	140
17 Sun.	Daytona Beach, FL	680
18 Mon.	Arrive Nashville 2 p.m.	
19 Tue.	Leave Nashville 2 a.m.	710
19 Tue.	Kitchener, Ontario, Canada	363
20 Wed.	Scranton, PA	356
21 Thu.	Toronto, Ontario, Canada	385
22 Fri.	Albany, NY	300
23 Sat.	York, PA	211
24 Sun.	Rochester, NY	935
25 Mon.	Arrive Nashville 3 p.m.	
26 Tue.	Practice with Sonny	
27 Wed.	10 a.m. Record with Sonny	
28 Thu.	Leave Nashville 10 p.m.	495
29 Fri.	New Philadelphia, OH	509
30 Sat.	Beloit, WI	277

Twenty dates, total miles driven, 12,218

May '66

01 Sun.	Indianapolis, IN (Butler Field House)	287
02 Mon.	Arrive Nashville 3 a.m.	
04 Wed.	Record with Milo at Monument	
05 Thu.	Leave Nashville 4 a.m.	443
05 Thu.	Pensacola, FL	359
06 Fri.	Jacksonville, FL	442
07 Sat.	Asheville, NC	659
08 Sun.	St Petersburg, FL	162
09 Mon.	Daytona Beach, FL Day off	
10 Tue.	Daytona Beach, FL Day off	379
11 Wed.	Columbia, SC	103
12 Thu.	Greenville, SC	168
13 Fri.	Knoxville, TN	113

14 Sat. Chattanooga, TN   134
14 Sat. Arrive Nashville 11 a.m.
16-19 Open   464
20 Fri. Greensboro, NC   77
21 Sat. Raleigh, NC   103
22 Sun. Winston-Salem, NC   436
23 Mon. Arrive Nashville 4 a.m.
23-26 Open   191
27 Fri. Birmingham, AL   101
28 Sat. Huntsville, AL   112
29 Sun. Arrive Nashville 11 a.m.
30 Mon. Open   475
31 Tue. Valdosta, GA   180

              Fifteen dates, total miles driven, 5,388

Jun '66

01 Wed. Panama City, FL   744
02 Thu. Travel day
03 Fri. Lynchburg, VA   218
04 Sat. Baltimore, MD   90
05 Sun. Hershey, PA   731
06 Mon. Arrived Nashville 6 p.m.
07 Tue. Practice with Sonny 2 p.m.
08 Wed. 10 AM Record with Sonny
09 Thu. Leave Nashville 7 p.m.   772
10 Fri. Rochester, NY   254
11 Sat . Youngstown, OH   247
12 Sun. Jackson, MI   512
13 Mon. Arrive Nashville noon
14 Tue. Leave Nashville 6 p.m.   769
15 Wed. Beaumont, TX Rodeo. HOT, 91
16 Thu. Beaumont, TX HOTTER
17 Fri. Beaumont, TX HOTTEST; Heat index 100+
18 Sat. Beaumont, TX Hot wave   769

19 Sun.	Arrive Nashville 6 p.m.	
23 Thu.	Leave Nashville	387
24 Fri.	Charleston, WVA	309
25 Sat.	Knoxville, TN	436
26 Sun.	Richmond, VA	614
27 Mon.	Arrive Nashville noon	

Fourteen dates, total miles driven, 6,852

VACATION (to Endicott, NY, and Canada), miles 2,800

Jul '66

14 Thu.	Leave Nashville	679
15 Fri.	Oklahoma City, OK	
16 Sat.	Oklahoma City, OK	
17 Sun.	Oklahoma City, OK	679
18 Mon.	Arrive Nashville 11 p.m.	
19 Tue.	Record sound track for film - *Nashville Rebel*	
20 Wed.	Filming at the Opry movie - *Nashville Rebel*	
22 Fri.	Leave Nashville 10 p.m.	558
23 Sat.	Shreveport, LA (Louisiana Hayride)	403
24 Sun.	Tupelo, MS	215
25 Mon.	Arrive Nashville 1 a.m.	336
28 Thu.	Urbana, IL	
29 Fri.	Day off - stayed in Urbana	277
30 Sat.	Belle, MO	444
31 Sun.	Carlisle, OH	310

Eight dates, total miles driven, 3,901

Aug '66

01 Mon.	Arrive Nashville 1 a.m.	
01 Mon.	10 a.m. Record with Sonny - Christmas Album	
02 Tue.	10 a.m. Christmas Album	
03 Wed.	10 a.m. Christmas Album	
04 Thu.	10 a.m. Christmas Album	
05 Fri.	Leave Nashville 6 a.m.	381

05 Fri. Gallipolis, OH	411
06 Sat. Altamont, IL	303
07 Sun. Hartford, MI	480
08 Mon. Arrived Nashville	
10 Wed. Leave Nashville 9 p.m.	941
11 Thu. Duluth, MN	414
12 Fri. Saint Ignace, MI	771
13 Sat. Arrived Nashville 1 p.m.	
18 Thu. Leave Nashville	836
19 Lindsay, Ontario Canada	211
20 Sat. Port Stanley, Ontario (The Stork Resort)	166
21 Sun. Oshawa, Ontario	
22 - 24 Open Days - stayed in Canada	525
25 Thu. Garden City, NY (Islip Speedway)	506
26 Fri. Lewisburg, WVA	352
27 Sat. Ashville, KY	236
28 Sun. Duquoin, IL - fair 40,000	220
29 Mon. Arrived Nashville 1 a.m.	
30, 31 - Sept 2 Off Days	

Twelve dates, total miles driven, 6,753

Sep '66

03 Sat. Left Nashville 7 a.m.	316
03 Sat. Pana, IL	351
04 Sun. Angola, IN (Buck Lake Ranch)	541
05 Sun. New Tripoli, PA	787
06 Mon. Arrived Nashville 2 p.m.	
07 Wed. Leave Nashville 10 p.m.	532
08 Thu. New Orleans, LA	512
09 Fri. Austin, TX	102
10 Sat. Waco, TX	180
11 San Antonio, TX	
12-13 Days off - Stay in San Antonio	210
14 Wed. San Angelo, TX	193

15 Thu.	Lubbock, TX	121
16 Fri.	Amarillo, TX	364
17 Sat.	Colorado Springs, CO (Sun 18th Open Day)	624
19 Mon.	Odessa, TX	1017
20 Tue.	Arrive Nashville 9 p.m.	357
23 Fri.	Anderson, SC	582
24 Sat.	Salisbury, MD	789
25 Sun.	Arrive Nashville	
29 Thu.	Leave Nashville 8 a.m.	1074
30 Fri.	Providence, RI	239

Fifteen dates, total miles driven, 8,911

Oct '66

01 Sat.	Trenton, NJ	198
02 Sun.	Dickerson, MD	655
03 Mon.	Arrive Nashville	
4-6	Days off	
07 Fri.	Nashville - *Ralph Emery* TV show WSM 4 p.m.	405
08 Sat.	Lima, OH	419
09 Sun.	Hammond, IN	23
10 Mon.	Chicago, IL TV show WBKB	469
11 Tue.	Arrive Nashville 7:30 a.m.	
13 Thu.	Leave Nashville 7 a.m.	798
14 Fri.	Allentown, PA	80
15 Sat.	Newark, NJ	92
16 Sun.	New Haven, CT	1272
17 Mon.	Travel day	
18-19 Tue. and Wed.	Mobile, AL	447
20 Thu.	Arrive Nashville 9 a.m.	
22 Sat.	Nashville -DJ Convention Nashville in Municipal Auditorium	
23-25	Days off	
26 Wed.	Leave Nashville 6:30 p.m.	834
27 Thu.	Mankato, MN	120
28 Fri.	Sauk Rapids, MN	865

29 Sat. Canton, OH		212
30 Sun. Detroit, MI		532
31 Mon. Arrive Nashville 2 p.m.		

Fourteen dates, total miles driven, 7,421

Nov '66

02 Wed. Nashville - *Bobby Lord* TV show WSM	
3-4 Days off	408
05 Sat. Charlotte, NC	244
06 Sun. Atlanta, GA	248
07 Mon. Arrive Nashville 2 p.m.	
07- 10 Days off	248
11 Fri. Atlanta, GA autography party	231
12 Sat. Winston Salem, NC	263
13 Sun. Norfolk, VA	705
14 Mon. Arrive Nashville 6 p.m.	
15-17 Days off	438
18 Fri. Roanoke, VA	289
19 Sat. York, PA	110
20 Sun. Cherry Hills, NJ	808
21 Mon. Arrive Nashville 5:30 p.m.	
22-23 Days off	333
24 Thu. Macon, GA	322
25 Fri. Greenville, TN	214
26 Sat. Paris, KY (I tape-recorded the show - only time ever)	373
27 Sun. Pittsburgh, PA	
28-30 Travel Days	2437

Twelve dates, total miles driven, 7,423

Dec '66

01 Thu. Los Angeles, CA

(Record Soundtrack for movie *Hillbillies in a Haunted House*)

02 Fri. a.m. Film movie *Hillbillies in a Haunted House*

p.m. show in LA - Shrine Auditorium

03	Sat. Film Pat Boone TV show	340
04	Sun. San Jose, CA	
05	Mon. Open day	330
06	Tue. Burbank, CA	64
	TV Show - *Swingin' Country* (Rusty Draper and Molly Bee)	
07	Wed. San Bernardino, CA	
08	Thu. Travel day	1076
09	Fri. Pueblo, CO	111
	(I drove over Wolf Creek Pass in blizzard - elev 11,000 ft)	
10	Sat. Denver, CO	
11-13	Days open	578
14	Wed. Carlsbad, NM	352
15	Thu. Grants, NM	141
16	Fri. Farmington, NM	403
17	Sat. Las Cruces, NM	45
18	Sun. El Paso, TX	1300
19	Mon. Arrive Nashville 11 p.m.	
21	Wed. 10 a.m. Record with Sonny	
22-31	Off until January 13	

Fourteen dates, total miles driven, 4,740

Just one day after I finished organizing our travel schedule for this book, I received a birthday card from Janice and Randy Sullivan, some fine folks we attend church with who were aware of our time with Sonny. They did not know I was writing this book. The card read: "I've been everywhere, man. Of travel I've had my share, man . . . I've been everywhere."

January 1967 turned out to be the most harrowing month of our entire seven years. We found ourselves smack-dab in the middle of what became known as The Great Chicago Blizzard of 1967. After performing in Lansing, Michigan, on the twenty-second, we had four restful days off. Bright and early on the morning of the twenty-seventh, we headed out for the short 118-mile trip to Port Huron, and got caught in the north side of the unexpected blast. When, after hours and hours and more hours we finally arrived in Port Huron, we discovered that the police had been on the lookout to tell us the show had been canceled. We were storm-stuck there for three days. Trying to get back on schedule, we left on Monday morning the thirtieth, driving southwest straight into blizzard-ravaged Chicago, which was about to be hit by a new four-inch snowfall. Our next show was on Wednesday February 1. We drove 1,203 freezing traveling-straight-into-the-wind miles away in Winnipeg, Manitoba, Canada, into the coldest, windiest weather, and no matter what we tried to do, we couldn't get the bus even close to warm. On the day of the show, historical records indicate it was 25 degrees below zero Fahrenheit with constant northwest winds (this was before the wind chill formula was developed in the late 1970s). Still driving west, our next show (on Feb. 2) was 359 miles away in Regina, and records for that day state we were driving into 25 mph northwest winds. Using the National Weather Service's wind-chill calculator, 25 degrees below zero with a 25 mph headwind calculates out to a wind chill of 57.5°F below zero. We were lucky if we got up to 40 mph all that day, which meant the cold factor was even worse. Even though all of us found everything in sight to wrap up with because the bus wasn't putting out any heat, we really felt the Arctic cold inside the metal monster. I was never so cold for so long in my entire life.

But we didn't stay cold for long—1967 saw three singles reach #1 on the Billboard country charts, and by year's end, the singles had held down the #1 slot for eleven weeks—more than any other country artist in that year. It was the beginning of the sixteen consecutive #1 singles.

SALLY MOHLER SNIPPET

The first time I saw Sonny James and the Southern Gentlemen was exactly fifty-one years ago today. It was at Ponderosa Park in Salem, Ohio. Until two weeks before, my mom and I knew nothing about Ponderosa Park or much about country music. Over the Fourth of July, actor Michael Landon of Bonanza fame was going to be there, and our neighbors asked us to go, and seeing it was only ten miles away from where we lived in Sebring, Ohio, we thought why not? At the time I was our neighbor's babysitter—and an "awkward" thirteen years old.

We really had a good time that day and started listening to country music a little bit more. My mom asked if I'd like to go back and who I'd like to see. At that time Sonny James' "I'll Keep Holding On" was popular. I told Mom I thought Sonny was pretty good, so on Sunday July 8 we went back to Ponderosa Park. We couldn't stay for the second show because we were going on vacation the next day, but our friends stayed and said that second show was something else. We knew we had to see them again. The next time was on February 5, 1966, in Akron, Ohio. So my mom and I, along with my best friend, headed out for the forty-mile trip to Akron.

I got to meet Sonny that time. I had an album for him to sign, and he asked my name and asked me to tear the cellophane wrap off the album for him. While I was standing there, he asked me to tear the wrap off a few more albums after that, and he talked to me the whole time. From that moment on he had me—we were hooked.

As luck would have it, Sonny and the Southern Gentlemen were appearing in Youngstown, Ohio, about five weeks later on March 12, so the three of us, Mom and my best friend and I, were off on another adventure only thirty-four miles away.

That time, my mom wanted to get an album to send to her cousin who lived in Czechoslovakia. At the end of their shows, the Southern Gentlemen sold their latest album, so my mom purchased it from one of them, Duane West, and my mom told him what she was going to do with it. Duane told her that she should find one of the other Southern Gentlemen, Gary Robble, and tell him because he was the same nationality. Now how strange was that?

That was the beginning of a life-long friendship with Sonny and Gary. We went to see Sonny whenever he was close enough until he retired in 1984. We were lucky enough to have a lot of good visits over the years and still kept in touch with both of them on holidays and birthdays.

It's good to know that Sonny James truly was a "Southern Gentleman."

SALLY MOHLER - *Sebring, Ohio (Written on July 18, 2016)*

CHAPTER 17

SEPTEMBER 1968 - DORIS' DIARY

1968 was a long blurry way from a whole lot of things. In the music business when you are on a roll and things are going "up and to the right," yesterday should quickly be left behind, because yesterday in the music business has very little to do with tomorrow. All that seems to matter in this business is next; next show, next week, next month, next release, next year—all that really seems to matter is that the arms of the future are always reaching out trying to pull you toward them.

By 1968 we had been traveling in the bus for two-and-one-half years; now we could carry an extra person, so we did every once in a while. My oldest son Greg, who was born in 1964, traveled with us on three different occasions when were out for one of those long week-ends (leaving Thursday and arriving back in Nashville on a Monday). On this extended trip in 1968 Sonny brought along somebody very special—Doris traveled with us for the first time. This would be her opportunity to reap the benefits of touring as it really was and not like what it was imagined to be. She would get to enjoy first-hand some of the non-amenities of home. It was to be a month-long trip that years later I would learn had more depth to it than I could have imagined. Along with my keeping an abbreviated journal, a journal that unbelievably no one was aware that I kept, Doris, some forty years later, informed me that she had written down her daily thoughts on that trip, then had typed them out when she got back to Nashville. Fortunately she came across it in some of their papers years later and presented me with a copy.

I invite you to accompany us on this special trip from September 9, 1968 through October 10, as I combine the information from Doris' diary along with a sentence or two from my journal preceding hers. It's a fun read, especially from a lady's perspective. These written comments will carry us just over 12,000 miles in a month's time, miles that will include twenty-one road shows, a network TV show, along with a bus breakdown somewhere in the middle of it all. Try to sit back and enjoy the ride.

Monday September 9, 1968 Left Nashville at 7 a.m. heading for Miles City, Montana — just as a stop-over, not a show date — drove literally 1,507 non-stop miles.

Doris wrote: *"As most trips start, this one is also early…and especially so because we didn't get to bed until midnight last night. It was 5:30 a.m. when we loaded the 'ton of luggage' it looked like we had, on the bus. Milo's turn to drive. (Later)…somewhere down the road. This first day is uneventful other than just riding and putting mileage behind us. We stopped in Chicago for dinner tonight [at Joes' truck stop], then back on the bus. By now all the boys had had their turn driving, and when I woke in the morning, they told me, I would be somewhere in Montana!"*

Tuesday September 10, 1968 Stayed overnight in Miles City, Montana

Doris wrote: *"I'm not used to a 'moving bed' and I was glad when daylight came so that I could see outside and get up. You haven't lived until you try to put on your 'face' while traveling on a bus. I think I'm healthier on one side than the other…they were right…we had a delicious breakfast in Fargo, North Dakota! I can't believe that this time yesterday I was in Nashville. I'm in the lobby of the Holiday Inn waiting for Sonny to finish 'phone calls and the boys have gone to town to do something or other. If my friend, Jo Walker, were with me, she would have just jumped out of her chair...a Dachshund like her 'Gretel' just pranced by following its owner. In the afternoon, after the stop for lunch, we are rolling along the flatlands of Dakota, with Glenn, Duane, Gary asleep, Sonny and me nodding riding along on the front seat...all of a sudden Milo and Sonny spot Antelope...you'd thought they had seen a man giving away thousand dollar bills the way they were hollering 'Get up guys', and all the fellas tumbling out of their bunks yelling 'What is it!!"...Milo stopped the bus, all get out and walked up a small hill for a better view and hoping Glenn can get a good picture...no picture, the antelope are too far away by now. Well, that's one way of waking up a dozing bunch of travelers! Today was another day to just ride and enjoy the wide open spaces. We checked into the motel about 9 o'clock tonight and was I ready for that bed that didn't move!"*

Wednesday September 11, 1968 Drove 286 miles. Stayed overnight in Bozeman, Montana

Doris wrote: *"Up at 7:30 to eat breakfast and be on the road ...we still have a long, long way to go, before we arrive in Cashmere, Washington, our first date. Passed through Billings, Montana, had a letter to mail that Sonny needed to get to New York...while he was doing that, the fellas looked at western wear and I stretched my legs walking around a few minutes.....Later.....at lunch time we stopped in a very, very small town to have a hamburger [Reed Point, Montana]. It was the only town for miles ahead and was the only place to eat in town...Big choice!...but that hamburger was good 'cause we were HUNGRY. There were two dogs there that were so pretty and the waitress said only the day before they had cornered a bob cat while hunting with their owners. The boys wanted their pictures made with them so Glenn did the honors. Today is still another day to ride and look at the beautiful flatlands and rolling plains and changing colors of autumn and put miles behind us on our way to Cashmere. Hurray, we sleep in a motel again tonight. This trav-*

eling 9 hours a day is not my cup of tea I don't think."

Thursday September 12, 1968 Drove 566 miles. Heading for Cashmere, Washington — first show date

Doris wrote: *"The alarm clock sounded like a fire bell this morning going off at 5:00! No one told me I was getting up at that hour!!!... whew and now I am told to be ready by 5:30...I barely made it. We have traveled all day and seen some beautiful country side...up into the mountains, down in the valleys and across the plains. As we drew close to Cashmere, the orchards started showing up...one town of Wenatchee, Washington, claims to be the Apple Capitol [sic] of the World, It is now much later in the day, we are at the motel, and the fellas are getting ready to go to the show. Sonny and the boys, Grandpa Jones and Hank Snow...And another long day has come and gone."*

Friday September 13, 1968 Drove 137 miles. Heading for Seattle, Washington

Doris wrote: *"We had a chance to sleep late this morning as we don't have many miles to make today. Sonny had met 'Tiny' last year on a show there. He lives in Cashmere and this morning we stopped by his place of business...a very, very large extraordinary fruit market... featuring, what else??...apples! But he has a little of everything...straw baskets, honey, candies, all fruits, things for children and grandma... and in between! Tiny is a remarkable man. He employs high school boys who are planning on attending college and pays them extra well in order to help with their tuition. They are real workers...so nice and clean cut. We really enjoyed our visit with all of them. When we boarded the bus to leave, there were apples, pears, candies, plums on it...Compliments of Tiny!! We made several pictures while here and hope they turn out good. Well, today wasn't just a day for beautiful scenery...it was Gorgeous! ... and sometimes breath taking...going over the Blewett Pass [elevation 4,124 ft] and Snoqualmie Pass [elevation 3,015 ft]. It has drizzled rain all day but it didn't mar the beauty of this unspoiled countryside...part of it goes through a national forest. Got to Seattle about 4:30, checked into the motel and Sonny changed clothes, got his uniforms, etc. together and met the boys at 5:30. They have to get to the auditorium, set up their P.A. system and get ready for two shows tonight. I ordered room service, ate a quick dinner, shampooed my hair, rolled it and went to sleep sitting under my dryer...! Our room overlooks the famous 'Space Needle' of the World's Fair. It is beautiful all lighted up tall in the sky with the lights of the city twinkling off and on below. At last the rain stopped."*

Saturday September 14, 1968 Drove 173 miles. Heading for Portland, Oregon

Doris wrote: *"After a HOT night's sleep, (the temp. was 80 degrees in the room and the hotel couldn't get it down because they were converting air conditioning to heat for the winter!)...we had breakfast in the room so that we could see the baseball game between Detroit and Oakland and see if Denny McLain can get his 30th win of the season. Didn't get to see it all as we had to drive on (in the rain again)...Duane drove into Portland, Oregon and found the auditorium. It is now 5:30 and all the instruments have been unloaded and everyone is getting ready to set up for the show...Hank Snow and his boys have just arrived. I will go inside tonight for the 7:00 show as we are parked right in the rear entrance of the building...it is really pouring now!*

Mr. Jack Roberts, the promoter of the show, gave me a center row seat. Grandpa Jones is on first, then Hank Snow and his band...Intermission... and then Sonny. It is certainly some kind of feeling to watch them work and hear the people applauding so much and having such a good time. After the first show Sonny told me to come back stage before I went back to the bus. Mr. Dave Pearl and David Miller of Capitol Records were with Sonny. They came to say hello and catch the show. I didn't get back to that bus until almost 11:00 p.m. because of all the 'howdying' back-stage. But the second show finally got under way and I tried to get some of my things a little more organized and not all over the bus. I read my book for a little while and must have fallen asleep because now the boys are loading up the instruments and there are people outside the bus and Sonny is signing autographs!...it is after 1:30 [in the morning]...we are now leaving for Vancouver, B.C....and people think entertainers lead such an easy going life...I'll travel all night on the 'moving bed' again. It is STILL raining...We have to leave to get there.

Sunday September 15, 1968 Drove 314 miles overnight. Heading for Vancouver, B.C. Canada

Doris wrote: *"I woke up this morning (for about the 10th time) and looked out of the bus window and all I saw are orange roofs (like mini Howard Johnson motels!)...It is actually a very pretty park and Gary said he got so sleepy he pulled into the park to wait until we could all get up and go through Canadian customs...We all made use of the park facilities and took in some of that nice fresh air even though it looked like it was going to pour again any minute. There were several other people parked in the park...house trailers, campers, station wagons, somebody else got sleepy too! After thirty or forty minutes of filling out forms and answering questions about the bus, at last we're on the way. We are in a hurry...again. It is always rush, rush, it seems on tour...we drove and drove and grabbed a fast breakfast (at noon!) and the group is on the way to the auditorium for the afternoon show to set up. At six o'clock this afternoon, Sonny called and we were going to evening services, but he was still at the show and the church building was clear across town and the services started at 6:00! He hurried back to the motel as soon as he could, we ordered a fast meal, swallowed his in two bites, and left in a puff of smoke for the second show at 7:30! There is no room on a tour for anyone who must eat at the same time every day or go to bed and get up at the same time...everything is all opposite from what I do at home! We are all 'travel weary' so plan to stay over in Vancouver tomorrow and break the trip up a little and get laundry, etc. done. Sonny and the fellas don't get back to the motel until 12:30 tonight...These are such long days and they work so hard on stage and by the time they all get to bed each night they are absolutely exhausted.*

Monday September 16, 1968 Open day for travel. Driving 705 miles. Heading for Red Deer, Alberta

Doris wrote: *"Well, another surprise. Sonny told me this morning we wouldn't have a day off! We have a seventeen hour drive over the mountains. It is five hundred miles as it is, but with the mountains it will take us all that time with the bus...and the rain! Mr. Wally Kiss of Capitol Records came to the room to say goodbye to Sonny and show him the wonderful review Billboard gave his new record BORN TO BE WITH YOU [newest release after Heaven Says Hello]. This was the first time they only reviewed one country record by itself, so it excited us a-plenty! Mr. Kiss is going to lead us out of town to Hwy. 1 and we are all on the way to Red Deer."*

Tuesday September 17, 1968 Arriving in Red Deer, Alberta

Doris wrote: *"Last night was the longest night in history for me on that bus. Everyone this morning has aches and pains...all night we couldn't drive over 45 miles per hour because of the narrow, winding, curving roads and all the boys have to look out for elk, bear, moose or whatever else is up in this wild and wooly country wandering across roads. Sonny had asked them before we went to bed to wake us up if they saw any unusually big elk or moose. He was determined I was going to see one of them up close. Sonny went back to bed but I couldn't get sleepy enough, so I sat up on the seats in front and wrapped a quilt around me and took me 'cat naps' while Glenn was doing his shift... well after flipping and flopping on the seat for what seemed an eternity, I went to the room in the back of the bus [located right above the diesel engine]. I think I must have just gotten stretched out when the bus came to a HALT and Gary and Glenn were hollering 'Get Up, Get Up', 'look on the side of the road' ...All of us who were asleep knocked into each other getting to the front of the bus and right on the side of the road is standing an ELK that looked as big as a moving van...with antlers you wouldn't believe...and not fifty feet from him was a cow and calf. She was almost as large as he, but without the antlers. From then on it was slow motion driving over those mountains by stopping every few miles to look at elk or moose, so we didn't get to Red Deer until around noon and checked into the motel. We all fell into those nice steady beds in our rooms, grabbed two hours sleep, showered, dressed and ate a quick bite and they left for the show…two again tonight. It is the same package of Sonny and The Southern Gentlemen, Dottie West, Grandpa Jones and Hank Snow and they will make the entire Canada tour. We saw the sun for a few hours today…but the clouds came back before too long."*

Wednesday September 18, 1968 Drive 106 miles to Edmonton, Alberta

Doris wrote: *"Well, last night coupled with the night's ride over the mountains just about ruined me. The night couldn't end soon enough for us even though Sonny is almost sick from exhaustion. He said his legs gave out on him on stage last night but he did something silly so people would think he was about to fall and went on with the show…even the boys didn't catch it. He didn't get back to the motel until 1:45 in the morning after those two shows and then everything bad about a night's sleep happened…the noise in the motel, no air conditioning, the bed was awful. Even though it is STILL raining and cloudy I was glad when we were up and dressed to eat. Sonny had several calls to make and then we checked out for Edmonton. The sun came up about an hour later!…We arrived in Edmonton around 3:00 p.m., were met in the lobby by two disc jockeys from the radio station who wanted Sonny for an interview… Sonny said fine, just give me about twenty minutes to get upstairs to the room, show the bellboy where to put the luggage, etc.…we did and just as the bellboy left, a boy was standing in the doorway wanting to know about Roy Orbison's boys dying in the fire at their home and asking us all about Roy. He said he was his Canada Representative for his fan club. Of course we didn't know any of the details so we weren't much help to him. Then the disc jockeys came up and the boy left, reluctantly, and Sonny made the interview and as they were winding up that one, another gentleman from another station appeared in the doorway and HE wanted an interview also…the Capitol man arrived in the middle of all this and after the interview, Sonny and I freshened up and went down to the dining room with Mr. Bill Maxim, the Capitol Records representative and had dinner. It is now 5:30 and the fellas have already gone to the audi-*

torium to set up the PA system. Sonny will ride over with Mr. Maxim. I told them goodbye as I was too pooped to go to two more shows. Sonny is really fighting a sore throat. Two shows a night, not getting to bed before 1:30 or 2:00 is really having its effect on his voice."

Thursday September 19, 1968 Drive 185 miles to Calgary, Alberta

Doris wrote: *"This motor hotel made up for the last two bad nights. The room was lovely, the temp inside was perfect, we had hot water (Sonny's complaint…not hot enough in some places [motels and auditorium dressing rooms] to shave!)…and the food was excellent and we enjoyed it in our room. But we woke up to the same weather forecast… rain. And it is 35 degrees…Brrr and the wind is blowing like crazy. On the way to Calgary we saw patches of snow. Speaking of patches, wonder how little 'Patches', our dog, is doing with Mom and Pop [Sonny's folks]. We are going to call them tonight. Arrived late in the afternoon, got some quick sandwiches while Sonny was getting ready to leave for the show, and the man from Capitol came by for him about 6:00 p.m.…Before he arrived, though, we got that call through from Alberta to Alabama… that's some long distance phone call. They were fine and Patches was too. Dottie's boys and Sonny's boys have been pulling little silly things on each other during this tour. Dottie's boys have played their joke on The Southern Gentlemen so tonight is the night Dottie's boys will get it! No, they are going to wait until the last show in Winnipeg in order to make them think they have forgotten all about the joking. While Sonny is gone I have rearranged suitcases and hangup bags…boy do they get in a mess. Wrote letters and cards but don't know when they will get mailed…also tried to bring this diary up to date. Two more shows tonight so Sonny will not get in until 1:00 again. Hope the rain stops tomorrow. I have yet had a chance to go 'window shopping' and look any of these towns over. We get to each place just in time seems like to grab a fast bite, go do a show and come back and gladly fall asleep. Sonny came in from the show tonight (I didn't go again…) and told me that between shows he was told Mr. Red Foley had died in Fort Wayne, Indiana from a heart attack. Sonny called the Associated Press in Nashville to verify it. 'Mr.*

Red' had been a great help to Sonny and so many others, for at one time Sonny appeared with him on the ABC-TV Ozark Jubilee and helped m.c. the shows once a month from Springfield, Missouri. Shirley Boone [Pat Boone's wife] is a personal friend of ours and we are sad for her tonight. She is Mr. Red's daughter."

Friday September 20, 1968 Drive 385 miles to Saskatoon, Saskatchewan

Doris wrote: *"From 10:30 this morning until 7:00 tonight we rode without stopping in order to arrive in Saskatoon for the show...to make it worse we couldn't drive over fifty miles an hour because we were in a driving rain, which later turned into snow and back to rain. Usually the group is at the auditorium and has the PA system set up and the other people on the show receive the benefit of it, but Grandpa and Hank will miss it tonight because it can't get set up until intermission as the show was about to start when we arrived...Dottie and Sonny are on the last half, I had to go to the dining room here in the motel as they don't have room service. Ate and ordered some sandwiches and pie to take back with me to the room so that Sonny would have something to eat when he comes in. It is cold in Canada day and night...am so glad that snow melted though. Today was just filled with riding. We wouldn't have had ANYTHING to eat the entire day except for Tiny...yep, we ate apples, candy and that was our 'big lunch'...thanks to Tiny! Sonny got back about 1:15 in the morning and he was more than ready to eat. Fell into bed about 2:00."*

Intermission

Saskatoon — you've just got to hear an unbelievable story and this is the place to tell it. My wife Thelma and I live in our second house a dozen miles or so west of Nashville just off an I-40 interstate exit. We had purchased a piece of land and built our first home just a couple of miles east of there in 1967. As is the case when things are really rolling along in the music business, you might have some other projects, but you hardly have time to really dedicate yourself to them. We had picked out a plan and the house was going up, suffering from only a few hitches here and there. Before I knew it our very first home was completed and ready for occupancy. My wife, now very pregnant with our second child, had moved us in. When the blue bus pulled up in front of our new home after an abbreviated tour, "Uncle Daddy" arrived and stepped up to the front door of the new place. I didn't even have to ring the doorbell to get in — Thelma was welcoming me with an "open-door policy," she proudly opened the door to invite me into our beautifully arranged new home — a place we really loved — and we loved it for nearly twenty-two years.

But as so often happens, time and space and "people-lution" (that's a song title from the album *A World of Our Own* that we recorded in 1968) sometimes interrupts long-range plans. Over time the traffic out here on that side of the interstate started to increase to the point where we decided to start looking for a new location, but still not far removed from the area — the region reminded me of where I grew up in upper New York State.

A few years later we found what we were looking for, and after twenty-seven years in the home where our three boys grew up — we made the move — a location just on the other side of the interstate — a development with just one entrance and a little over three dozen homes in it.

It's a Saturday morning about 10 o'clock and I am at the stop sign leading out of our area ready to make a left turn and head toward the interstate. An SUV-type vehicle is coming from the left, the interstate side, with his right blinker on and he turns into our street and starts motioning to me. I caught his drift; this happens every now and then on our street, so I backed up from the stop sign as he made his way out of his vehicle over to me, asking as he walked if I could give him some help on directions.

It really went like this — "Yes Sir, could you help me. Are we on the right road to Dyersburg?" "Yes you are — I have a truckers Rand McNally map right here (a carryover from the road days). Let me show you where you are right now." I got over to the Tennessee page, found Dyersburg (which is about 170 miles west of Nashville) and started to run my finger along the map page to show him with more than simply words.

"Relatives or friends over there?" "Just friends in Dyersburg. We are on a horseshoe kind of vacation visiting a number of old acquaintances, and this is just one of them on the way." "Nothing like old friends. Where's home base to you?" "Oh, we're from Canada, a place way out in western Canada." "That's really beautiful country out there." "Oh — you've been out there?" "Yes I have — where out there are you from?" "From a place you've probably never heard of." "Try me" I responded. "Saskatoon. Saskatoon, Saskatchewan." "Beautiful place." "You've been there?" "A couple of times." "Really — what kind of work are you in?" "Well, it was probably over 30 years ago, but we did some shows out there." "Trade shows?" "No — I was in the music business at the time, and we were there a couple of times." "Who were you with?" "Well, our vocal group The Southern Gentlemen was with Sonny James and…" "Sonny James?" "Yes." He turned to his wife sitting in their vehicle across the road and hollered, "Margaret — this is one of Sonny James' Southern Gentlemen!" Wide-eyed he then turned back to me and said, "I don't believe this — we saw you in the late 60's when you were there. I don't believe this."

I wish I had taken down his name. We shook hands, he turned his vehicle around as they both waved — turned left toward the interstate, and were gone. But I am sure of this — for the rest of his life he will tell that story a thousand times or more. It's been one of my favorites to tell. You've noticed — I just told it here again for my umpteenth time.

Intermission Ends

Saturday September 21, 1968 Drive 167 miles from Saskatoon to Regina.

Doris wrote: *"We got up this morning and actually took our time dressing and eating breakfast as we only have 167 miles to go today...I love these little surprises like this! I thought we were in for another 'long chase across the plains'...that comes later I'm told. Since we have had rain for the last eight days, you can bet I say 'hurrah' for the manufacturers of Hair Spray. We arrived in Regina tonight about 5:00 and checked into the motel. The boys went ahead and ate and took off in the blue [bus] toward the auditorium. Sonny went later with Mr. Ron Andrews, a disc jockey from the radio station here, who met Sonny at the motel to do an interview. While the two men were cutting their interview, I went across the street to a big store that sold about everything and got some little articles...(like a scarf for my head...oh, this wind and rain!). Came back and got Sonny a quick bite at the motel and took it back to the room so he wouldn't be absolutely empty during both shows. After they left, I ate and then shampooed my hair to get that ton of hair spray out of it, dried it and got the clothes laid out for tomorrow. Sonny came in again about his usual 1:00 time. Only two more show dates in Canada and then we will cross back into the States. Good night all!"*

Sunday September 22, 1968 Drive 380 miles to Winnipeg, Manitoba

Doris wrote: *"Happy birthday to Sonny's 'Mom' in Alabama. We had a tree planted in the yard of the office at Nashville to celebrate the occasion. Helen and Bob Neal supervised it for us since we are rather far away. We drove all day without stopping again in order to get to Winnipeg for the show. If touring was like this all the time, Sonny would not tour, because the time of the shows and length of driving in the States allows he and Milo to attend services either on Sunday morning or night, but it hasn't happened up here. Tonight the boys played their joke on Dottie West's band...they put sneezing powder on the moustaches her boys wear in a comedy number and also put some 'alum' on the cigar her husband, Bill uses on the same number. The sneezing powder wasn't too successful, but the alum was!...Glenn got a picture of Bill just as he put that bitter cigar in his mouth and what a face!!...they had to keep on playing. Everyone got a big laugh out of it and then Dottie and her boys got back at The Southern Gentlemen by having one of her boys dress up as a girl and run across the stage at the end of Sonny's show. This is as far as the fun goes, because no one bothers any of the instruments or would hurt the show in that way ever. Since this is the last show in Canada, both groups of us ate Chinese food together and finally about 2:00 a.m. we are headed for Great Falls, Montana and Dottie is headed back to Nashville."*

(And so began one of the most extreme stretches of traveling that any of us ever did — the main recipients of the miles that lay ahead were Huggins [Glenn] and myself.)

Monday September 23, 1968 Travel day 838 miles to Great Falls, Montana

Doris wrote: *"Would you believe I have a 'code in muh node'?? ever since yesterday...yes, it was still raining and got my head a little wet I guess. We all stayed awake last night until we arrived at the border and went through customs so we didn't get to sleep until 3:30 this morning. Feeling stuffed up and hot and cold and waking up every little while hasn't given me the best rest in the world. We stopped for diesel sometime this morning and had to check some wiring on the bus...we got us some breakfast and ate it on the bus and the sun was out for a little while and then...it turned cloudy. We stopped in Watford City, North Dakota to get some cough medicine and aspirin for my cold, for Sonny to make his call to Bob [Neal] and for Milo to check the bus. We made this little town a busy place! We have a seal leaking on the bus and this town has no facilities...so we have to make it to Great Falls [454 miles] by driving very slow and every time we saw a truck stop or station that sold this 'grease' we put some in, because we didn't know how much the bus had leaked, etc....and we weren't taking a chance on it going 'dry' on us and burning something out. We should have known...this is 'Blue Monday'...This is why there has to be a day off now and then in order for things like this to happen! And give time to get it fixed...just glad they didn't have a show tonight because Sonny would be ready to collapse for sure. As it is, we are all about ready for the 'Funny Farm'. "*

Tuesday September 24, 1968 Great Falls, Montana [we drove through

Great Falls just 13 days ago]

Doris wrote: "*Milo and Sonny have located a place to have the bus repaired...only it is not a leaking seal...it is a major repair job, only because of a little cog with a broken part. Sonny called the Flxible Bus Company in Ohio to have the parts flown in. The show tonight was a birthday celebration for Radio Station KMON in Great Falls, Montana, with Sonny, Connie Smith and Charlie Pride. Our bad luck even rubbed off on Connie...she and her husband flew in for the show, but her guitar and stage clothes didn't arrive! She and Jack had to perform in their street clothes. These last two days of the tour we want to just forget!...*"

Wednesday September 25, 1968 238 miles to Billings, Montana [Doris & bus in Great Falls]

Doris wrote: "*After phoning for the parts they did not arrive...We will be without the bus for two days as it is jacked up at the International Harvester Company with men waiting to work on the bus just as soon as the plane arrives today from Ohio. Sonny had to rent two station wagons to make the next two days of show dates...Oh, is it ever a job trying to think of everything to get off the bus to take with them for the next two days. After loading equipment, uniforms, suitcases, etc. etc. there is room for two boys in one front seat of [one of]]the station wagons and three boys riding in the front seat of the other station wagon...they are filled to the brim! I'll be staying in Great Falls while they go to Billings for the show. The parts will be here this afternoon and the men will get the bus back together. After the group left about 1:00, I went to down town Great Falls to finally look around one of these places...after about two hours I had looked at all there was to look at, so came back to the motel. Wrote Cards and letters and hope against hope that the men are working hard on the bus so we can leave early in the morning.*"

Thursday September 26, 1968 317 miles to Rapid City, South Dakota [Doris & bus in Great Falls]

Doris wrote: "*Would you believe that those parts have not arrived yet!!! I had called earlier to the airport and was told a flight from*

Cleveland at noon would have the parts on it and would arrive in Great Falls at 4:30. I made a special trip out to the airport to pick it up and take it personally to Mr. Imker, who is waiting (has been for two days!) to repair the bus. Got to the airport and was told there wouldn't be a flight until 6:30 that night!...and then it might be late...! The next flight wouldn't be until midnight tonight...You know which one it arrived on of course. Sonny had Milo call me at 10:30 tonight. Milo said Sonny was trapped back stage and couldn't get out to the phone and he called to tell me to go on to bed as no one was standing by at midnight to work on the Bus, but would get on it first thing in the morning. So that saved me a trip to the airport at midnight. This afternoon after returning from the airport I stopped at a new shopping center about two blocks from the motel and looked around it and ate lunch and wandered in and out of the stores. Came back to the motel, ate, and read, watched television, and then off to bed, hoping to get up early in the morning and go get those bus parts...!

Friday September 27, 1968 281 miles to Casper, Wyoming [Doris & bus still in Great Falls]

Doris wrote: *"I was thrilled this morning when I called Mr. Imker to see if he had called the airport regarding the parts...He said, 'We have it and the bus will be ready by noon'...Hallelujah!...I won't soon forget my stay in the 'Electric City' and especially all the nice people at International Harvester who have helped us. The weather sorta flopped back to bad again, after two days of sun, and it is cloudy, damp and windy. Glad I did all my wanderings yesterday as today is no day to be out. Glenn and Gary are driving one of the station wagons back here after the show in Casper, Wyoming to get the bus and ME, and we will make a long drive to Salt Lake City, Utah in time for the show tomorrow night. Mr. Imker brought the bus to the motel and I put everything on it I knew I wouldn't need, plus some packages of Gary and Glenn's and Duane's where they had shopped. Off to bed."*

This is my (Gary's) recollection of that evening show. It was the "best of luck" and it was the "worst of luck." In the three days before we arrived in Casper we had already burned up the roads for 1,398 miles. On September 27 we woke up and drove 281 miles to Casper knowing two of us were going to have to take one of the station wagons and roar on back to Great Falls right after the show to pick up Doris and the bus. Huggins and I volunteered.

It's one of those moments you can't really explain but it actually happened just like this. One of the restrictions Sonny had in his contract was that we would not be booked by promoters in facilities where alcohol was consumed, or where there was dancing. We arrived at the auditorium, set up our sound system, set up Sonny and Milo's amp on stage, and then as always, while still in our street clothes, we sold our souvenir books. When we had finished that routine we went to our dressing rooms and changed into our stage outfits. Little did any of us know that they didn't sell alcohol in the place, but they did allow folks to bring their "brown paper bags" with their favorite nourishments in them.

It was obvious what favorites they brought - because by the time we were introduced as the closing act the front row for sure had downed too much of whatever, and they were somewhere out there in distillery heaven, making us and the entire crowd aware of just how rowdy someone in that condition could be. We stepped on stage and did our opening number amidst all the frivolity. Sonny, aware by that time of what was coming down, made the most gentlemanly statement he could about what was written in his contract, and we respectfully ended our show after just one number. Now I don't know if Sonny got paid or not for that show — he never discussed anything about it with us. To this day I wish I had paid more attention to what he said to the crowd, but my attention was fixed on the wild and crazy guys on the front row. Without question it was the "best of luck moment" as it gave Huggins and me about a forty-minute start on our trip back to Great Falls — which for harrowing was the "worst of luck."

Huggins and I took one of the station wagons and following a day in which we had already logged 281 miles, we took off full-tilt around 9:30pm on a 555 mile trek with a half-moon in the night sky above us, driving like determined maniacs, on those two-lane roads (this was well before the interstate system had been completed). Off to the left and right all night long there were eyes, eyes and more eyes, mostly, it seemed, off to our right. When you took the number of eyes we saw and divided by two Huggins and I estimated we saw at least 250 antelope as we literally hotfooted our way back to Great Falls. Thankfully, never one time did one of those two-eyed dangers jump out in front of the vehicle.

Saturday September 28, 1968 6:30am

Doris wrote: "*The phone rang about 6:30 and it was Glenn and Gary. They had arrived and were ordering breakfast. I was already up and dressed because I was anxious to get gone! We left Great Falls at 7:30. . .*

Back to my story. When we arrived we had to unload all the stuff we had in the station wagon and load it into the bus, load all that Doris had with her, jump into the bus around 7:30am, and head out.

Saturday September 28, 1968 7:30am 660 miles to Salt Lake City, Utah

By this time Huggins and I hadn't had any bed rest for twenty-four hours, and had already logged 2,234 miles in four days, with 660 miles to go to get to the show in Salt Lake City.

Saturday September 28, 1968 406 miles to Salt Lake City, Utah

While Huggins and I were on our way, Sonny, Duane and Milo were heading out to drive their measly 406 miles to Salt Lake.

For the three of them in the station wagon, it was just another ho-hum day on the road. For Huggins and me, it was a day where fatigue was beginning to take its toll, and neither one of us took to one of the bunks for rest — while one of us drove the other sat up in the front seat, and in between nods kept asking one another "are you doing OK?" To save time we didn't stop to change drivers — we knew our ETA would be pushing the envelope, so to save time we switched off as the bus was rolling down the road.

Back to Doris ". . .*and arrived in Salt Lake at the Valley Music Hall auditorium at 7:10 and people were already arriving for the show. It had been sold out for almost two weeks. I stayed on the bus because I was not dressed to go inside and didn't feel like it anyway...still have this cold. Sonny brought the Capitol representative and his wife out to the bus to say hello and later, Al Edwards and his wife Shirley. He is a disc jockey we have known for some time. Also Bob Neal was at the show tonight. He had flown in and had been with Sonny on the two previous nights (but I didn't know it). Did Sonny and the boys ever enjoy working the show tonight! The acoustics were perfect and everyone could see without a pole blocking their view. It is a theatre in the round type auditorium. It was just great. We left immediately after the show, ate a sandwich while the bus was being filled with diesel. It is a long, long trip to Pueblo, Colorado, over mountains and have two shows, one a matinee, which makes it really rough...*"

Back to me . . . Doris didn't allude to it but we arrived just twenty minutes before show time and thankfully we didn't need to set up our sound system. Huggins and I didn't have time to clean up — the bus didn't have a shower or drinking water — so we did a spit wash, as folks in Milo's hometown would call it (it's not what it sounds like), and put some Noxzema on our faces in order to make shaving tolerable, did the masculine facial thing, swished some mouthwash around (we did all this as the bus was rolling down the road), ran into the dressing room as soon as we got there, jumped into our stage clothes, and headed off to headline the show (a picture of us actually on stage that night is in the second picture section).

Incidentally, even though Doris indicated it was a "theatre in the round," that doesn't nearly describe the actual sensation when you were on stage. It was a circular auditorium where the stage spun slowly around (the only other stage like that where we performed was in Owings Mills, Maryland, where we were contracted for five consecutive days in September 1967). For Huggins and me, our heads were still going around and around. All my life I have had to deal with a touch of vertigo, so after that thirty-six hour wild and wooly stretch

without bed rest, and now with the stage going round and round —
well, that was anything but fun for me, no matter how great Doris
thought "the boys enjoyed it."

Sunday September 29, 1968 644 miles to Pueblo, Colorado

We left immediately after the show in Salt Lake City and drove 644
miles to do a matinee and evening show in Pueblo, Colorado.

Doris wrote: *"We arrived and checked in, in time for the group to
clean up and rush to the auditorium. I got a pleasant surprise because
Larry Rushing and his wife, Nancy, live in Pueblo and he is the Minister
for one of the congregations here. Was a little late for the night service
but nevertheless enjoyed hearing him. Afterward, Larry, Nancy and
another couple wanted to go to the show, so I asked to be dropped off
at the motel and enjoyed a visit with Trina, of K-Bar-T Roundup and
Linda Osteen, who does the art work for Sonny's [fan] club. They had
been to the Matinee that day and Sonny had made arrangements to
meet them at the motel so I could say hello. Linda's Mom and sister were
also along. We visited about forty minutes and they had to start back
home as it was getting pretty late and they had to drive to Lamar [120
miles]. I ordered a quick sandwich and went to the room and went to
sleep!! It was almost 1:00 before Sonny got in, exhausted, and it wasn't
long before both of us were 'sawing logs' sound asleep."*

Back to me . . . after Huggins and I had covered 3,533 miles in
seven days, the last 2,140 covering three crazy days without any bed
rest — finally we were stretched out in real beds and "out like a light,"
on our way to being normal again, while Sonny and Doris were simply
sawing away.

Monday September 30, 1968

Off day for travel heading for Fresno, California (only) 1,220 miles
away. Today we would climb twenty-four miles up to Wolf Creek
Pass, elevation nearly 11,000 ft., and then nineteen miles back down
the other side. We had been over this same route two years earlier in
December, 1966 heading from San Bernardino, California to Pueblo

when we hit a monstrous blizzard at the pass. That 1966 trip two years earlier was one of the most harrowing experiences we ever had, and it happened to have been my shift to drive at the time.

Doris wrote: *"We drove today and I mean drove... We must be all the way to Fresno, California by tomorrow night. Over the mountains and down in the valleys and over every other kind of terrain that you can take a bus. After spending quite a while pulling hills and coming down the other steep side, we had to stop and let the brakes on the bus cool off.*

This is beautiful country...some national forest but I forgot the name of it...we made some pictures while we were cooling brakes and taking a five minute stretch. And this is all we did today, ride and look, look and ride, and keep putting those miles behind us far into the night before I finally gave up and went to bed."

Tuesday October 1, 1968 Arrive at Fresno, California.

Doris wrote: *"Woke up half a dozen times all night and was glad when it was daylight enough to get up! I have been moving for the last 20 hours and I'm weak kneed from not walking. We got to Fresno in the late afternoon, checked into the motel and Milo, Sonny and I had a meal leisurely and didn't have to gulp it down. The boys left and after working with the air conditioning for a while, had to call in someone to fix it...and after all the ritual that you go through getting ready for bed, I finally made it...after being in the bed a few minutes I thought sure it was moving! I just couldn't quit seeing that road before my eyes. No need to tell that when Sonny came in from the show, he was ready to hit the 'sack' too."*

Wednesday October 2, 1968 219 miles to Hollywood, California

Doris wrote: *"We all had breakfast and then started the four hour trip to Hollywood where the group will be doing the Joey Bishop Show tonight (taping it for tomorrow)...have to be at rehearsal at 6:00 p.m. so we had some moving around to do...getting uniforms pressed and instruments checked and everybody ready to go. The show is filmed at 8:00 and Sonny got back to the motel around 10:00. It came up a terrible thunder storm and lightening hit several trees and rain slicked freeways caused several bad accidents and at least two people were killed. Glad we weren't driving anywhere to a show tonight. When Sonny got back, he ran to the coffee shop and got us something to eat and brought it back to the room. We watched some of those crazy local television shows out here while eating and part of the Bishop show and fell asleep."*

Thursday October 3, 1968 Day off — stay in Hollywood, California

Doris wrote: *"We had no breakfast this morning. Sonny needed the sleep and we're meeting some people for an early lunch anyway at the Brown Derby Restaurant...first time for us to be in the main dining room. Bette Rosenthal, Ray Harris, Seymour Heller and Lee Karsian, the agency that represents Sonny along with Bob Neal. Bette is the associate member. Bette and I got acquainted over what was supposed to be a 'good' salad that Mr. Heller chose!...oh me. The men talked about business and everything else. The rest of the meal was better than that salad...wish I could remember the name so as to tell people not to order that. After lunch and all the goodbyes, etc., Sonny and I looked at several places for some sweaters he wanted but couldn't find any in his size. We stopped by the market and got some fresh fruit to take back to the room with us. It is several hours after breakfast now. Sonny is not feeling a bit good and I'm not feeling the best in the world myself. So glad we made no commitments to see anybody tonight so that he can rest as much as he will! Later I went down to the ice cream parlor on the corner and got several different kinds of ice cream to taste...(they only have 26 kinds to choose from!)...got Candi-Date; Banana-Berry; and just in case we didn't like either of these...good old peppermint! We watched Sonny on the Joey Bishop Show tonight and he sang his new record, Born To Be With You, and also did a medley of Young Love, Take Good Care of Her and Heaven Says Hello, talked with Joey, then off camera during a commercial break, both went down to the audience to say hello. The show doesn't go off here until 1:00, so we're late again getting to sleep. Some man doing pantomime [Marcel Marceau] took up so much time all the other guests were cut short of their scheduled time. Frank Fontaine*

'Crazy Guggenheim', only got to do one of his two songs scheduled but at least Sonny got to do both of his numbers."

Friday October 4, 1968 32 miles to Anaheim, California

Doris wrote: "*We got up early this morning because Sonny has several appointments today at Capitol, lunch at 1:30 with Larry Scott and Bill Wardlaw of KBBQ Radio. Rushed back to the motel and got packed because Sonny has to leave at 3:00 to get to Anaheim at 5:30 and so the boys could go on to the civic auditorium and set up the equipment for the show. This is the first time they have played out there…usually the shows are held at the Shrine Auditorium in downtown Los Angeles. Sonny was supposed to call me back tonight but I know he got tied up with the people who were meeting him, and they have to pack and leave immediately after their part of the show for the drive to Oakland (San Francisco) and so I went to bed about 11:00 because I didn't feel he would call that late.*"

Saturday October 5, 1968 396 miles to Oakland, California

Doris wrote: "*I got up this morning, don't know what time…there is not a clock around! Dressed and ate and came back…the phone was ringing…it was Sonny. They arrived in Oakland after an all-night ride and he was having to make some sort of personal appearance in the Bay area that afternoon, so didn't have much time to talk. I didn't go on these last two dates with them as Sonny wanted me to stay in Hollywood and rest up for the long hard trip home to Nashville. I sure didn't argue! This has been the most tiresome tour he has been on in years and it's a good thing it has just about come to a close or we would all have to 'Cancel out' because of sheer exhaustion. I went up on the 'Boulevard' as the natives refer to it and walked and looked at the stores…and the people!… Sorry, but it is a scream…some of the get ups would win First Prize at the Halloween Ball. I looked and walked and relaxed just taking my time until my feet decided they were through for the day; stopped in a restaurant, had an early dinner to rest my bones, got a taxi back to the motel.*"

Sunday October 6, 1968 81 miles to Sacramento, California

Doris wrote: *"Got up, dressed, ate, and went to see all my friends at Hollywood Church where we attended when we lived here. Some have moved away, but some of them were still there. Enjoyed seeing and talking with them. After services, Mrs. Ruby and Mrs. Bonham and I had lunch where they have lunch every Sunday and then went by the ice cream place and got ice cream; took it along with all the other things like plates, spoons, napkins and cakes and cookies they had made to the Nursing Home for the Aged. They go there every Sunday afternoon from about 3 to 5 o'clock and treat the patients who are able to come to the dining room to eat. The 'helpers' take refreshments to those unable to get out of bed. Boy, it is pitiful and it makes you appreciate the fact you can move around still. After we left there, went by Mrs. Bonham's so I could say hello to her husband who is ill also; however, he is not bedridden. We hurried and just made it back to church before it started at 6:00. We have really been moving today! I enjoyed it so much…it was nice to be able to do something for somebody. I also enjoyed it because Mrs. Ruby always takes her little toy poodle with her every Sunday; she is Patches Mother!…'Lady' stays in the car during church; during lunch (Mrs. R. brings her scraps); and then during the hospital visit. She took her home before the evening service as it was getting chilly and 'Lady' is expecting again and she was tired enough to sleep now. She is so tiny…how did Patches get to be twice her size!!"*

Monday October 7, 1968 Day off — stayed in Sacramento, California - The bus to Bakersfield 178 miles

Doris wrote: *"Didn't do anything today except pack all my suitcases like they should be…or should say pack that ONE suitcase. I put everything I possibly could on the bus the other day when Sonny left [with the boys for Bakersfield] so that I wouldn't have much to get on the Greyhound bus with. I'm to catch it today and ride up to Bakersfield to meet the group to do the last show tonight, then we head for good old Nashville!…*

Tuesday October 8, 1968

Doris wrote: *I checked out of the motel and took the taxi to the bus station. Brother, you can't imagine the four hippies who were clustered together off in the corner, such costumes. Then after I got my ticket, went over to sit down and there was a man about half drunk or doped, didn't know which, who sat there and sang and muttered and got up and down and made a phone call, came back, sang and muttered some more, then went out the door...! The hippies' bus came before mine, thank goodness and they loaded on to it. Mine came and it was welcomed!*

Tuesday October 8, 1968 Bakersfield — ready for trip home to Nashville.

Doris wrote: *Uneventful ride to Bakersfield [278 miles]...just dozing and looking at the country side...Just as we got to Bakersfield and about to turn a corner, a BEAUTIFUL blue bus turned the corner from the other direction...! Guess who!!!! Pulled into the bus depot and as I was getting off, Glenn and Duane were coming across the walkway to meet me. As we walked back toward the street, another bus pulled up in front of where Sonny's bus was parked...it was Merle Haggard and his group!...they saw Sonny's bus and stopped to see what was the matter. Merle lives close by and was just starting out on a tour. After we said hello to Bonnie and the boys in the band, Merle left and we went to the auditorium to set up for the show. I met several people tonight, either disc jockeys and their wives or local entertainers, or fans who have met Sonny and the Gents from time to time. We will be leaving right after the show tonight for good old Music City, USA, so won't be any need of continuing this diary because we are going to ride day and night until we get back home to Tennessee.*

The next tour I pick to take won't be this mixed up and long rides, and two shows a night and all these other unexpected events that I got on the trip!"

[We headed out after the evening show for the 2,022 mile non-stop trip to Nashville. Arrived home Thursday the 10th at 10 p.m.]

[Home for 2 days — left early the morning of the 12th for a 550 mile trip to our next show in Warren, Ohio]

259

1961 - Carole and Lyman Smith, Sonny, and Budd King. Carol was a long-time co-writer with Sonny. We recorded forty of their songs.

Early 1963 - Sonny and Nat King Cole - Capitol Records Hollywood Recording Studio.

September 1962 — Our quartet's 1952 Chrysler Crown Imperial limo that we came to Nashville in. Picture taken in Ono, Pennsylvania

May 1963 — Record sleeve SONNY JAMES RETURNS TO CAPITOL.

1964 August 15 — First time to appear with Sonny - Grand Ole Opry.

Bob Neal of Bob Neal Talent Agency, Sonny's long-time manager.

1964 35-foot Flxible just before it was purchased.

December 1966 Denver, Colorado L-R Lin, Sonny, Duane, Gary, and Milo.

1967 First CMA Awards Show - co-hosted in Nashville by Sonny and Bobbi Gentry.

1967 July 5 - Mike Douglas TV show in Philadelphia. Gary between Patty Duke and Sonny.

1968 September 28 - Theater in the round - Salt Lake City.

1967 Gents and Sonny at a Texas rodeo. Sonny's favorite picture of us.

1967-1969 - Single record jacket for "Room in Your Heart."
L-R Milo, Duane, Sonny, Lin, and Gary.

1967-1969 -Album cover for True Love's a Blessing
L-R Milo, Duane, Lin, Gary, and Sonny

1967-1969 - Album cover for Need you
L-R Gary, Sonny, Milo, Duane, and Lin.

1967-1969 - Album cover. Born To Be With You.
L-R Gary, Duane, Huggins (Glenn), Sonny, and Milo.

1967-1969 - Album cover.
First live recording done in the
Houston Astrodome.

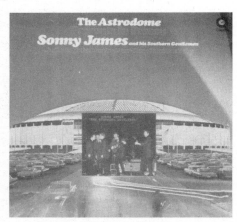

1967-1969 - Single "My Love,"
L-R Milo, Gary, Sonny, Duane,
Huggins (Glenn).

1967 — Sonny and Dizzy Dean.

1969 — Sonny and Ed Sullivan.

1970 - Sonny and Glen Campbell.

1970 — Sonny and George Burns.

1970-10-17 Capitol Records Show in Nashville.

1971 - February Apollo 14 flag from flight. Our music went to the moon.

1976 - Sonny playing his Martin D-28 on a show.

1973 - Sonny and Marie Osmond - holding awards for her single "Paper Roses."

1994 - Gents at their 2nd reunion in Pueblo Colorado. L-R Claude Diehl, Gary Robble, Lin Bown, Duane West, and Glenn Huggins.

2007 - Walking the red carpet.

2007 - The last time the Gents would perform together.

1996 - One of Sonny and Doris' highly anticipated Christmas cards.

2006 Hall of Fame Plaque.

2009 - Terry and Fredia Dillard with Sonny, picture taken behind our house.

2013 - October 13 CMHOF ceremony in Nashville. Sonny, Barry Gibb, and Greg Robble.

2014 - December - Sonny's last and largest Christmas card. Sent to DJ Terry Burford at KZHE in Magnolia, Arkansas. L-R Sam Austin, Terry, Roy Alphin, and Dave Schon.

2014-10-24 - Nina McKay — ninetieth birthday surprise. Don McKay wrote about his mom's special moment in the book's introduction.

2018 - John and Janet Panagos in the Hackleburg Independence Day Parade.

Milo Liggett — Sonny's long-time bass player.

Milo and Sonny performing live. My favorite picture of the two of them.

BRADLEY STUDIOS
In 1955, brothers Owen and Harold Bradley built a recording studio in the basement of a house on this site. They added another studio here in an army Quonset Hut, producing hits by Patsy Cline, Red Foley, Brenda Lee, Marty Robbins, Sonny James, and others. Columbia Records purchased the studios in 1962. The studio established its reputation in the music industry with hits by stars including Johnny Cash, Bob Dylan, Roger Miller, George Jones, and Tammy Wynette.

Plaque in front of the Quonset Hut on 16th Ave S. Nashville, Tennessee.

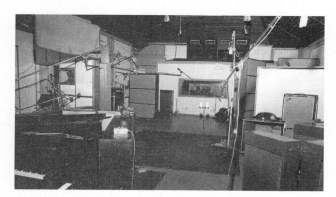

The Quonset Hut in Nashville where we did most of our recording sessions.

CHAPTER 18

SONNY'S R&B MAINSTREAM MERGER

In 1969, *Billboard Magazine* named Sonny James Country Music's Artist of the Year.

Following the musical formula he made his own, and with the influence of Nat King Cole's success, two weeks after taking on The Southern Gentlemen, Sonny recorded "You're The Only World I Know," which was released in late November 1964. While "You're The Only World I Know" was climbing the country charts, Sonny and The Southern Gentlemen were in the Columbia Recording Studio in Nashville on January 18, 20, and 21, recording, "'*Til the Last Leaf Shall Fall*," the only religious album Sonny would ever do. Two days later on January 23, 1965, "You're the Only World I Know" would reach #1 country, and surprisingly finding its way to #91 on the pop charts and remaining the #1 country song for four consecutive weeks through February 13, 1965.

Sonny and The Southern Gentlemen were immediately contacted, and flew up to New York City to film *The Jimmy Dean Show* on Friday, February 26. ABC aired the show six days later on Thursday, March 4. It was the first network television show Sonny had done in about six years, and the first one ever for The Southern Gentlemen. Only six months into this new venture, Sonny, Milo, and The Southern Gentlemen found themselves on a journey that would ultimately place them near the pinnacle of country music history.

Even though that was so, Sonny was not about to get caught up in the trap of pop music again. Steering himself totally away from anything of the sort, Sonny did a medley of four songs while sitting on a barrel of some kind, surrounded by The Southern Gentlemen as they blended their voices into one microphone. It's always tickled me, and now that the clip of that show has made its way to YouTube, to again hear Jimmy as he introduces us doing "I'll Keep Holding On," say to Sonny, "You wanna go back to your barrel ..." Here, just two months before turning thirty-seven, and backed up by a vocal group who was fourteen years his junior, Sonny was again satisfied to be known as that country boy Southern Gentleman from Hackleburg, Alabama.

In March 1965, after introducing the song on *The Jimmy Dean Show,* "I'll Keep Holding On" would peak at #2. Similarly, "Behind the Tear" would achieve #1 status in October of 1965, with the Cole approach leading the way.

In November 1965 Sonny and The Southern Gentlemen, for the first time, recorded a rhythm and blues song, Adam Wade's "Take Good Care of Her." Released in the spring of 1966 during the stride of the American Civil Rights Era and without fanfare it became Sonny's third #1 since we joined him, reaching that spot in June. This single recording made Sonny the first country artist to record and deliver an R&B song into the country music mainstream.

Just one month after recording "Take Good Care of Her," we were back in the studio recording "Take Me Back," an R&B song which had been a top twenty hit for Little Anthony and the Imperials; however, this recording was never released as a single, and therefore never reached significance on the country charts. It, however, was always one of my very favorite songs that we recorded.

Though R&B material seemed to fit perfectly, Sonny went three years and thirty recording sessions before we recorded another one.

Sonny's timing during our seven years with him was incredible, and by 1969, he felt the time was right to commit himself to record R&B — and he did.

During this highly successful run of sixteen consecutive #1 hits, beginning in 1969, of the next seven singles — five had previously been moderately successful releases for soulful R&B artists Ivory Joe Hunter, Brook Benton, Clyde Otis, and Jimmy Reed. Those five songs were "Since I Met You Baby," "It's Just a Matter of Time," "Endlessly," "Empty Arms," and "Bright Lights, Big City" — all of which reached #1 on the Billboard country charts.

From the inception of the R&B genre in 1949, through 1971, when Sonny's last such recording tapped the top of the charts, no other country artist ever achieved such success with R&B material. The next time a country artist reached #1 with an R&B song would be April of 1976.

Sonny James and The Southern Gentlemen stood alone for twenty-seven years as true innovators — broadening the limits of country music through this unique adaptation of great R&B songs.

LYNDA FRATZKE SNIPPET

I was born, and have lived in Pierre, South Dakota, since childhood. There was always music in our home since my mom had an extensive record collection. She played records so much that when I was just two and a half, Mom wrote in my baby book that I liked "Hound Dog" by Elvis. My sister Kathi and I played her records so much that certain songs just became part of us.

Watching singers perform on TV was another one of my great rewards out there in the country. The only trouble was, we could pick up only one television channel, and on Sunday nights we would faithfully watch *The Ed Sullivan Show*, transmitted, of course, on CBS. One Sunday night when I was about eleven I saw Sonny James and The Southern Gentlemen perform "Running Bear" on his show, and instantly I became a fan.

Forty years rolled by. It was an ordinary day at my job as the assistant manager of the Holiday Inn Express in Ft. Pierre. The phone rang, and I answered it with the usual: "Holiday Inn Express, Ft. Pierre—this is Lynda. How can I help you?" The caller said, "This might sound a little strange. I'm not calling for a reservation; I'm writing a book, and I need just a moment of your time to get some information." Now I was intrigued. He continued, "Is this the same Holiday Inn that was in Pierre in 1969?" I explained that no, this was a different one in a new location, but that the original building was still standing. It had been sold a couple of times, and was now called the Pierre Inn and Suites.

Our conversation continued; the caller said he had searched for the Inn on Google Maps, stating it looked like the one he remembered from forty-seven years ago, and he wanted to make sure. Curious, I asked, "What were you doing in Pierre back then?" He replied that he had been traveling through the area with a group on their way to Iowa, and they had stopped there for Thanksgiving dinner. I asked, "What kind of group were you in?" He said, "Are you at all familiar with Sonny James?" Oh my! My new friend introduced himself as one of the Southern Gentlemen. We talked uninterrupted for a least twenty minutes more. This much excitement rarely ever happens in Pierre!

A few weeks later, Gary called back, requesting my help. He was scheduled for a radio interview with Terry Burford at KZHE in Arkansas, and he wanted to surprise him. The day came; I was so excited to help! I was listening online as I waited on the phone while Gary told Terry about Thanksgiving at the Holiday Inn in 1969, and his quest to see if the Inn was still there. When he got to the part, "So I looked up the number, dialed it, and heard ..." I chimed in with "Holiday Inn Express, Ft. Pierre—this is Lynda. How can I help you?" It worked - Terry was speechless for a moment! I tried to do my best imitation of a not-so-excited person. Being live on the radio like this was something I will never forget!

LINDA FRATZKE - *Pierre, South Dakota*

CHAPTER 19

#1 STREAK — SIXTEEN IN A ROW

	SONG	(RECORDED)	(REACHED #1)		
1967	"Need You"	06/25/65	04/22/67	#1	1
	"I'll Never Find Another You"	09/01/65	08/05/67	#1	2
	"It's the Little Things"	09/01/65	11/18/67	#1	3
1968	"A World of Our Own"	10/31/67	01/20/68	#1	4
	"Heaven Says Hello"	11/01/67	06/01/68	#1	5
	"Born to Be with You"	07/18/68	12/14/68	#1	6
1969	"Only the Lonely"	11/21/68	03/08/69	#1	7
	"Running Bear"	01/17/69	06/14/69	#1	8
	"Since I Met You Baby"	01/17/69	10/04/69	#1	R&B 9
1970	"It's Just a Matter of Time"	11/05/69	02/14/70	#1	R&B 10
	"My Love"	01/17/69	05/16/70	#1	11
	"Don't Keep Me Hangin' On"	02/18/70	08/08/70	#1	12
	"Endlessly"	02/20/70	11/28/70	#1	R&B 13
1971	"Empty Arms"	07/23/70	04/10/71	#1	R&B 14
	"Bright Lights, Big City"	04/28/70	07/24/71	#1	R&B 15
	"Here Comes Honey Again"	05/11/71	11/06/71	#1	16

RAYMOND MOONEY SNIPPET

My first recollection of hearing Sonny James was in 1957 on the radio in our kitchen in Rutland, Vermont, when I first heard his version of "Young Love." Another version of "Young Love" came out at the same time, but I knew Sonny's version was much better. Little did I realize when I was ten years old how popular Sonny James would become.

Flash forward to 1970 when I was a member of the City of Rutland Fire Department and a full-fledged Sonny James fan. His hits of "My Love" and "Don't Keep Me Hanging On" had me hooked, and I was buying his albums for home and eight-track tapes for my car. Imagine my delight when I found out that Sonny James and The Southern Gentlemen would be appearing at the Champlain Valley Fair in Essex Junction, Vermont (about seventy miles north of Rutland), on September 4, 1970. I managed to talk four other fellow firefighters and a good friend (all country music and Sonny James fans) to chip in and buy box seats in the center front row to see and hear our idol perform. So, on a Friday afternoon, we started north to the fair. But the closer we got, the darker the skies got. And when we arrived not only had the skies opened but the storm was turning into what we call a "gully-washer." When we got to the ticket booth, we were told that we no longer had our center box seats because Sonny and the Gentlemen were taking it over. They would have drowned on the stage and were doing their first performance in our box! But, we were given the six seats in front of the box, separated by only a railing! Sonny James was within touching distance of us, not across the racetrack on the stage. I think Sonny had been told of the situation because at some point he thanked us for our hospitality. After that, the rest was a buzz because I was seeing Sonny James singing in person in front of me. We had the best seats in the house that evening! After the performance, Sonny autographed an album I had brought. I still have it framed in my cellar family room forty-six years later.

I saw Sonny two times after this. At the Hartford, Vermont High

School, Sonny was introduced by Rex Marshall who was a television personality when I was a kid. Rex was the Reynolds Aluminum ad man and was also the announcer Sunday nights for Mr. Peepers with Wally Cox. He had relocated to the area and was a radio personality with a show called *The Country Club*. He was instrumental in getting Sonny and the Gentlemen to appear in Hartford. Anyway, my wife Judy and I brought my mother along, and Mom became an instant Sonny James fan that evening. She bought an album and had him autograph it (as did I), and thereafter talked about how handsome and polite he was, and watched him whenever he was making an appearance on television. I bought her many of his future albums, and she was a fan until she passed at eighty-nine in 2003.

The last time I saw Sonny was in 1978 at the Rutland Fairgrounds, where he appeared along with Cal Smith who had a big hit with "Country Bumpkin." At thirty-one, I was still in awe of him. At the end of the show, there was long line of autograph seekers, and I didn't do what I now know I should have done. I wished now I had thanked him one more time for allowing us to have the *best seats in the house*!

RAYMOND MOONEY - *Rutland, Vermont*

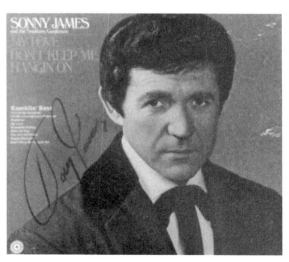

Signed album cover Raymond Mooney has had displayed in his family room since 1970.

CHAPTER 20

APOLLO 14 — 1971

"It's been a long way, but we're here."
—ALAN SHEPHARD AS HE STEPPED
ON THE MOON ON FEBRUARY 6, 1971,

For the Apollo 14 flight to the moon, a request was made for Sonny James and The Southern Gentlemen's music to accompany the astronauts.

The following is first a brief list of facts about the mission, and second is the actual transcript of a special tape Sonny made to accompany the men on their flight.

Apollo 14 was the eighth manned mission in the United States Apollo program, and the third to land on the Moon. It was the last of the "H missions," targeted landings with two-day stays on the Moon with two lunar EVAs, or moonwalks.

Commander Alan Shepard, Command Module Pilot Stuart Roosa, and Lunar Module Pilot Edgar Mitchell launched on their nine-day mission on January 31, 1971, at 4:04:02 p.m. local time after a forty-minute, two-second delay due to launch site weather restrictions, the first such delay in the Apollo program.

Shepard and Mitchell made their lunar landing on February 5 in the Fra Mauro formation—originally the target of the aborted Apollo 13 mission. During the two lunar EVAs, 42.80 kilograms (94.35 pounds) of Moon rocks were collected, and several scientific experiments were performed. Shepard hit two golf balls on the lunar surface with a makeshift club he had brought with him. Shepard and Mitchell spent 33½ hours on the Moon, with almost 9½ hours of EVA.

In the aftermath of Apollo 13, several modifications had been made to the Service Module electrical power system to prevent a repeat of that accident, including a redesign of the oxygen tanks and the addition of a third tank.

While Shepard and Mitchell were on the surface, Roosa remained in lunar orbit aboard the Command/Service Module Kitty Hawk, performing scientific experiments and photographing the Moon, including the landing site of the future Apollo 16 mission. He took several hundred seeds on the mission, many of which were germinated on return, resulting in the so-called Moon trees. Shepard, Roosa, and Mitchell landed in the Pacific Ocean on February 9.

APOLLO 14 FLIGHT TAPE

"It's good to be riding with you—Stu, Alan, and Ed. And my group The Southern Gentlemen and myself, we've picked out some songs that, as we ride around together, we thought might help you pass the time of day or night depending on the time that you're listening to this.

And some of the songs I think you'll remember and unless I miss my guess a couple of you were probably going with that special girl when I first sang this song. If I can get Wayne [White], my drummer, over at the other side to start me off — Wayne just a little bit of this one about half way through — OK? OK.

Song — "Young Love"

Since that song, man that brings back memories even to me. Well, since that time we've done, I think, about every kind of song you can think of. All kinds of tempos, happy songs, blues songs, and a few comedy songs mixed in. If you've seen us do any of our television shows, we always include maybe one or two of our happy songs and I thought now would be a good time maybe to have one of those toe tappers that we sang so often. So here's one that kinda gets up and moves a little.

Song — "Endlessly"

You know rumor has it, Stu, that you're some kind of a singer. Well, anyway, the group and I have decided that we would include a song that absolutely is no problem at all for anyone to sing, so this is our big chance here where the neighbors aren't around to complain about singing. As a matter of fact, Ed, you and Alan — it would be a good idea for you to join in and kind of give support to Stu — give him that good harmony. He may have a recording contract waiting for him.

You all might be the next male Andrew sisters — wouldn't that be something? We'll kick it off, and you guys join in. OK? All right guys, now really sound out. As Lawrence Welk would say — ah one, ah two, ah one two three . . .

Song — "You Are My Sunshine"

Ahh — you never sounded better. What a group. You gotta admit — we're loud. Right? But occasionally we do settle down and do what is known in the trades as we call it — a secretary song. Now you have terms for your different expressions in engineering and the flights that you take and the different things that you become involved with. Well, we have this kind of talk in the music business. So this is what is commonly known as a secretary kind of song — one that just moves kind of easy — and these are the main songs that are really bought by the people, I guess because they have that kind of soft tone feeling to it, so I thought we would include one of these.

Song — "Born to Lose"

Since all of you are living in Houston now, I don't know if I might have had the opportunity of seeing you in the audience or maybe you've been to some of the appearance I've done there in Houston, but last year I did an album at the Astrodome, and I think that was probably one of the most exciting things that I've probably ever done. It's my understanding that it's the only album that's ever been recorded from the Astrodome. And you kind of get a feeling of loneliness as you know if you've ever gone to any of the football or baseball games there. It's such a huge place, and we were right out in the middle of the Astrodome and we had something like twenty-five- or thirty-thousand people — I've forgotten. But one of the songs that really had a great feel to it, at least from the feeling that we got from the audience — clapping their hands and singing along with us and everything — it had kind of had a western atmosphere about it. It's an Indian type song about Running Bear. And I thought I would do this song simply because if one of you were at the show, you can recall the enthusiasm that the audience got from this number. So I thought we'd do this on the tape.

Song — "Running Bear"

You know, all of my group that tours with me over the country and records with me and does television shows with me, every time that there has been a space flight, I think, we have all sat around, we watch it with enthusiasm as much as anyone else, and I, for one, am a nut on this kind of thing because when it comes to getting the coverage looking and all the magazines and photos, the color photos particularly that were made, I've always, ah, thought and imagined, you know, what it would be like in makin' one of these flights, but I think if I would get anything from it I would think that, particularly when I see the things that you fellas experienced in making a flight such as this, I think that it would probably strengthen the belief of any one person. And I think to express that I've, ah, worked up a couple of arrangements on a couple of songs that I wanted to particularly sing for you and to wish you my best. I hope one of these days that I might meet each of you personally—and I want to thank you for the ride. Good luck.

Songs - "Just a Closer Walk" and "How Great Thou Art"

September 14, 2018 email to Christopher Roosa—son of Apollo 14 Astronaut Stuart Roosa: "Hello again, Christopher—Would you or the Roosa family have a problem if I used the transcription of the tape Sonny sent along with your dad on the flight."

September 27, 2018 email response, "I think it would be great to include the story in your book. My father often talked about that tape in his speeches.

All the best,

Christopher

BRIAN JASPER SNIPPET

My wife Scarlette and I were enjoying being a part of the first ever Elton John Expo to be held in Atlanta, Georgia in mid-August 1994. We had traveled south from Kentucky to meet some music icons who actually recorded and produced the classic Elton John albums and singles from the 1970s. Among them was one of my heroes, producer extraordinaire Gus Dudgeon. Dudgeon — one of Rock's greatest men behind the controls. It was recordings by these people that sold tons of records; Rock classics like the standard "Your Song," "Daniel," "Don't Let The Sun Go Down On Me," and so very many more that are a part of our music consciousness.

At dinner on the night of eighteenth, the room was full of excited fans ready to explode with enthusiasm and keen to talk about all things Elton. The room was charged with the presence of Gus Dudgeon, who cast the image of John Lennon himself in his dress, speech, and mannerisms.

He'd not only known John Lennon and Elton but also recorded these two giants of music live at Madison Square Garden. Gus, a figure who cast a mighty shadow, was a little bit unapproachable by most, clean shaven with his clear framed Lennon glasses, dress shirt, and slacks.

His caustic wit and that British accent were amusing but also a little intimidating. It was a strange situation for them as they'd never been in a room with a bunch of true fans, maybe 100 people who like myself, owned everything Elton, and largely to their surprise, were totally knowledgeable.

Gus, his wife Shelia, and my wife Scarlette, and I were seated close to each other at the hotel's restaurant—so close that our chairs were nearly touching. I casually leaned over to Gus and told him I was writing songs with Sonny James. He retorted—"The Sonny James? 'Young Love,' Sonny James? I said, 'Yes, and the 'Running Bear' and 'Since I Met You Baby'—Sonny James.'

Gus was checking me—"Johnny Preston did 'Running Bear.'" I said 'yes, but Sonny had a huge seller with it, too.' His mouth literally then dropped open as he lost it and became a little bubbly: "I have 'Young Love' on my jukebox back home in England." We were instant pals. Fans dropped by our table after Gus and Shelia had left, and asked me: "What in the world did you say to him? He looked astonished!"

That weekend we talked, sang songs, laughed, and thoroughly enjoyed our time together. It was to be the only time we spent with Gus and Shelia Dudgeon. Five years later, they lost their lives in a tragic automobile accident. But always I will wonder what became of that jukebox with the Sonny James record on it.

BRIAN JASPER, *who is from Somerset, Kentucky, wrote songs with Sonny for thirty years and was co-writer on the last single Sonny recorded in 1986, a single that was never released titled, "Guess Again."*

CHAPTER 21

THE BEE GEES

So today is tomorrow. Winters are summers.
And the end of the rainbow is here.
End of the Rainbow

—BY BARRY GIBB, STEPHEN GIBB, ASHLEY GIBB

And it ended like it started: the first major show the Chordsmen did was three months before joining Sonny as The Southern Gentlemen, and was in the old Madison Square Garden in May 1964. The third-from-the-last show we did was on June 4, 1971, in the new Madison Square Garden. For all of us, everything would change. Sonny would take on replacements as our vocal group slowly peeled away. His streak of consecutive #1 hits would continue for another two songs. Five months after we left, the last in that streak of sixteen in a row would hit on November 6, 1971, both recorded with us before we departed.

Our vocal group headed off in opposite directions. Our first tenor Lin Bown and our bass Huggins (Glenn) would eventually take up residence in Colorado — many miles from each other. Our baritone Duane West would move to Shelbyville, Tennessee, and I would stay in our same house in Nashville for another twenty-three years.

Strange as it may sound, our vocal group didn't sing a note together for the following eighteen years, until our first reunion in 1989. However, we did find ways to do what we loved to do — harmonize. Lin and his wife Vicki along with a third individual (Charlotte Dock, and later, Hermine Stearmen) would sing as the New Hope Singers for twenty-one years, primarily in churches in the Midwest, with some trips carrying them to all four corners of the USA. Duane would do freelance vocal background work before permanently joining the Jordanaires as their baritone in 1980, when Hoyt Hawkins died. Huggins would join a chorus for a spell, but a serious back ailment and over twelve back surgeries way too early in his life, would put a clamp on his activities and would take away his ability to do very much. I would find a spot in our church, singing the third part with our music director Paul Eby and his wife Martha Ann. Thank goodness for them — it satisfied my harmonizing itch.

But it was never enough. In the mid-seventies, I found the cure for the deep harmonizing ailment I was actually suffering from, and it came, interestingly enough, through my oldest son Greg, who has been mentioned many times before in this writing. When it came to this part in the story, it would take more than my journal, the detailed discography, and Vivian's autograph book — the internet would ultimately become the over-riding source we would rely on.

It was December 1976 — Greg was twelve; Barry Gibb was thirty, and the nonidentical twins Maurice and Robin Gibb were all of twenty-six when Greg asked his mom for a Beach Boys album for Christmas. By some weird mistake, they ended up with the album *Children of the World* by the Bee Gees. Little did any of us know what that would lead to some twenty-eight years later.

Greg adopted them as the new vocal sound for our family. Our other two sons, Dale and Page — no so much. Greg even had a life-sized poster of them on the inside of his bedroom door; I would find myself in the finished basement of our home wearing headphones, listening to their songs over and over and over again—our love of their music never waivered.

In the mid-eighties when he was twenty-two, Greg went to work for Senators Coaches located in Corinth, Mississippi. Greg had traveled with us on the bus a number of times back in the late '60s, and no doubt had caught a serious case of the touring bug, with the music business becoming his life's work until his mid-thirties. Until then, Greg had spent his entire adult life primarily working for tour production manager Jake Berry, continuously touring about 330 days each year with all the top rock and pop artists of the 1980s and 90s. Artists such as Eric Clapton, Aerosmith, AC/DC, Metallica, and The Rolling Stones are just a small sample of those he worked for in tour production, and why he was generally absent from our lives for over fifteen years. Through that entire period there was one group that eluded him — The Bee Gees. The Brothers Gibb rarely did lengthy tours, primarily because of what was understood by Greg to be Barry's unfortunate back issues.

In 1989, this changed when the Bee Gees released the album *One*, and a US tour was scheduled. At that time Greg was touring with Eric Clapton and working closely with Warren Poppie in great anticipation. Warren lived and worked out of Los Angeles; his wife Sally worked in the offices of the Hollywood management company that was handling the Bee Gees. When it came time for ink to hit paper, wouldn't you know it - the Bee Gees production contracts went in another direction. Greg would not be on the Bee Gees tour. But if you know Greg much at all, you know he's a serious and very appreciative Bee Gees listener. Warren's wife Sally didn't miss the opportunity to get Greg a tour jacket — denim, with a large retro Bee Gees logo across the back. It has been kept in pristine condition, unworn, with the tag still hanging off the sleeve.

The door had been closed tight on that story for thirty years, when unexpectedly, it swung wide open again. It was 2013. Greg became aware that Barry Gibb would be on The Grand Ole Opry on Saturday night, October 26, as a guest of Ricky Skaggs. Greg made a quick call to Sonny to see how he might possibly get him backstage to meet Barry. Sonny made a couple of calls, but unfortunately the policies had changed at the Opry, so the long-standing ability to casually hang out backstage was no longer an option. At that moment, Greg decided to try to get tickets for the Opry performance; he made a call and secured them.

As for Sonny, he really felt bad that he couldn't make this simple request from Greg work out. On short notice, Sonny invited Greg to be his guest at the upcoming Hall of Fame Medallion Ceremony on Sunday October 27 — Greg hadn't been to this event since Sonny's induction in 2007. Greg, who loved doing things like this with Sonny (who enjoyed having Greg by his side), accepted. As an afterthought, Greg asked Sonny who the inductees were, with Sonny responding Kenny Rogers, Bobby Bare, and Jack Clement. In that second, Greg realized why Barry was in town, and it suddenly all made sense — Barry was actually in Nashville to sing "Islands in the Stream" with Dolly Parton during Kenny's part of the Medallion ceremony; a song Barry had written and produced for the two of them. As Greg told me, he said to Sonny, "We're going to meet Barry Gibb at the Medallion Ceremony, no doubt about it." Sonny was beyond thrilled to realize he would be the catalyst for this opportunity after all. It just so happened that Dolly had been in a minor accident, and would not be performing with Barry during the ceremony. In her place would be TG Sheppard's wife, Kelly Lang, doing "Islands in the Stream."

It's a tradition that at the end of every Medallion Ceremony, the Hall of Fame members in attendance, along with everyone who performed during the ceremony, gathers on stage to sing "Will the Circle Be Unbroken." As the official ceremony came to a close, all those previous inductees congregated out of sight as they prepared to take the stage to sing that closing number. Sonny was standing with them; TG came from the far end of the line over to Sonny and asked "Have you met Barry because he wants to meet you?"

Research after the fact would bring to light what the common bond was. In the '50s throughout much of the English-speaking world, pop music was simply American country-influenced music. The young Brothers Gibb later acknowledged they would sing in the style of the Everly Brothers and add a third part. In one of the Gibb's earliest performance promotional photos, they were dressed in stage clothes their mother had made for them, wearing white shirts and Southern Gentleman ties (second section of pictures).

With the song sung, and the event over, it took only a couple of minutes for Sonny and Barry to migrate toward each other and finally meet at center stage. Sonny called out for Greg to come up and told Barry he had a close friend with him who was really looking forward to meeting him. Long after the theater had emptied, Sonny, Barry, Greg, Barry's son Stephen, with Barry's wife Linda nearby, were still sharing stories, laughs, and smiles.

Even with decades of wondering if this moment would ever occur, Greg would be the first to say the true thrill was seeing his lifelong friend Sonny being appreciated for his accomplishments in history. It was a colorful collision of respect, influence, and deep musical tethers all converging under the umbrella of a historical event. Nobody spoke of the influences and relationships and successes they shared between themselves. It was all simply in the moment, so simple and beautifully kind. He's wondered if it perhaps meant more to Barry than we could have ever imagined. But that's exactly what it seemed to be. Then, Stephen and Greg graciously stepped aside to allow the photographers to document this memorable moment between two icons of pop and country music.

For the rest of the evening Sonny was super-excited, and boyishly happy. Doris would tell Greg numerous times over the next couple of years how Sonny was so happy that night. It was a memory she held onto for as long as she could. It no doubt gave her great comfort and helped her see him in her memory with nothing but smiles, full of energy, being unable to stand still.

The Barry Gibb / Eric Clapton / Sonny James Connection

How does Eric Clapton fit into the story of Sonny and The Bee Gees? We know Barry Gibb knew Eric Clapton at least by February 1,

1968. The Bee Gees and The Cream (Eric's group) were photographed together in Copenhagen, Denmark in a hotel lobby, with Eric seated on a sofa directly beside Maurice and Barry Gibb. The relationship between Barry and Eric is undoubtedly a fascinating story in itself. From what we know, it was Eric who first suggested to Barry that the Bee Gees should head to Miami for recording and inspiration. This resulted in the brothers not only recording in Miami, but moving there when it became the hub of their career's greatest successes. For a short time during the late 80s, the Bees Gees and Clapton even formed a collaboration together under the name "The Bunburys."

A phone call Sonny received sometime during 1993 takes things a step further. As the story was related to me by Brian Jasper, Sonny's long-time co-writer (see the previous snippet), Sonny received an invitation from Clapton to fly over and go fishing with him. Apparently Eric had taken the time and interest in inviting not only Sonny, but also Don Williams ("I Believe in You," "Tulsa Time"), for some downtime together. We don't know if Don made the trip or not, but during those years, Sonny simply didn't enjoy globe trekking and took a pass on the invite.

So, with taking a bit of history and adding a good measure of kindness, we were unexpectedly surprised when Clapton released his first-ever Christmas album in October of 2018 and discovered it included a song which Sonny had written with John Skye, titled "Christmas in My Hometown." Sonny had first recorded it in 1954, and then again with us in 1966 for his *My Christmas Dream* album on Capitol.

This song had surfaced every once in a while over the years, most notably in 1996 when The Hallmark Channel produced a Christmas movie starring Tim Matheson, Melissa Gilbert, and Travis Tritt, with Tritt singing the song. Initially the movie was to be titled *Christmas in My Hometown*, but eventually the title was shortened to *Holiday for Love*.

For Eric Clapton to have chosen to record and release a song Sonny had written so long ago is an enormous honor for Sonny's memory. For Eric to have chosen this song, which so defines everything in life that was ultimately so near and dear to Sonny — his beloved hometown folks in Hackleburg, Alabama — is so far beyond being honored that it's like being remembered for exactly who Sonny was, and is, to so many.

FAYRENE WHITMAN SNIPPIT

As I am sitting in my living room, I am thinking back to some precious memories I had as a child living in Hackleburg, Alabama. Times like around mid-September when the Hackleburg schools would let out for two weeks so that the farmers could get their cotton fields harvested, almost everyone picked cotton to make money to buy their winter clothes. I remember a truck coming by at 6:00 a.m. and picking up all the students who would be picking cotton. We would all pile up on the trailer on top of the cotton that we had picked the day before and ride to the cotton fields.

At the end of the week, we would all get paid. Our mother would put all of our money together, and on Saturday we would walk a mile from our house to Loden's Clothing Store. The thing that I remember most is when Sonny would bend down and fit us with some new shoes. While we were with Sonny, getting fitted, his mother, Della, would wait on Mother and sell her material, thread, and so on, as mother made all of our clothes. But I can't leave my buddy Pop Loden out. I can still taste the bubble gum and candy that he would give me—but I had to sit on his knee to get it.

Every year during the Christmas season, Pop and Mom Loden would have a Santa Claus at their store. Mother would get us dressed up, and we would walk that mile to their store to see Santa (we walked because we didn't have a car). I remember the time that one of my sisters said, "Santa looks just like Daddy." Turned out she was right—our Daddy, Charlie Holland, was Santa. A few years later, Mother let the secret out and also told us that when Daddy was through being Santa each year, Pop Loden would always make it worth Daddy's time and give him a pair of overalls as payment. Pop and Mom Loden were very kind-hearted and humble people. I could see where Sonny got his kindness and humility from. The name Southern Gentleman could not fit anyone else any better. Sonny was truly that.

Some years later we moved fifteen miles away to Haleyville, Alabama. Then the news got out that Sonny would be opening a furniture store in Haleyville. On May 2, 1970, they had the Grand Opening, and Mother and I went and we got to see Sonny again. That was really special to us. We did not have a TV, but our neighbors did, and we heard that Sonny James was going to be on *The Ed Sullivan Show* the following weekend, so we went over to the neighbors and watched it. Oh how we loved seeing our shoe-fitting friend on TV.

And oh, how I wish I still had that pair of shoes that Sonny fit on me when I was just four years old. Some things stick in your mind forever.

FAYRENE WHITMAN - *Haleyville, Alabama*

The Loden's store 1950 - Fayrene Whitman's father dressed as Santa surrounded by children at Christmas time.

CHAPTER 22

HACKLEBURG

*"Can't tell what's ahead, but whatever it is,
I'll still be Sonny James of Hackleburg when it's all over."*
—Sonny's response to a question by Dallas, Texas reporter
Tony Zoppi on February 10, 1957

"Rain fell lightly on the side-by-side footstones of tornado victims
Alven and Ida Powell at Cedar Tree Cemetery. Across the highway,
a big CAT excavator dug debris where the Piggly Wiggly once stood"
wrote *Birmingham News* writer Mike Oliver in 2011, a few weeks after
the storm had torn Hackleburg apart.

"'He was the postmaster, and she was his assistant,' said eighty-three-year-old Miss Clifford Wise, standing over the Powell gravesite on this recent drizzly day. 'They had a lantern and were found dead up against a tree—they were trying to get to their storm cellar.'" "That was sixty-eight years ago; the date chiseled into the marble markers was April 12, 1943. The day a tornado destroyed the town."

Hackleburg in 1943 had decreased in size from when Sonny was born fifteen years earlier. At the time of that '43 tornado, its population had dropped from around 600 in 1928 to right at 500. Where Sonny was, or what he was doing at the time of the tornado, we will never know. The Loden family might have been working out of one of those previously mentioned radio stations or back home on their farm, located about six miles south of Hackleburg on Hwy 253. Whatever the circumstances — he never talked about it. When Sonny was on *The Ed Sullivan Show* in early 1957, Whitey Cochran, long-time resident and four-time mayor, remembers Mr. Sullivan asking him on the air what the population of Hackleburg was. Sonny responded, "Counting the chickens and everything? — 483." Shortly after that, Barney Shackelford, two-time mayor of Hackleburg, remembers front plates on cars around town that read, "Hackleburg—The Friendly City—Population 483" — a tribute to Sonny's math (chickens included).

"Hackleburg was named, so the story goes, for those devilish 'hackle burrs' that flustered early sheepherders by doggedly locking into the fleece. Many residents have lived here for generations and are not in a hurry to leave. Despite the history, the burr under the saddle of the town for the last three generations has been those vicious, unconscionable tornadoes.

"Now the cemetery is absorbing a new round of tornado victims . . . The EF5 storm that roared through the town [of 1,400] at 210 mph destroyed 10 businesses, 180 homes, and sadly took the lives of 18. The new markers will have one thing in common—they are being prepared with a shared date: April 27, 2011."

Each year on the first Sunday in May, "Decoration Day" is observed at Cedar Tree Cemetery. On that special day, family and friends make their way to the cemetery and place flowers on their loved ones graves. "A big, white marble headstone marks the graves of Archie and Della Loden," said Miss Wise, the cemetery treasurer, "'There's a spot waiting for Archie and Della's son, Sonny James.'"

But this year would be different—75 percent of Hackleburg was no more, and May 1 was more like "devastation day." People were being encouraged to stay away until clean-up measures could bring a sense of safety to the area.

Three weeks after the tornado had done its worst, Fayrene Whitman and her husband Billy decided to head on over to see the town she so remembered from her childhood. At the time, Fayrene and Billy were living in Haleyville, Alabama, which was about fifteen miles away. Preparing in advance to observe "Decoration Day," Fayrene had already made some silk flowers to put on her parents' graves, and the grave of their baby girl they lost in 1962, only seven weeks after her birth. Now three weeks later, when they arrived and went to the cemetery, they noticed that miraculously only one tombstone had been blown over by the tornado; however, in spite of what nature's forces had done to bring Hackleburg to its knees, the town's people had risen up, and three-fourths of the over twelve hundred graves already had new flowers on them.

In the middle of town at 309 S. Main was a two-story building housing a business named Shackelford Heating and Cooling. The building still has the original name Loden's in faded white paint visible on the red brick between the two windows on the second floor.

"The Loden building had been built like a fortress sometime after the 1943 tornado, obviously with lessons learned from that storm sixty-eight years earlier. It is one of the very few buildings in this small downtown area to survive this latest blast from Mother Nature.

"The structure originally housed a store owned by Mom and Pop Loden, parents of Jimmie (Sonny Boy) Loden, better known as country music hall-of-famer Sonny James.

"Across the street from the Loden building, hardware store owner Tim Bishop said he plans to stay. Indeed, customers were finding him one day last week, even though he's selling his wares out of a trailer behind the heavily damaged building until he can rebuild with the help of insurance money. The store, built at the turn of the century and whose discolored bricks show where it had been repaired after the 1943 tornado, will be demolished.

"For the past twenty-five years, Shackelford Heating and Cooling has occupied the Loden building, and its owner is uncertain about downtown's survival. 'I hate to see it go, but I don't see business coming back here,' said Phillip Shackelford, fifty-six, as he cut sheet metal to make heating and air ducts. Nearby, his seventy-eight-year-old mother, Jean, cut insulation with a razor-sharp utility knife.

"But for the moment, Shackelford, like Bishop across the street, seems busy—both in a line of work in high demand as town residents rebuild. 'Business is good,' Shackelford said, slicing another piece of sheet metal."

Three years after the tornado had torn the town apart in April 2011, Sonny phoned his cousin Randy Jackson in Hamilton, Alabama, a town located twelve miles south of Hackleburg. Sonny made some friendly talk and then, according to Randy, he changed his tone and said, "Randy, would you do me a favor—when the time arrives would you come to Nashville and pick me up and take me home?" At first Randy, the owner of Hamilton Funeral Home in Hamilton didn't get it. But then the words settled in. And when that day came, Randy, as he had promised his long-time friend a few years before, honored that commitment—he made the solemn trip up to Nashville and drove his friend back home for the last time.

It was around 11 a.m. on September 26, 2017 when my oldest son Greg and I made our second somber trip to Hackleburg. This time, our first stop was at the cemetery to visit Sonny's resting place, a place after one and a half years of being apart, Sonny and Doris would be side-by-side once again in just a couple of hours.

We then dropped by the Loden building just across the way, initiating a visit with the owners Phillip and Carolyn Shackelford and his spry eighty-six-year-old mom Jean.

When the tornado came through the town in 2011, the Shackelfords told us they were four and a half miles away at their home just south of town on Prospector Road. Phillip's mother, Jean Shackelford, told us they saw the tornado "laying trees down easy" as it made its way toward town before releasing its enormous fury flat-out.

We then made our way from the Loden building to Cedar Tree Street to view the house that Sonny had built for him and Doris around 1962—a modest one-story, 2,100 square foot, three bedroom white brick home—one of the houses to survive the tornado. In the mid '60s, Sonny invited Thelma and me and our young son Greg to come to Hackleburg and stay with them for a few days. In the early '70s, Sonny sold that house and moved to a home in Nashville, but his heart never moved with him.

In 2017, due to the tornado, the old Church of Christ building had been wiped away and replaced by a new structure just south of town. Also gone were the cedar trees that had once lined the road shielding the cemetery. For the first time in years, Sonny's old house now had a clear view of the cemetery across the street, a visible reminder of the town's roots.

Following the drive over to Cedar Tree St., Greg and I made our way to the new church facility for a lunch kindly prepared by ladies of the church before the 2 p.m. service started. It was beautifully Doris from beginning to end.

Three weeks later, Greg and his wife Lisa, and their thirteen-year old twins Bennett and Lauren, were on their way back from a getaway in Florida. Going out of their way, Greg took his family by the cemetery and sent me a picture of the grandkids standing by the Loden plot—the most recent flowers were still there, their wilted heads bowed in reverence.

"Cedar Tree Cemetery is a place where the names on the headstones can also be found on nearby town streets—Cantrell, Clay, Mixon, Ray. It's a place where generations of families are buried, and gravesites are awash with flowers."

After getting better acquainted with those wonderful folks from

Hackleburg and spending final moments at Sonny and Doris' gravesite, I was taken back, once again, to the Christmas album and the song "Christmas in My Home Town."

> Oh I'd love to spend this Christmas -
> With the folks in my hometown
> Just to have the gang around -
> Friendly folks in my hometown.

> My heart is winging homeward
> As the snow comes falling down
> Oh I'd love to spend this Christmas
> With the folks in my hometown.

And so now and forever more Sonny and his beloved Doris will get to spend Christmas after Christmas with the folks in his hometown.

Some weeks after the April 27 storm, Mike Oliver, a writer for the *Birmingham News,* spent time in Hackleburg, and on July 12, 2011, a 1,600-word article was printed in the paper. Six years later I came across the piece, and with Mike's written approval, I integrated my work into his, with the above chapter being the final result.

You can read Mike's entire story at:

http://blog.al.com/spotnews/2011/07/alabama_tornadoes_devas-tated_h.html

Mike can be reached at: Mike Oliver/The Birmingham News/ AL.com

BARB DAY SNIPPET

Like so many of us, I became a fan of Sonny James in my early teens. I poured over the *Country Song Roundup* articles, and studied the album liner notes to learn everything I could about him. He was intriguingly different from other country singers. His singing, with its precise pitch, clear enunciation, and sincere emotion caught my attention. Sonny's guitar playing, especially on "A World of Our Own" and "I'll Never Find Another You" was thrilling in that "turn-the-record-player-up" way. His songs were clean and decent, and he had such a good reputation. Sad to say, I never had a chance to see him in person.

Unfortunately, the ups and downs and twists and turns of life tend to re-arrange one's priorities, and Sonny James got left behind on a sharp curve somewhere on the road into adulthood. He was a memory, a glowing light in the rearview mirror when I looked back on my teen years. Then, on Feb. 23, 2016, I read in the newspaper that he had died. I cried.

While searching the internet for more information, I discovered the Official Fans of Sonny James Facebook page, and joined it. One day I posted the statement "I wish Sonny had written his memoirs." That post got several likes. Soon afterward, I received a private message from Southern Gentleman Gary Robble, asking permission to call me. When the phone rang, I was shaking because I was going to be speaking with *a really important person*. The trembling stopped when I realized I was chatting with a really friendly, everyday guy. It was a fun conversation; we even found that we had some similar interests and experiences. For example: I had attended Bible college to become a teacher; he went to ENC to study for the ministry. My college, Baptist Bible College of Pennsylvania (now Clarks Summit University), was founded in Johnson City, New York, just seven miles from where Gary grew up.

Maybe two or three weeks later, Gary called me back. He had decided to go ahead and write a book about Sonny and The Southern

Gentlemen. He needed a proofreader and someone to bounce ideas around with, and would I like to help him? I was over-the-moon excited to help! Can you believe it? An ex-elementary school teacher and homemaker in Massachusetts meets an ex-Southern Gentleman and insurance agent in Tennessee on Facebook, and they work together electronically to write a biography of Sonny James!

Email and Voice-Over-Internet made this book possible. These chapters have been sent, corrected, discussed, sent back, re-sent, recorrected, rediscussed, and re-sent back and forth until the electrons cried for mercy.

I have an even greater respect for Sonny James now that I know so much more about him than I did as a teen.

Sonny didn't write his actual memoirs; but I feel genuinely honored to have had a part in documenting his legacy to country music history.

BARB DAY — *Greenfield, Massachusetts*

CHAPTER 23

FINAL COMMENTS

*It's hard to take someone who lives in your heart
and put them in a book.*
—LEE ROBERTS

On February 22, 2016, I was faced with that moment we all hope
never comes — the moment we never forget. The phone call came,
one of a series that had come my way in the previous month, but
this one had that tone of finality about it. It turned out it was to be
our moment — Sonny's and mine. I entered the room, and when the
time seemed right, I made my way around and placed my right cheek
against his. For one of the few times in our relationship, I softly said
all the words. With my parting thank you, and as I started to move
away. I looked again at his face, and watched as a tear rolled down
his left cheek. Twelve hours later, the phone rang again. It was all so
right — so right.

So in all these pages, I failed to tell you how he died. I opted instead
to tell you how it all happened and how he lived. Dying once is just

once, living principled through the myriad of life's ups and downs and disappointments is the true measure of a man. Great lives never go out — they go on.

A man can get sidetracked in the music industry by the lure of popularity and self-importance and easily lose sight of the lasting significance of life itself. In Johnny Cash's book, *The Man in Black,* Johnny mentions Sonny on four different pages. I purchased the book five years ago and took it by Sonny's to read Johnny's quotes from pages 77 and 78. The back story is that this was Johnny's first public appearance after his first record had been released, and he was on a show with Sonny in Covington, Tennessee.

Johnny said he knew about Sonny's committed life and said he had to talk with him because he sensed the "pitfalls and temptations" he would face. When Johnny faced Sonny with the question, Johnny quoted Sonny as saying, *"I am not just an entertainer who became a Christian. I am a Christian who chose to be an entertainer. I am first a Christian."* That's what Johnny said he remembered hearing Sonny say, but in truth that's how Sonny lived — what he was first and foremost.

So for all those classic male country artists of the 1960s who paved the way for today's new batch of singers, for those same artists who got a complete song in a single take, even though it might have happened on take 12, to all those artists who were obliged to sing on key when they recorded, this book pays tribute to the one who left us on February 22—George Washington's birthday. Understanding him as I do, I am sure he found in his professional career that spanned thirty-one years, and in his personal life, that portion of peace we all seek but few in the music business rarely ever find. Not only did Sonny find it in his career, but Sonny and Doris found it in their love for each other—a vow said once in 1957 that lasted fifty-eight years and seven months.

No longer can you ride into Nashville on a logging truck, pull up in front of a record company office, go inside and sing a few songs, and get a recording contract.

No longer can you offer the head of a record company what will become a No. 1 song to their label's main artist in return for an on-the-spot contract for the no-name vocalist singing on the demo.

No longer do today's stars have backing groups whose names are as memorable as those of the '60s—The Texas Troubadours, The Cherokee Cowboys, The Strangers, The Wagonmasters, The Buckaroos, The Twitty Birds, The Tennessee Three, The Southern Gentlemen and others. If you were to ask folks the names of the men who were in these groups, most would struggle to name even a few. To all of those long-forgotten names who helped to establish and maintain the careers of the artists they worked the road with, I dedicate this book to you.

And to WSM on-air personality, Eddie Stubbs, who came to Hackleburg, Alabama, on Saturday, February 27, 2016, to pay his respects as the sole representative of Music City USA; thank you from the bottom of our hearts.

> "Today, as the funeral service was in its final moments in Hackleburg Alabama, as an instrumental from "The Guitars of Sonny James" filled the high school gym, the funeral directors rolled away the flag-draped casket containing Sonny's earthly remains. Two of the original remaining members of The Southern Gentlemen in attendance [Milo Liggett and Gary Robble] immediately strolled along behind the casket as it was rolled down a long hallway. It was a subtle reminder that they had backed him up for many years and were taking the final walk with him. They went as far as they could go; as far as any of us could go. What a powerful image seeing those dedicated friends of Sonny James, The Southern Gentlemen."

> Ted Burleson
> Hamilton Church of Christ
> 2376 Military Street South
> Hamilton Alabama 35570

As for the lead singer of The Southern Gentlemen who toiled over this manuscript as a labor of love for months that turned into nearly three years, not many people will think much about him after this, and only his family will know what the few remaining years of his life will offer. For those few the actual yearly journals will remain in his family's possession, journals which were the original foundation for this published work, thus fulfilling Rick Hall's February 24, 2016 comment, "I pray history recognizes the legacy." I pray it does. I also pray I have.

ED SULLIVAN SHOWS

January 20, 1957

<u>Sonny James</u> / Fess Parker / Ivory Joe Hunter
Sonny James - "Young Love"
Ivory Joe Hunter (at piano) - "Since I Met You Baby"
Betty Johnson - "I Dreamed"

June 22, 1969

<u>Sonny James & The Southern Gentlemen</u> "A World of our Own"
[Running Bear]
Flip Wilson --Jackie Mason --Karen Wyman --Hal Frazier --Georgia
Tech Glee Club
[my (Gary's) dad with us]
Audience bows: Guy Lombardo

January 11, 1970

11-Jan-1970 CBS Sun (repeated 26-Jul-70)
<u>Sonny James & The Southern Gentlemen</u>
Ike & Tina Turner Revue, Tiny Tim & Miss Vicki, Flip Wilson

(comedian), Stiller & Meara (comedy team) (Jerry Stiller & Anne Meara), Karen Wyman, and Vino Venito (sword balancer) (Tiny Tim & Miss Vicki had married a month earlier on December 11, 1969 on the Johnny Carson Show as 40 million viewers tuned in.) Highlights:

> --Ike and Tina Turner Revue - medley: "Proud Mary" and "Bold Soul Sister"
>
> --Tiny Tim with the Enchanted Forest (an all-female band) "Earth Angel."
> www.youtube.com/watch?v=TT8t0VxZXEM
>
> --Tiny Tim sings a medley of old-fashioned love songs to his wife, Miss Vicki.
>
> --Flip Wilson (stand-up routine) - talks about his preacher, Reverend Leroy, and the preacher's wife (who, after shopping, tells her husband, "The Devil made me buy this dress").
>
> --Sonny James "Free Roamin' Mind" and "It's Just A Matter of Time." "Free Roamin' Mind" is at
> www.youtube.com/watch?v=b9qKzCSBiyM
> "It's Just a Matter of Time" can be found at
> www.youtube.com/watch?v=DegZTLMCRh0
>
> --Karen Wyman (seventeen-year-old singer from the Bronx, NYC) "Time and Love."
> www.youtube.com/watch?v=e29xiKLneQU
>
> --Carter & Lynn (Adagio dance duo from Detroit, Michigan)
> --Audience bows: Miss Vicki's parents; Tiny Tim's parents; and The Kessler Twins.

May 10, 1970

<u>Sonny James & The Southern Gentlemen</u> "My Love" "Waterloo"/ The Jackson Five/Don Rickles (comedian)/Ella Fitzgerald/George

Carlin (comedian)/Roger Williams (pianist)/Peter Gennaro (dancer)/ Marilyn Michaels (celebrity impressionist)/Gino Tonetti/Clint Eastwood (on film)

September 25, 1970

From Memphis, Tennessee, at the Memphis Blues Baseball Ball Park Sonny James & The Southern Gentlemen "Endlessly" "Tennessee Waltz"/Arthur Godfrey/The Johnny Mann Singers with Thurl Ravenscroft "Tony the Tiger/Mr. Grinch"/Judy Ford (Miss America 1969, her skill, a trampolinist)/Dave Manfield (helicopter stunts)/ Loretta Lynn/ Archie Campbell.

DISCOGRAPHY 1964 — 1971

DATES SONGS WERE RECORDED

SONNY JAMES AND THE SOUTHERN GENTLEMEN YEARS

August, 15 1964 The Southern Gentlemen did their first show with Sonny

September 1, 1964 Sonny James + Mixed group of singers
I'M GETTING GRAY FROM BEING BLUE unissued
YOU'RE THE ONLY WORLD I KNOW   Reached #1 - February 1965
WISH I HADN'T HAPPENED

The Southern Gentlemen record with Sonny for the first time
'Til the Last Leaf Shall Fall — Sonny's one and only religious album

January 18, 1965 Sonny James & The Southern Gentlemen
IF I HAVE WOUNDED ANY SOUL
THE BIGGER WE ARE
WHEN THEY RING THE GOLDEN BELLS
HE'S EVERYWHERE

'TILL THE LAST LEAF SHALL FALL
DOES JESUS CARE

January 20, 1965 Sonny James + Mixed group of singers
I'LL KEEP HOLDING ON (JUST TO YOUR LOVE)
BEHIND THE TEAR   #1 - August 1965
I'M GETTING GRAY FROM BEING BLUE

January 21, 1965 Sonny James & The Southern Gentlemen
(Recorded five more songs for the religious album)
AN OPEN FIELD
HE
BE WITH ME LORD
HOW GREAT THOU ART
PEACE IN MY SOUL

March 15, 1965 Sonny James + Mixed group of singers
DO WHAT YOU DO, DO WELL
IN MY BLUE ROOM
EVEN THE BAD TIMES ARE GOOD
WHEN I'M GONE

March 17, 1965   Sonny James + Mixed group of singers
JUST ASK YOUR HEART
RUNNIN'
INVISIBLE TEARS
THREE DAYS OUT OF OMAHA
THREE IN A ROOM

June 25, 1965 Sonny James + Mixed group of singers
I'LL NEVER BE ANYTHING BUT IN LOVE WITH YOU
NEED YOU, #1 — April 1967

July 7, 1965 Sonny James + Mixed group of singers

TRUE LOVE'S A BLESSING #1 — October 1965
YES OR NO
WHAT MAKES A MAN WANDER

Only The Southern Gentlemen record with Sonny — no mixed groups

July 8, 1965 Sonny James & The Southern Gentlemen
IN MEMORY OF LOUISA
ALL MY LOVE, ALL MY LIFE
THERE'S ALWAYS ANOTHER DAY

July 9, 1965 Sonny James & The Southern Gentlemen
TONIGHT I FOUND MY TRUE LOVE
SHACKLES AND CHAINS
I TRULY DO

September 1, 1965 Sonny James & The Southern Gentlemen
I'LL NEVER FIND ANOTHER YOU #1 — August 1967
IT'S THE LITTLE THINGS #1 — November 1967
ON AND ON
I'LL TAKE CARE OF YOU

November 24, 1965 Sonny James & The Southern Gentlemen
TAKE GOOD CARE OF HER - R&B #1 — June 1966
SOMETHIN'S GOT A HOLD ON ME - R&B

November 26, 1965 Sonny James & The Southern Gentlemen
THE LAST TIME
SHE BELIEVES IN ME unreleased

December 8, 1965 Sonny James & The Southern Gentlemen
ROOM IN YOUR HEART #1 — September 1966
IT'S GONNA RAIN SOME IN MY HEART
WHEN YOUR WORLD STOPS TURNING

December 10, 1965 Sonny James & The Southern Gentlemen
I GET FOOLED, DON'T I?
LOVE ME LIKE THAT

December 17, 1965 Sonny James & The Southern Gentlemen
ON THE FINGERS OF ONE HAND
DON'T CUT TIMBER ON A WINDY DAY
TAKE ME BACK - R&B

March 2, 1966 Sonny James & The Southern Gentlemen
230 54080-14 THERE'S NO WAY TO GET THERE FROM HERE ST 2703
231 54081-9 RED MUD ST 2703

March 2, 1966 Sonny James & The Southern Gentlemen
232 54085-30 I LET HER DOWN SOMEWHERE ST 2703
233 54086-14 A TREE OF BIRDS ST 2703

March 8, 1966 Sonny James & The Southern Gentlemen
WHERE DO WE GO FROM HERE
TIMBERLINE

March 9, 1966 Sonny James & The Southern Gentlemen
I'M HAVING A HARD TIME (GETTING OVER YOU)
FOR RENT
EVERYTHING BEGINS AND ENDS WITH YOU unreleased

March 10, 1966 Sonny James & The Southern Gentlemen
HOW MANY TIMES CAN A MAN BE A FOOL
SHE BELIEVES IN ME

April 27, 1966 Sonny James & The Southern Gentlemen
YOU ARE ALL I LOVE rejected
THE FEATHER OF A DOVE
WE'RE ON OUR WAY rejected

June 8, 1966 Sonny James & The Southern Gentlemen
YOU ARE ALL I LOVE
LOVE IS A LIGHT
GIVE ME TIME

CHRISTMAS ALBUM
August 1, 1966 Sonny James & The Southern Gentlemen
DO YOU HEAR WHAT I HEAR
LITTLE DRUMMER BOY

August 2, 1966 Sonny James & The Southern Gentlemen
A POCKETFUL OF MISTLETOE
MY CHRISTMAS DREAM
SILVER BELLS

August 3, 1966 Sonny James & The Southern Gentlemen
BAREFOOT SANTA CLAUS
THE STAR STILL SHINES
SILENT NIGHT/THE FIRST NOEL

August 4, 1966 Sonny James & The Southern Gentlemen
WHERE THE TREE IS
CHRISTMAS IN MY HOMETOWN
CHRISTMAS LETTER
CHRISTMAS ALBUM FINISHED

December 21, 1966 Sonny James & The Southern Gentlemen
EVERYTHING BEGINS AND ENDS WITH YOU unreleased
SHE BELIEVES IN ME unreleased

April 5, 1967 Sonny James & The Southern Gentlemen
I'LL FOLLOW YOU unreleased
GOODBYE MAGGIE, GOODBYE

April 6, 1967   Sonny James & The Southern Gentlemen
BACK DOOR TO HEAVEN
DON'T ASK FOR TOMORROW
I KNOW

April 11, 1967   Sonny James & The Southern Gentlemen
HAWAIIAN WEDDING SONG
IN WAIKIKI
WE'RE ON OUR WAY

April 12, 1967   Sonny James & The Southern Gentlemen
AN OLD SWEETHEART OF MINE
RALLY 'ROUND YOUR LOVE unreleased
LOVE IS A HAPPY SONG

May 5, 1967   Sonny James & The Southern Gentlemen
SCARS
DOG
TODAY IS THE END OF THE WORLD

August 15, 1967   Sonny James   no BGV
THE JOURNEY
CLOUDY FOLLOWED BY TEARS
MISFORTUNE'S CHILD

October 24, 1967   Sonny James   no BGV
WHAT A SHAME
DISCOVERIES AND INVENTIONS
LIKE THE BIRDIES FLY

October 24, 1967   Sonny James   no BGV
I'LL DO THE SAME THING FOR YOU
THE BLUES CAN'T KEEP A GOOD MAN DOWN
WHERE FORGOTTEN THINGS BELONG

October 24, 1967   Sonny James & The Southern Gentlemen
A THOUSAND TIMES A DAY
TODAY WILL BE MY DAY TO LIVE
PEOPLE-LUTION

October 25, 1967   Sonny James & The Southern Gentlemen
A MIDNIGHT MOOD
I'VE BEEN KEEPIN' BUSY WITH THE BLUES
WALKIN' WITH THE BLUES

October 31, 1967   Sonny James & The Southern Gentlemen
HEAVEN ON EARTH
THE ONLY ONES WE TRULY HURT (ARE THE ONES WE TRULY LOVE)

October 31, 1967   Sonny James & The Southern Gentlemen
A WORLD OF OUR OWN #1 — March 1968
MISERY AND ANGRY
FAIRY TALES

November 1, 1967   Sonny James & The Southern Gentlemen
CAN THIS BE ME?
LET ME LIVE AND LOVE WITH YOU
LOVE ME LIKE THERE'S NO TOMORROW

November 1, 1967   Sonny James & The Southern Gentlemen
A WEB OF LIES
MORE THAN EVER
HEAVEN SAYS HELLO #1 — August 1968

November 7, 1967   Sonny James & The Southern Gentlemen
SONG FOR SHARA
ABOVE AND BEYOND (THE CALL OF LOVE)
HERE I STAND (AND IN MY HAND I HOLD A RING)

February 13, 1968 Sonny James & The Southern Gentlemen
NO OTHER ARMS, NO OTHER LIPS
EVERYTHING BEGINS AND ENDS WITH YOU unreleased

April 16, 1968 Sonny James & The Southern Gentlemen
SHE THINKS I STILL CARE
DON'T BE ANGRY
IT'S OVER

April 17, 1968 Sonny James & The Southern Gentlemen
CRAZY ARMS
'68 ROCK ISLAND LINE
I FALL TO PIECES
CLINGING TO A HOPE

July 18, 1968 Sonny James & The Southern Gentlemen
BORN TO BE WITH YOU #1 — December 1968
RAMBLIN' ROSE

November 20, 1968 Sonny James & The Southern Gentlemen
OUT OF THIS WORLD
THAT'S WHY I LOVE YOU LIKE I DO #1 — May 1972
AMAZIN' LOVE

November 21, 1968 Sonny James & The Southern Gentlemen
ONLY THE LONELY #1 — March 1969
EVERYTHING BEGINS AND ENDS WITH YOU unreleased

January 14, 1969 Sonny James & The Southern Gentlemen
IT'S WORTH IT ALL
KEEP ME IN MIND
WHERE DID MY LOVE GO

January 15, 1969 Sonny James & The Southern Gentlemen
MEAN OLD MISSISSIPPI
SHE WILL I KNOW
WAKE UP TO ME GENTLE

January 16, 1969 Sonny James & The Southern Gentlemen
ROSES ARE RED (MY LOVE)
FOOL NO 1

January 17, 1969 Sonny James & The Southern Gentlemen
RUNNING BEAR unreleased
SINCE I MET YOU BABY   R&B #1 — October 1969
MY LOVE #1 — May 1970

February 11, 1969 Sonny James & The Southern Gentlemen
ISLAND OF DREAMS
EVERYTHING BEGINS AND ENDS WITH YOU

February 18, 1969 Sonny James & The Southern Gentlemen
SOMEHOW YOUR NAME COMES UP AGAIN
KEEPER OF MY HEART

February 19, 1969 Sonny James & The Southern Gentlemen
DOWNFALL OF ME
THIS WORLD OF OURS
I'VE JUST GOT TO KEEP ON KEEPING ON

March 20, 1969 Sonny James & The Southern Gentlemen
RUNNING BEAR unissued

March 26, 1969 Sonny James & The Southern Gentlemen
ALL THE WAY TOGETHER
RUNNING BEAR #1 — June 1969

March 27, 1969 Sonny James & The Southern Gentlemen
FREE ROAMIN' MIND
I'LL WATCH OVER YOU

June 4, 1969 Sonny James & The Southern Gentlemen
I'LL NEVER FIND ANOTHER YOU
BORN TO BE WITH YOU
THE MINUTE YOU'RE GONE/TAKE GOOD CARE OF HER/HEAVEN SAYS HELLO/
IT'S THE LITTLE THINGS unreleased
JUST A CLOSER WALK WITH THEE
HOW GREAT THOU ART
YOUNG LOVE
THE ASTRODOME ALBUM

June 4, 1969 Sonny James & The Southern Gentlemen
DEEP IN THE HEART OF TEXAS
THE EYES OF TEXAS ARE UPON YOU
I'M MOVIN' ON
'68 ROCK ISLAND LINE
TRUE LOVE'S A BLESSING
TRAIN SPECIAL '69
RUNNING BEAR
SINCE I MET YOU, BABY

November 5, 1969 Sonny James & The Southern Gentlemen + 3 Jordanaires
IT'S JUST A MATTER OF TIME   R&B #1 — February 1970

November 6, 1969 Sonny James & The Southern Gentlemen + 3 Jordanaires
YOU'RE THE REASON I'M LIVING
WHAT AM I LIVING FOR

November 12, 1969 Sonny James & The Southern Gentlemen + 3 Jordanaires
TRACES
WATERLOO

February 18, 1970 Sonny James & The Southern Gentlemen + 3 Jordanaires
HAPPINESS BOUND
DON'T KEEP ME HANGING ON #1 — August 1970
WOODBINE VALLEY

February 19, 1970 Sonny James & The Southern Gentlemen
ONE DAY BYE AND BYE
HAPPY MEMORIES
REACH OUT YOUR HAND AND TOUCH ME

February 20, 1970 Sonny James & The Southern Gentlemen
BLUE FOR YOU
KISS IN THE SUNSHINE
ENDLESSLY R&B #1 — November 1970 #1 ALBUM

July 21, 1970 Sonny James & The Southern Gentlemen
YOUR CHEATIN' HEART
I CAN'T STOP LOVING YOU

July 21, 1970 Sonny James & The Southern Gentlemen
ANY TIME
YOU ARE MY SUNSHINE
I WALK THE LINE
TENNESSEE WALTZ

July 22, 1970 Sonny James & The Southern Gentlemen
KING OF THE ROAD
HE'LL HAVE TO GO
YOUNG LOVE
SUNSHINE GIRL

July 22, 1970 Sonny James & The Southern Gentlemen
BORN TO LOSE
STILL WATER RUNS DEEP

LOVE IS YOU

July 23, 1970 Sonny James & The Southern Gentlemen
JUST KEEP ON THINKING OF ME
IT KEEPS RIGHT ON A-HURTING
EMPTY ARMS   R&B #1 — April 1971

July 23, 1970 Sonny James & The Southern Gentlemen
FOR THE LOVE OF A WOMAN LIKE YOU
AS IF I DIDN'T KNOW unreleased
I'M IN LOVE WITH YOU
A LOVE THAT WILL NOT LET YOU GO unreleased

April 27, 1971 Sonny James & The Southern Gentlemen
OUT OF SIGHT, OUT OF MIND
ONLY LOVE CAN BREAK A HEART #1
TRUE LOVE LASTS FOREVER

April 28, 1971 Sonny James & The Southern Gentlemen
PLEDGING MY LOVE
BRIGHT LIGHTS, BIG CITY   R&B #1 — July 1971
JESUS KNOWS

May 11, 1971 Sonny James & The Southern Gentlemen
TAKE CARE OF YOU FOR ME
MIRACLES STILL HAPPEN
LOUISIANA BAYOU

May 11, 1971 Sonny James & The Southern Gentlemen
SOMETHING'S GOT A HOLD ON ME   R&B
HERE COMES HONEY AGAIN #1 — November 1971
SURPRISE, SURPRISE

May 12, 1971 Sonny James & The Southern Gentlemen
I WAITED TOO LONG
AMI ESPOSA CON AMOR unreleased
GOT YOU ON MY MIND AGAIN unreleased
HE HAS WALKED THIS WAY BEFORE

May 13, 1971 Sonny James & The Southern Gentlemen
CLINGING VINE
LORD, YOU KNOW HOW MEN ARE
ACHIN' THING CALLED LOVE
TIME'S RUNNING BACKWARD FOR ME unreleased

In total The Southern Gentlemen did 73 recording sessions with Sonny.

In the beginning, other than on the religious album, Sonny used a mixed vocal group on 6 sessions. Starting on July 8, 1965 and thereafter he only used The Southern Gentlemen.

Three of the Jordanaires joined us on four sessions recording eight songs (Gordon, Neal & Ray) (November 5, 1969, November 6, 1969. November 12, 1969 and February 18, 1970)

The Jordanaires did nine recording sessions with Sonny before The Southern Gentlemen joined him in August 1964 totaling twenty-one songs. The first session was on April 15, 1957 and concluded with the last one on April 10, 1964. Six of those nine sessions came in a three day period in 1957. April 15 (two), April 16 (two) and April 17 (two)

Only one of those twenty-one songs charted - Lovesick Blues #15 country (1957) — didn't chart pop, this was Sonny's second follow-up release after Young Love.

The Anita Kerr singers did two sessions with Sonny totaling five songs on RCA (October 11, 1961 and January 8, 1962). None of the songs they recorded with Sonny charted.

My Sincere Thanks to Seven Very Special Folks

Suzanne Cummings..................................Terry Dillard
Richard Custer......................................Don McKay
Barb Day...Greg Robble

and especially my Southern Gentlemen Brother
Milo Liggett

Couldn't have done it without all of you.

Gary Robble